When Swan Lake Comes to Sarajevo

When Swan Lake Comes to Sarajevo

RUTH WATERMAN

CANTERBURY
PRESS
Norwich

© Ruth Waterman 2008

First published in 2008 by the Canterbury Press Norwich
(a publishing imprint of Hymns Ancient & Modern Limited,
a registered charity)
13–17 Long Lane, London EC1A 9PN

www.scm-canterburypress.co.uk

British Library Cataloguing in Publication data

A catalogue record for this book is available
from the British Library

ISBN 978-1-85311-865-4

Map by John Flower

Typeset by Regent Typesetting, London
Printed and bound in Great Britain by
MPG Books Ltd, Bodmin, Cornwall

Contents

For the musicians of the Mostar Sinfonietta,
who have so generously allowed me into their lives

Some names and identities have been changed for reasons of privacy.

Thanks are extended to Architect Manfredo Romeo and General Engineering of Florence, Italy, for information about the reconstruction of Stari Most (www.gen-eng.florence.it/starimost); and to Accord International and the George Bell Institute (www.georgebellinstitute.org.uk) for their financial contributions towards travel expenses.

Deep within me, I know that part of the artist's job is . . . to create a dream . . . to create images from the depths of the imagination, and to give them form whether visual, intellectual or musical . . . images of vigour for a decadent period, images of calm for one too violent, images of reconciliation for worlds torn by division. And in an age of mediocrity and shattered dreams, images of abounding, generous, exuberant beauty.

Michael Tippett

Introduction

I had never been to a post-war country before, though I'd often wondered what happens after the guns are silenced and the media moves on. Encountering Bosnia as a musician rather than as a diplomat or social historian or journalist, I didn't know how to understand the long uncharted path away from the days of violence.

This is an account of my personal journey, of my experiences and thoughts in the order in which they happened, with all their incompleteness and contradictions and misunderstandings. In a chaotic country, one experience after another piles up, feelings sometimes follow facts at a remove, and the sense of it all emerges only gradually, if at all. In choosing to write without the benefit of hindsight, I have attempted to give a flavour of what it was like to walk in the aftermath of war, to breathe the Balkan air.

At first there was a vague thought of making a radio programme (which was in fact broadcast on the BBC), so I took a tape recorder in case people wanted to tell me their stories. I was startled, and touched, by the number of acquaintances and strangers who, without invitation, started to talk of their experiences both during and after the war. It seemed part of a deep need to speak, to have someone hear them, especially an 'international' as I was called. What they said was so extraordinary that I continued to record them during my subsequent visits. So this book is partly an act of witness, offering the voices of individuals as they revealed not only the details of their lives, but also their courage, despair, bewilderment, resilience and humour.

Ruth Waterman
June 2007

Stari Most

The famous bridge of Mostar was built in 1566 by the Ottoman Turks under the architect Hajruddin. The slender white stone bridge called Stari Most – Old Bridge – became the symbol of the town. Flanked by two white towers, it consisted of a single, almost circular arch.

On 9 November 1993, during the Bosnian war, Stari Most was destroyed by shelling.

In June 2001, after two years of scientific and archaeological research, reconstruction of the bridge was begun in accordance with the original methods, with stone from the original quarries.

Funders included UNESCO, the World Bank, the European Bank for Reconstruction and Development, and the governments of Italy, France, the Netherlands, Turkey and Croatia. The project involved an international committee of experts, as well as German, French, Turkish, Bosnian and Croatian engineering firms. The reconstruction cost 15 million Euros.

The new Stari Most was opened on 23 July 2004. It is now a UNESCO World Heritage site.

Length: 28 metres
Width: 4 metres
Height above river (at average water level): 20 metres
Load bearing arch: 80cm height, composed of 111 rows of voussoirs (arch stones)
Average stone block: 40x80x100cm
Composition of bridge arch and elevations: tenelija stone (local limestone)
Composition of pavement: krečnjak stone (hard marble-like limestone)

July 2002

'Would you be interested in becoming involved with the Mostar Sinfonietta?' An email out of the blue.

Mostar.
The bridge.
The violence.
The streams of refugees.
The quiet after the war.

What would it be like to go into that quiet?

I replied, 'Yes.'

A week later, I was standing in my kitchen holding the phone to my ear, trying to take in numbers – numbers of violinists (3), violists (1), oboists (nil); numbers of displaced, killed, returned (too large to absorb); of schools, music therapists, budgets, dates. And behind the numbers, an immensely kind voice and a generosity that honeyed the numbers and drew me on.

Ian Ritchie, concert consultant and music promoter, was telling me about the Mostar Sinfonietta, which he initiated together with composer Nigel Osborne of Edinburgh University. He told me that it's a small chamber orchestra with a core of thirteen players, augmented by a few international volunteers. It was formed just after the Bosnian war to provide music education for the whole region, as well as to play concerts and bring music to children with special needs and those still traumatized by the war. Mostar is virtually a divided town, he says, but the ensemble is the only body to be completely inclusive, with members from all communities.

I was immediately struck by the thought that the orchestra is perhaps helping to reinforce the new peace, to rebuild the community. And it would be wonderful to be involved with that. If nothing else, I could support the musicians and encourage music to recover its voice there.

'During the summer, the Mostar Sinfonietta will be in Croatia to provide music for theatre productions of *King Lear* and *Medea*. Perhaps you could bring some chamber music and do some coaching for a few weeks?' I jumped at the idea. It would be an introduction to the players, to be followed by a visit to Mostar later on in the year. I made sure to pack my copy of *Lear* together with some Schubert quartets and Scott Joplin Rags.

Reconstruction of Stari Most

Soil on site is firmed, condition of roads improved, area fenced.
Scaffolding erected around tower walls.
Cleaning of joints in tower walls, damaged stones repaired or
replaced, joints re-pointed, injection works started.
Drilling for foundation for the crane.
Dismantling of remaining pavement, measuring and numbering of
stones for later reassembling.
Repair of abutment wall, replacing damaged stones and injecting
grouting.
Archaeological excavations. Fifteenth-century wooden bridge dis-
covered.

Thursday

It's deliciously cool after last night's oppressive heat. As I wander
from the hotel to the dock at seven in the morning, I take in the
pale blue Italian sky, the deserted waterfront and the vast stretch
of water that is the Adriatic. I flew into Trieste last night and am
about to cross the sea to reach the tiny island of Brijuni, just off
the Croatian coast. But the wind is picking up and I'm told by the
shipping supervisor that the ferry is delayed due to the 'Bora'. The
'Bora' – I remember this wind from Virgil, wreaking havoc on
battles in Roman times, and here it is, still rattling its sabre. While
I'm waiting, I sit at an outdoor café drinking strong rich coffee,
and the wind blows colder and the sea wakes up and the steep cliffs
at the back of the town seem to press in.

I think about meeting the Bosnian musicians and how they are
all survivors of war. About how it seemed incomprehensible that
such brutality could erupt in Europe at the end of the twentieth
century. About the choice of plays – *King Lear* and *Medea* – both
exploring to the bitter end the themes of disintegration, of conflict,
of family hatreds, of revenge. About being among people for
whom these are red-hot issues. About the idyllic island of Brijuni.

After a four-hour crossing, I step off the ferry onto a small stretch of paving that separates the seafront from a couple of modest hotels shaded by oleander bushes. There is an old building right at the water's edge with strange curling gables and moss clinging to its walls, but apart from these signs of human cultivation, the island looks untended and lush. I wait for a few minutes until a young man bounds towards me, takes one look at my violin case, and offers his hand. 'Ruth?' he says in an unmistakable Scottish accent.

He introduces himself as Aidan Burke, the manager of the Mostar Sinfonietta. His boyish face and fine light-brown hair make him look all of eighteen years old, but he must be older.

'There are no cars on Brijuni so is it OK to walk you to where we're all staying?'

I think I'm going to enjoy this – twelve days without traffic. Aidan leads me away into the woods where a fifteen-minute walk takes us to some low, oblong buildings that look like army barracks. Evidently they *were* army barracks when Tito used this island as his summer base. The whole island is now a national park, the presidential palace tucked away somewhere in its centre.

'When you've settled yourself, would you like to come down to the canteen for a coffee and we can chat?'

'Thanks, that would be lovely.'

We sit at one of the large Formica tables that look out onto the water. It is very hot. There's a spacious open terrace and a slope of grass leading down to the sea. In a nearby field, a few enormous stags are grazing.

Aidan tells me he plays the viola and was completing his degree at Edinburgh University when one of his professors, Nigel Osborne, invited him to spend some time in Bosnia, giving creative music workshops for schools and youth groups. The Sinfonietta grew out of those activities, and Aidan found himself falling in love with the country, staying on and eventually taking the role of orchestra manager.

I want to ask him lots of questions, about the orchestra, and life in Mostar, and about the work here on Brijuni.

'Last things first. It's a tough schedule here,' he says. 'At night, there's the performance, at the moment, it's *Lear*. We've three more of *Lear*, then a few days' break, and then *Medea* starts. We have to get to the mainland first, so we leave here at about five in the afternoon. We don't get back until about 1 a.m. And then there are always rehearsals during the day. Sometimes just the musicians, you know, to tidy up things that maybe went a bit astray the night before. And now, we're already rehearsing the music for *Medea*. Maybe you can help. I mean, if you would come to the rehearsals, it would be really helpful to us.'

'Of course.'

'And then there are rehearsals with the actors, which can go on for hours. So people are pretty tired. Today is our day off, no rehearsals and no performance.'

Aidan leans back in his chair.

'You know, I've brought some chamber music with me,' I say. 'Ian thought the musicians might like to play and be coached, though it looks like there's not much spare time.'

Chamber music is manna for musicians. Neither alone with your instrument nor lost in the glorious sound of an orchestra, but just making music with a few colleagues. The perfect intimacy.

It's also ideal for teaching and learning the skills of being a musician.

Aidan hesitates. 'I'm sure some of them will want to work with you. I do, for a start,' he laughs.

'Well, we can talk about it tomorrow. So tell me about the Sinfonietta. How do you manage when there are so few musicians in Mostar?'

He explains that in the beginning, they had to bring in guest musicians – from the UK, from Germany – but that now, as the ensemble gets better known, and with the emergence of advanced students from the Sarajevo Academy of Music, they are almost able to stand on their own feet.

'We have many of the cream of the Academy students working with us, and of course, that's always been one of our aims – to provide a platform for talent.'

He smiles.

'You know, I am proud that we are a cross-community orchestra. Which means that the musicians come from all areas of Mostar, which means that they come from all the different ethnic or religious backgrounds. We never planned it that way, never tried to make it that way, that's just happened that way – we've always made it a priority to look for people who have the talent and the desire and the will, and the initiative actually, to find us and come and work with us.'

It 'just happened'? How can that be so? I want to ask Aidan to go back to the beginning, to tell me how such an ensemble, integrated in defiance of the new norms of separation, could be born without hard labour. But he is in full flow so I let him continue.

'I was talking to some of the members of the orchestra, they were saying that they found it difficult to cross the boundary, the road that divides East and West – Mostar's not divided by the river, it's divided by what was the front line during the war, just to the west of the river. Anyway they felt that some people wouldn't join the orchestra because they would feel afraid to go into the other part. But I think today it's a lot better than it was a few years ago. A few years ago, I myself got worried crossing the divide and I'm not even from here, I wasn't in the war, I don't particularly have any interest in this . . . in what one person might call a religious conflict, another would call a power conflict, another would call . . . you know . . .'

He goes on to tell me about a car bomb that exploded in Mostar shortly after he'd arrived, apparently in protest against a proposal to unify the police force. The international community is not only providing peacekeeping troops, but has a mandate to oversee the rebuilding of civil institutions. 'Suggesting a federal police force was a bold step, one of their only big steps until that point, because the police were completely separate – they still are. And so someone, or various people, weren't happy, and they made a huge car bomb. Some people were killed, many people were injured, the side of a building was blown off in just one sheer blast. And that was late September '97.

'Today things are a lot better, but sadly it seems that politically we still remain divided, in Mostar. Even though it's supposedly a Muslim–Croat Federation, what that ends up meaning on the bottom line is that the so-called Muslims are holding one side and the so-called Croats are holding the other side and they kind of, just keep each other happy and try and make sure that they just stay in power, at whatever cost. I'm saying 'so-called' because nobody – hardly anybody – is a pure Muslim or Croat or Serb, there was so much intermarriage.'

As we chat, some of the musicians wander in and I'm introduced to them. They smile politely but move away quickly: they want to relax, and anyway only a few speak English. I'll meet them properly in good time.

Then two bearded men walk by and casually sit down at a far table.

'Oh, there's Gloucester!' says Aidan.

My mind whirls. I must look startled.

'Over there,' he continues. 'With Lear.'

Shakespeare's characters are alive and well in former Yugoslavia.

'Another coffee?' I ask.

I go up to the counter and request a *kafa* and a *čaj* (pronounced chai), two words I made sure to learn on the boat earlier today. There's something oddly nice about the word for tea being so similar to the cuppa cha of my native Yorkshire.

Now Aidan fills me in on the Ulysses Theatre, saying that it is just over a year old and based in Croatia. But it gathers its actors and designers, costume-makers and musicians from the whole region, including those who had to flee to more distant countries during the war. Under the circumstances, this is a courageous act, and a political one too.

'Working with them is one of our many different threads. You know, we do a lot with children, with youth choirs, some dancing groups, and of course the schools' music project. But *King Lear* is an absolutely fantastic initiative with Rade Šerbedžija, one of the greatest actors of former Yugoslavia. He really is unbelievable. OK, I'm still fairly young, but I've never worked with actors like this, ever.'

It was his professor, Nigel Osborne, who brought the

Sinfonietta into partnership with the Ulysses Theatre. 'The director said, we want you to compose the music and Nigel said fine,
done, as long as the Sinfonietta is going to be the ensemble. And
they said fine. So we have a lot to thank Nigel for. But it's not just
Nigel, there's a huge number of people, for example Ian Ritchie
who had a very strong, energetic and creative impulse from the
beginning and remains very much on board. There's too many
people to name I'm afraid, just so many generous people who have
donated their time and their skills to come and work with us, and
this continues. And this is the reason that we've succeeded and got
to where we are. And why we're still going.'

The evening brings my first chance to see the orchestra in action.
They are all ages, men and women, and all Bosnian except
for Aidan, an English cellist and an English clarinettist. There's
evidently no cellist or clarinettist in Mostar. I'm astonished that
Aidan seems to speak fluent Bosnian. It used to be called Serbo-
Croat, but since the war, Serbia, Croatia and Bosnia have taken
the language and wrestled it into three different ones by emphasiz-
ing the regional differences. A bit like Scouse or Yorkshire
suddenly being classified as 'not English'. I haven't been able to
find a Bosnian phrase book, just a Serbo-Croat one. I'm not sure
how I'll be able to learn which words are acceptable to Bosnians.

The Sinfonietta is rehearsing some music written by their bass
player which sounds very much like folk music – simple harmonies,
Eastern European rhythms. Intonation and ensemble are often a
problem, but it seems that everyone is just getting acquainted with
the music, and the focus is on cleaning it up. The rehearsal goes like
most of the rehearsals I've attended all over the world: somebody
stops playing and starts talking, someone else starts talking at the
same time, voices are raised, usually in good humour though not
always, and even though it seems to teeter on absolute chaos,
things do get done. It's nice to witness a rehearsal where I can't
understand a word that anyone is saying.

There's a television in the room, and a number of children are
either watching it, listening to the music, or dancing around. I
notice that *West Wing*, the series set in the White House in
Washington DC, is playing (without the sound), with Croatian

subtitles. The White House on Brijuni. Actually not so far-fetched, as the white stone used to build it was quarried in Yugoslavia.

Before I go to sleep, I spend a few hours reading *King Lear*. I need to memorize the shape of the plot if I'm to follow it in Croatian. The play is long and I'm only halfway through. Tomorrow, I'll be able to read much more.

Vocabulary learned today
čaj – tea
kafa – coffee
bez šećera – without sugar (otherwise handfuls are poured in)
hvala – thank you
molim – please

Friday

I wake up and wonder where I am.

When I come down to breakfast, everyone greets me with a quick '*dobar dan*'. As I look around, I'm acutely aware that the people here have suffered, but I can't see any signs of it in their faces or their posture. It's not like in other countries, where people are stooped from centuries of hardship. But as time goes on, I hear comments like, 'When I was a refugee in Vienna . . .' or 'When I was out of work for a year in Slovenia . . .' Some now live in the UK, the US, Holland; many are displaced within former Yugoslavia; most are questioning whether to return, where they belong. Aidan points out a singer from Chechnya and adds in a whisper that her husband is missing. She is here with her eleven-year-old daughter, already becoming a tall beauty, who chatters in Russian and English to everyone she meets. There are younger children too, and they seem well-loved, not spoiled, but valued.

This morning I sit in on a rehearsal for the music for *Medea*, making the occasional comment when invited. The leader of the orchestra is a young woman of real beauty. Her fine features and dark eyes exude a quiet radiance and a kind of peace that comes perhaps from having suffered and accepted. Her name is Rada – she moves gracefully and her laugh is gentle. Sitting next to her is a Russian, a middle-aged man called Vassili who, I can see, plays excellently. Next to Aidan is Suzana, a dark-haired motherly woman who is the wife of Ivica, the bass player. Of these, only Ivica speaks English, so for the moment, I have a wordless acquaintance with them. As for the others, they are also nameless.

Before lunch, I join a yoga class that is offered to the actors and musicians, and after lunch, Aidan succeeds in rounding up a string quartet. We find some space in the lobby and I take them through the Schubert Quartettsatz, suddenly a refreshing draught of purity in this humidity and heat. The actual playing of it, however, is decidedly ragged. Rather than tackling any of the detail, I decide to plough on to the Scott Joplin Rag which soon has everyone smiling. I see that we'll have to work hard on capturing the irresistible rhythm of ragtime. But at least the ice has been broken and they can take away the music to practise it.

This evening, I go to see my first *King Lear* in Croatian. The performance takes place on another island, so first we have to take a small ferry to the mainland, to the pretty village of Fazana, where the audience gathers on the dock. At 7 p.m., the musicians begin playing pseudo-Strauss waltzes on the pier as the audience piles into three boats; the Duke of Burgundy says a few words to introduce the King of France who regally boards one of the boats, and we all set off for Mali Brijuni – small Brijuni. This is an uninhabited island, and the first sight that greets us as we disembark is the Fool, a burly actor, sitting half-naked in a hammock, glaring at everyone. And then one notices a black horse, walking elegantly round a field, its rider immaculately dressed in Habsburg army uniform. This *Lear* is set in the Habsburg Empire, hence the waltzes.

It's very disorienting to be faced with this play, in Croatia, set in the time of the Habsburg Empire. For a start, the language of Shakespeare feels so intrinsic to his plays that I can't quite accept that they are viable in any other language. But the actors clearly feel that they own Shakespeare just as much as the English, and judging by their performances, they do. The production has great energy. The audience is visibly moved – there is laughter as well as tears. Of course, I can't understand a word, but I'm able to follow the action, at least during the parts I've read.

Different scenes are set in different sites on the island, and as the audience walks from one place to the next, there is an excited buzz of conversation. Much different from the interval chatter in a theatre. Sometimes we stand, but for the long scenes we are seated on raised benches fixed on scaffolding in the courtyards of a huge ruined fort. The decision to place *Lear* in a fortress that was built by the Austro-Hungarian Empire is inspired. Brijuni was the summer home of the Habsburg emperors and then of President Tito. So the ruined fort is the perfect symbol for a centre of power that has twice suffered the violent loss of its power.

It's an extraordinary experience, watching *Lear* in Croatian, sitting under the stars on a deserted island, with four hundred people who have come from all over former Yugoslavia. I'm wondering how they can endure the spectacle of violence, jealousy, chaos and despair, all resulting from the deliberate division of a kingdom that takes place in Scene 1. It starts with Lear striding purposefully into view, holding a map of his kingdom and declaring his intent to divide it between his three daughters. It ends with each daughter raising an army and fighting the others, in an uncanny echo of the three factions who fought over Bosnia. Tonight the atmosphere is alive with the ghosts of the recent past, and at the end, there is hardly a dry eye.

After the performance, as the boats take the audience back to the mainland, we have to wait until a boat returns to take us directly to Brijuni. The company sits exhausted in front of a hut that functions as a tiny bar, most drinking beer or water or, as in my case, tea. The journey back is magical, the boat cleaving the black water, the sky patterned with stars, the rogue shapes of the land sliding quietly by.

When we get back to base, we all eat supper, even though it's after 1 a.m. But then we haven't eaten since lunch.

Vocabulary learned today
dobar dan – good-day
mali – small
nikada – never ('thou'lt come no more, never, never, never, never, never' – final scene, *King Lear*)

Saturday

Six hours' sleep is not enough for me, so I go back to bed after a breakfast of cereal, yoghurt, eggs, sausage and rolls. At least that's what's set out on the main table, but I can only face the yoghurt. When I re-emerge, Ivica the bass player asks me to help him with the Joplin, so we play it together and he eagerly writes down all the chords for guitar. He is one of the older men in the ensemble, tall with a gaunt square face, slightly abrupt manner and ready smile. He tells me that he lost his bass during the war and took up the guitar. Now he likes to play both instruments.

As soon as we finish, I dive into *Lear* again and read all afternoon until I finish it. I won't be able to remember the order of all the scenes, but I decide I'm going to see it again tonight.

As I'm downing a quick cup of coffee, the flautist in the Sinfonietta approaches and introduces herself.

'Hello, I'm Selma,' she says. 'I spent some years in England. It's nice to meet you.'

She looks to be in her twenties and has a soft, pleasant face. I invite her to join me and she chats fluently in English. It turns out that she's a flautist with a degree in engineering, a rare breed indeed.

Selma

I wanted to be electronics engineer, that was my dream when I was in high-school. I always loved my flute because I had it as a hobby, but I had it in school as well. I had been part of the music school, and also normal school, with lots of subjects. Went basically to two schools in the same time. Then I moved to England in '92 with the war, and got a place in Durham University. In engineering.

I was an asylum seeker but it seemed no one was really looking at my case for very long time, for three years no one even touched my case. So, people in Durham were really nice, they even kept my place for an extra year.

It's very strange how I became a musician. In '98, first time after six years, I came back for holiday. That was the first possible time I could come and see my parents. I saw the director of the music school in Mostar and she said look I've got all these flute students and I've got no one to teach them, there's absolutely no one in town who could take over these students. So if you come back I would like to give you a job. I wasn't even having an interview! But she knew me since I was a little girl. So I took a job opportunity. I really wanted to come back but the idea of not being independent financially didn't really make me happy. Even though my parents were prepared to help me find my way around and to pay for everything that I need and I could stay with them and all this. So I decided to come back in October '98. Took the job, started with sixteen hours a week, now I'm on twenty-two hours, so it's quite a lot.

You should have seen the Sinfonietta a year or two years ago. It was almost impossible to have a concert because we didn't have enough musicians. People in West Mostar two years ago, they were basically threatened by their own directors that if they come to help us playing concerts they would lose their job. So Vassili is the first one that broke the ice and came to work with us. He didn't lose his job because he's good enough and he's not from here, he's from Russia, so they don't look at it that way. It is slowly moving forward. It's going to take a very long time until we make Mostar Sinfonietta recognized everywhere, but I think we're slowly getting there. And we had really a few successful seasons, especially summertime, here in Brijuni, and the year before as well.

You know, when I think about what happened here, I still can't understand. I mean the war, and the camps. We had this experience before in Europe, with Hitler and his concentration camps, and it's repeating. I studied history from these books same like these people who organized all terrible things here. We had the same books, they didn't change for fifty years. You cannot change the history. If it was people that didn't have a chance to learn about these things, maybe, I could say, OK – it's not OK – but I understand in a certain way. But these people particularly . . .

'Selma!' One of the musicians is beckoning.

'Oh, it's time to leave,' Selma says, jumping up. 'Sorry, I must get my flute.'

'It's OK, we'll continue another time.'

On the way to Fazana, I lean on the boat-rail and look out towards the horizon. Ivica joins me. He thinks that *Lear* is too violent. 'There is no need to show the murders, or even to have any murders, in a play. It is corrupting,' he says.

Seeing it once more, I'm surprised by how familiar it feels. I can identify immediately all the characters as they enter, and I'm no longer shocked by the multiple deaths, or the lewdness of Regan – though I'm still shocked by the blinding of Gloucester, which is excruciating. At the moment of the attack, a powerfully bright light is shone directly at the audience, effectively blinding us. After five seconds, the attack is over and the light goes out, but now all we can see is darkness while our eyes adjust to normal lighting. So we are twice blinded, once by light, once by its absence. And then we see Gloucester stumbling in his permanent blindness. Tonight, at the moment of violence, someone close by me yawns audibly. Then someone else titters. I remember Ivica's comment about the violence and I understand the instinct to disassociate from it.

In the final act, as Lear descends inexorably into despair, I gasp with the rest of the audience as a shooting star glides high in the sky. It is bright and large and it travels slowly.

It is Lear's birthday, or rather the actor's, Rade Šerbedžija, and he seems genuinely surprised when the orchestra strikes up Happy Birthday during the bows. The cast and audience join in the singing and the tragedy of King Lear scuttles away into a corner of our minds. But Rade's Lear is unforgettable, a confident king raging and floundering and degenerating until he is completely broken. And at the moment when he is broken, he has nothing but his humanity.

After the show, I ask him if he's in the next production of *Medea*.

'No, I'm not.'

'Lear is enough,' I suggest.

'Lear is too much,' he says and smiles.

During the boat journey, Aidan comments that some of the stories of people here are so heartbreaking that it's too much for him. I wonder what he has just heard. I stare at the wake as the boat slices cleanly through the water.

Vocabulary learned today
brat – brother (*King Lear*, Act 2 Scene 1, 'Brother!' Wicked Edmund ensnares his own brother with deceitful fraternity. The hatred of an unfavoured son.)
kako ste? – how are you?
dobro – good

Sunday

Exhausted again. These late nights are taking their toll.

Today there is time for some lengthy coaching on the Schubert quartet movement. I work mainly on encouraging the players to move physically in order to communicate with the others. I ask each of them to practise leading and following. 'It's not just the first violinist who leads while the rest of you sit immobile,' I say. 'Each player has a responsibility to give energy, to contribute to the whole.'

Aidan translates.

'Each of you should be aware of what the others are playing, and not only the main melody. If you have an accompanying pattern, see if anyone else has the same pattern, so that you can mesh them together. Or maybe you have a dialogue with another instrument. Using your body to show what you are playing can stimulate everyone's aural antennae.'

In the end they all become more active and engaged, not only in their own line but also in the other lines as they are drawn into how the parts fit together. And the music sounds transformed.

It's the last night of *Lear* tonight, and I debate with myself whether to see it yet again. Three times in three nights? Can I stand the long unfolding of catastrophe yet again?

On the other hand, how can I pass up the opportunity? After all,

I've heard the great works of music countless times, and the re-listening creates the comfort of familiarity – the 'ah yes' of the opening of Eine Kleine Nachtmusik or Beethoven's Fifth – together with the delightful surprises of the sounds and parallels and subtleties not noticed before, the unfamiliar pushing up through the familiar. And there's always more to notice, to respond to, the unfurling of dimensions we haven't yet experienced or even guessed at.

Tonight's performance begins as usual with the waltzes on the waterfront. But once on the boats, the musicians start playing some light jazz, with one of the violinists singing up a storm à la Ella (Fitzgerald). I'm persuaded to join in, so I grab a violin and play Monti's Czardas with Ivica accompanying me on his guitar. It's nice how musicians everywhere seem to know that tune. The audience can't believe their luck – or am I just imagining it? There's an extra electricity in the air, a 'last night' excitement.

As we settle onto Mali Brijuni, I feel inexplicably involved in the production. Even though my brain is not involved in process-ing the words, my eyes seem to catch something new in every scene. It's a busy production, with too much happening on the set to have registered consciously at first sight. Rade has an even greater range of colour and dynamics, especially in the soft, broken-voiced phrases, '*Nikada, nikada, nikada, nikada, nikada*' . . . never more . . .

At the end, the cast comes out for their bows and stands in a long line as a few speeches are made. There is also a moment's silence for the boat's captain who had died in an accident a few months ago. Now there is no avoidance of the moment, no shuffling or discomfort. There are many tearful eyes, and a feeling of sadness – about the boat's captain, about Lear, about coming to the end of the run.

While we wait at the little bar as usual, the actors and musicians exchange hugs of congratulation and comfort. And then the singing starts. Lear and Gloucester and wicked Edmund raise glasses and, arm in arm, launch into a boisterous medley of folk-tunes. Some of the string players get their instruments and strum along and soon everyone has joined in the singing. Aidan tells me that the songs come from all over former Yugoslavia, from all the regions that so recently fought each other.

The singing doesn't stop when we climb onto the boat, but continues with a stream of local pop tunes, as if all the intensity of *Lear* night after night needs to be melted into music.

When we arrive on Brijuni well after 1 a.m., I see to my amazement that all the tables have been moved out onto the terrace and a huge feast set up. There's an outdoor grill with chicken and kebabs, platters of vegetables (courgettes, aubergines, potatoes, and some I don't recognize), rice, pasta, and two enormous cakes with *Kralj Lear* written in icing. Plus unlimited wine. Plus a dish of tinned tuna, perhaps to remind us of how we normally dine.

We fill our plates and wineglasses and settle down round the tables. There are speeches, and toasts, and when we've eaten and drunk, there is more music. The orchestra sets up their stands, and plays the folk-tunes that it was rehearsing a few nights ago. I'm roped in to playing along, sight-reading in 7/8 while unruly bars of 3/4 and 3/8 flash by at great speed – not exactly second nature to me, especially after a few glasses of wine. Then Ivica suggests that we play Monti's Czardas, as we did on the boat. We've played only a few bars when the actors start grinning and clapping and whistling and suddenly there is a tremendous surge of energy. When we finish, the applause and yelling and cheering continue for an embarrassing length of time . . .

Still the music doesn't stop, with Rade and his children now singing and dancing around the main table. All the children still seem to be wide awake and enjoying the high spirits. Someone even gets *onto* the table and sings. Though the wine is still flowing, nobody is unpleasantly drunk. This is the way to celebrate, with feasting and singing. I don't think I've ever played music *after* a performance; eating and drinking, yes, but no music-making.

At 4 a.m. I'm desperate for sleep but everyone urges me to stay up. 'At least for the dawn. You must stay up till dawn.'

Suddenly at about 5 a.m., it begins to lighten, no spectacular sunrise, just a grey muddy light over the water.

Vocabulary learned today

zbogom gospodine – farewell sire (admittedly not a very useful phrase, but I didn't learn it deliberately. *Zbogom* seems to be Croatian, as opposed to Bosnian.)

kralj – king

čekaj – wait (often heard addressed to children)

hajde – hurry up (often heard addressed to children)

Monday

This schedule is punishing. After three days of performances, plus rehearsals for *Medea* during the day, I'm struggling to stay awake, and I'm not even playing the show. I can understand why most of the orchestra is reluctant to have extra coaching in chamber music. I get up early to see off those who are leaving for Mostar today. There will be just a core of five musicians left for *Medea*.

While I wait with Ivica and Selma and the others at the little dock, someone starts talking about the war, saying that it was started by the West, that western countries gave money to Milošević and Tudjman to buy weapons so that they could break up Yugoslavia.

'And they use small bombs so that people were killed, but houses in cities are not destroyed.'

Newsreels of streets reduced to rubble flash across my mind's eye, but I simply ask, 'Why would they want to do that?'

'So then when war finished, western foreigners can buy buildings.'

Before I can absorb this, the conversation moves on, and I try to catch what I can.

'We in towns we couldn't believe what's happen.' – 'But people living in country, they are uneducated, they have passion, and they drink and getting more passion.' – 'Yes, so when recruiters come they promise exciting things and uniforms, and money, they join militias and start whole thing.' – 'The people in cities are more thoughtful, they respect each other. In the country, people are different.' – 'The Jews were not attacked, they help everyone. With medicine and food, where they can.' – 'Not like the gypsies. They just left.' – 'I like Jews because they helped, and also because they believe in education, they make something of themselves.'

The boat has arrived.

'You will come to Mostar?' asks Ivica.

'*Da*, I hope so,' I say.

'Sinfonietta is very important, very important. It was maybe dangerous to cross bridge to other side to rehearse, but I do it. I don't mind danger. More important to play music together.'

He asks me to please bring some music for bass because it's hard to find teaching material in Bosnia. I'll try to remember.

This afternoon, I go for a brief swim. The nearest beach is very stony, not only the natural white Croatian stone, but red stone too, red stones with ridges – I'm puzzled until eventually I find one that has 'Italia' carved into it: building waste! The water is warm, though refreshingly cool compared to the air, and salty and buoyant and calm.

Then I meet Medea. As I'm walking back up the hill to the barracks, a striking dark-haired woman approaches and starts to speak to me enthusiastically in Croatian. 'Sorry – *Engleski*!'

'OK,' she says in an American accent, 'I just wanted to say thank you for last night – you played with so much fire!'

She is Mira Furlan and has a wonderfully warm smile. I hope we can find time for a relaxed conversation at some point.

It feels strange that there's no *Lear* tonight. A few of the musicians take advantage of the evening off to go over to Fazana to improve on our culinary lottery and have a leisurely dinner. At a normal time.

We find an unpretentious café on the front and indulge in some delicious seafood and a couple of hours of small talk.

'You know,' Aidan says, 'it's hard to believe I've been living in Mostar for five years now.'

'That's a long time,' I say, 'considering it was only supposed to be a few months. How much have things changed since you first arrived?'

'Oh I really feel there's a very big difference to what it was then, just a general atmosphere in the street – that's the real pulse in Mostar, very much on the street.

'There was an incident a year ago when the international community tried to expose a lot of the corruption that's happening, so they raided the bank that they thought was doing all the laundering. Immediately there was a huge demonstration, and all of the exit/entry points between East and West Mostar were blockaded with burnt cars and things like that. But that was the first time anything had happened for a long time. Since then, nothing much to speak of has happened and I hope it continues that way. Apart from the occasional drunken shooting or a hand grenade here or there or whatever.'

He pours himself another beer.

He appears to take it all in his stride, but I wonder how this violence has affected him. On the way back to Brijuni, I get the chance to ask him.

'For me, yes, that was something to really think about. For the locals it was just "oh something else again" sort of thing, and "when is it going to stop", or "we've had enough", or not even, just trying to deal with it, they don't have much choice, you know?

'Your average Mostarian is caught in the middle, and that's not a very nice political divide to be caught in the middle of. I would say that the majority of Mostarians just want to get back to having a fairly sane and normal life, and I think they're already a long way along that road. People are starting to return home, to their houses that they were turned out of some nine/ten years ago. Some of the houses just ended up being empty once they'd been looted, some of them ended up being occupied by others, who may have been refugees themselves, depending what happened. In some cases some guys would just try and have four or five different houses. They'd try and get some people from abroad to come and live in them and pay money and whatever . . . But things do feel like they're being normalized, very slowly, in a kind of difficult, fragmented manner.'

Aidan seems to have a big heart. Always focusing on the Mostarians, being sensitive to their situation.

He turns to me. 'You're probably asking yourself why I've stayed so long. I suppose it's because I just love the place, and I love the people. Especially the people.'

Vocabulary learned today
naravno – of course
do vidjenja – goodbye

Tuesday

A decent night's sleep – seven hours in a row.

Nobody wants to rehearse today, so after breakfast, I wander down to the quay and past the hotels towards the beach. The path leads through a grassy area and suddenly there are table-tennis tables, in the open, on concrete bases. This is my game. But then I see that there's only one net, and I'm staring at it when a young Adonis emerges from a beach hut – would I like to play? He's in charge of the tables.

'*Naravno.*' Of course.

This is fun. We each win a game. He wants me to come back so that we can attract other players to come and play. 'I want people to play. No good if no-one plays.'

I join the Chechnyan singer for lunch. She looks to be in her forties, a little plump, and with dyed blond hair. Her name is Birlyant and her daughter Asya is with her. There is also Darko, a typographer from Ljubljana, Slovenia, who has designed all the posters and other printed material for the theatre.

Birlyant talks haltingly in Russian so that Darko can translate for me. She waits until her daughter has wandered away from the table before telling how the Russians came and crushed the Chechnyans, how her husband, who was a theatre director, was taken one day from the street and never heard of again. She talks about mass graves and how she cried for months. Then she herself was threatened so she had to leave and now she lives in Georgia with her two daughters. But the Georgians don't like the Chechnyans and there is no work. Her husband's family sends her money. I look at her. Her eyes are weary, but she has a sweet smile.

This afternoon I give a two-hour lesson to Rada. She is largely self-taught, she says. Her style is lyrical, smooth and gentle like her personality, but she needs to develop a more solid technique. I sense that she is also shy about playing, and you can't possibly play the violin while hiding in the wings – the instrument needs embracing. So I encourage her, I speak to her confidence so that she can play with more freedom. And then I focus on some technical points, because it's hard to have confidence when you know very well that your technique is unreliable. It's a productive couple of hours and I hope that during the next few days, I can reinforce what she has achieved. I often wonder about the usefulness of one encounter, since I now teach mainly master classes rather than weekly lessons. Perhaps the most I can expect is to have deposited a valuable nugget, preferably one that can expand its reach over time.

Meals are not good today. Lunch is watery soup followed by plain pasta with grated cheese; and supper is simply chips and mashed carrots. But there are plums to finish off with – and suddenly a plum tastes magnificent. Salads are always set out, but after a few days of coleslaw, beetroots and cucumbers, even they don't inspire much enthusiasm, especially when they've been sitting out for hours, a feast for the flies. One of the musicians has been taken to hospital with food poisoning, and there seems to be a question about drinking the water here. Perhaps it's better not to.

Though mealtimes are no gourmet affair – or perhaps *because* they are not – we spend hours at them, chatting in at least four languages: Croatian/Bosnian, English, German and Russian. For me, it's a chance to talk to people about their lives and they all want to tell me their stories. And everyone has a story to tell: of upheaval, exile, danger, bereavement, family strife, economic hardship. And intense bewilderment.

This evening I'm sitting with Darko. When I ask him how he thinks it possible that Yugoslavia had descended into such bloodshed, his immediate response is, 'The media.'

I ask him to explain.

'After Tito died, the heads of each regional parliament wanted to keep their power, and get even more power, and the best way to do that was to split up the country, to make independent states. So they agreed to divide Yugoslavia, yes they agreed, the Serbs and the Croats, and each used the media to spread lies about the others. You read these lies day after day and week after week, and eventually people start believing them.'

Ah yes, the media, as essential for dictatorships as for democracy.

'Now,' he continued, 'the politicians are all the old Communists and there's no effective opposition. Because the intellectuals left the country or stayed out of politics or couldn't get power. So the elections don't really give a choice, they're between the former Communists.'

Another perspective. I want to hear what more people have to say.

As we are sitting out enjoying the evening air, one of the stags that normally gather round the back of the kitchens gingerly approaches the dining area. Suddenly it rears up onto a table, sending everything crashing, then it races off, startled.

Vocabulary learned today
dobro veče – good evening
laku noć – goodnight

Wednesday

This morning I help with a rehearsal for *Medea*. The musicians are going through the Chechnyan songs that Birlyant will sing. She sits in the middle but doesn't sing; she just looks at the floor, shaking her head and mumbling '*ne, nyet*'. Her face is deeply sad and I can't tell if this is the mood of the songs or her reaction to the sounds being made. Probably both. And maybe the songs themselves carry a burden of sadness for her.

As the musicians continue to struggle with the music, I gently ask her to sing, to show them how she would like it to sound. She shakes her head again, saying a word that sounds close to 'tragic'. We don't seem to be making any progress, so I take my violin and play how I imagine the music might go, drawing on some faraway memories of Eastern European harmonies, of the sound of the steppes, of misery, of loneliness. Her eyes widen with surprise and pleasure, '*Da da da*', and I feel something has been released. She gradually opens up and allows herself to sing, though her deep voice is nearly inaudible. It sounds almost strangled.

This afternoon, I play table-tennis with Darko for almost an hour while his young daughter runs around the trees and sometimes picks up the ball. I think that she's impressed by the slamming. Then we all go swimming. I'm glad for these times of simple relaxation that buffer for a while the vague, pervasive tension.

Rada has asked me to help her with Mozart 29th Symphony which the Sinfonietta will play in their next programme, so I give her a long lesson on it. And we also go over the Chechnyan song that she had so much difficulty with this morning. She grasps the mood much better now and is able to produce a richer, more concentrated sound. Her capacity to absorb my suggestions quickly means that we are able to cover a fair amount of material. We discuss fingerings and bowings and articulations and other minutiae of violin-playing. This instrument never gives up on its demands.

I begin to read *Medea*. There are portents on the first page that this will not end well (as if one didn't know). I admire intensely the courage of the company, as well as the spectators, to confront issues that are still alive. The problem of revenge – whether to, when to, how to, how not to – no doubt troubles many people here. And elsewhere.

Supper: tinned corn only. The cuisine has definitely reached a low point.

Vocabulary learned today
Hrvatska – Croatia
HRT(!) – Croatian Radio Television

Thursday

I'm feeling much more relaxed. Last night there was a huge storm and today feels fresher, though the heat is already building. When I come down to the canteen, there is a sign taped to the door. Someone explains that the water is now unsafe to drink, that the local paper is reporting that the water in the whole of Istria is polluted, that maybe there has been an accident (industrial? military?).

No-one wants to work today, so this morning I spend time with Rada and her two young children by the water. As she keeps an eye on them, she tells me, in a kind of pidgin German, about how she tried to get out of Bosnia during the war, how she went every day to the checkpoint and was turned back, how she pleaded with the soldiers to let her through, every day, how one day they said yes, and she made her way to Vienna to become a student. She mostly attributes her personal survival to luck – taking one road instead of another, small random decisions. But it's clear that there is also enormous tenacity.

'Now Mostar is much better, but still there's some tension. Everything was fine before the war, no tension at all. I can't understand how this started, all the animosity. It was the politicians who created the hatred and the violence. That's really so. Now it's hard, there's little work and little money. We always want the old times, they were better, but of course we know that they can never return, we can't go back.'

The same bewilderment, the same questioning.

She tells me that her violin bow is not good and if I come across a better bow, can I please contact her and she will try to save some money to buy it. I say I'll keep my eyes open.

Later I take a walk with Birlyant and Asya who want to see the parrot. We've been told that it talks, but when we approach its cage, it prefers to be sitting pretty and silent near the bars. So we try to engage it in conversation, saying *dobar dan* in various parrot voices. All of a sudden it offers, *Kako ste?* And how are you indeed?

Satisfied, we go off into the fields and Birlyant tells me (through Asya's translation) that she is very happy to be here, because when she is in Georgia, she stays at home all day and is sad. Then she says that she will teach me some Chechnyan tunes that I can play on the violin. And she suddenly stops walking and turns to me and starts to sing, her voice now resonant and coming from a deep place – one woman singing to another in an open field, singing of the land she yearns for. A voice of exile floating on the warm air that carries it away through the trees.

A moment I will never forget.

This afternoon I explore the island. It seems to consist of forests, stony beaches, meadows cropped by herds of deer, some spectacular Roman ruins, the remains of a huge Byzantine fortress, and a beautiful fifteenth-century church from the time when Brijuni was ruled by the Venetians. It smells of the sea and of vegetation. There are pink and white oleander blossoms, cedars, holm oaks, holly, pines and cypresses; lots of birds – peacocks, seagulls, sea-swallows; a herd of zebra, little black squirrels, and huge rabbits. I see a dinosaur's footprint, and an olive tree that's reputed to be 1,600 years old.

It's been a treasure island for archaeologists who've found remnants of human habitation going back to 200 BC. There's a tiny archaeological museum with stunning fragments of frescoes and many beautiful Roman pots and glass vials. And another small museum dedicated to Tito, who came here first in 1947 and spent six months of every year here. There are many photographs of him with the local fishermen and members of his staff; then come the photos of him with statesmen and royalty – Khrushchev, Nehru, Queen Elizabeth – and film stars – Sophia Loren, Richard Burton, Elizabeth Taylor. There's also a room full of stuffed exotic animals. Tito was fond of animals so guests often brought him gifts of lions, ostriches, monkeys, zebras, even a wallaby, and when they died, he had them stuffed.

I sit by the sea before supper and Lear's five-year-old daughter comes to me and starts chatting. She played a very small part in *Lear* and evidently has one in *Medea* as well. She tells me with utmost seriousness and poise that, in real life, everyone will die, just like in *Lear*, some from old age, some from illness, and some when very young. The only moment in *Lear* which she couldn't bear was the blinding of Gloucester. And *Medea* has too much screaming, she says. A five-year-old speaks . . .

I feel like working this evening but everyone seems tired. There is absolutely nothing to do here at night. Even taking a walk is pretty impossible because it's pitch black outside, and the few street lights don't get switched on now that *Lear* has finished. No *Lear*, no lights.

I'm not the only one with energy. Two children start fighting and screaming in the entrance to the canteen. I go to see what's happening and two of Lear's children are doubled up in pain. It seems that they've been really pummelling each other though they each deny wanting to hurt the other. The older one quickly recovers her composure and transforms into a little lady. She talks about the theatre and says that she loves being on stage. 'It's like going into another world. Reading too takes you into another world. I love reading.'

Tonight I finally manage to collect my emails from a computer in the office upstairs. It's strange to make contact with my usual life – from the moment that I arrived on Brijuni, I've felt completely disconnected. Also disconnected from life here. Perhaps it's because I don't have enough of a role. I'm on the periphery, almost an intruder. I wish I could contribute more and be more a part of the community, but there's not much room for someone new, especially someone not intimately involved in the productions.

I drink coffee with Darko. He says that he's separated from his wife. 'It's all right. She wants to go back to Belgrade. I want to stay in Ljubljana.' The displacement of war.

Friday

Today I rent a bicycle. I'm not a bicycle person, but it's fun to speed through the woods and I'm tired of walking to and from the harbour. I zip down to the hotel to buy batteries for my tape recorder, but they don't have any. They promise to order them in from Fazana by 11 a.m. So I coach some of Mozart 29 again and find myself bringing up almost all the points I mentioned the other day. Frustrating but by no means the first time that has happened.

Down to the hotel again at 11 a.m. – no batteries. 'There aren't any batteries in whole Fazana.' I hop on the ferry to Fazana, find batteries, also buy water and two bananas, which I eat immediately, and return to Brijuni, all in an hour.

Lunch turns out to be a real meal for a change – calamari with spinach and potatoes. I sit with Selma and she soon comes back to the subject of the war.

Selma

That's a sad story, and you don't believe it – in Europe, in the twentieth century. And the saddest thing from all is, all these people who were signing openings of these concentration camps are still walking free around Bosnia, still practising politics some of them, it really makes you sick. No-one's even trying to take them to Hague.

And they are really educated people, you just don't get it. If it was anyone without one day of primary school, some stupid idiot, never had the opportunity to live in a mixed area, you would understand. If he was living only with his own people, you would understand. But these were people from the cities, who were actually having these odd, ridiculous, fascistic ideas, and have just something against your name and your surname. My family wasn't practising Muslims at all. Only thing that we had of Muslim religion was our name and surname. And that was the reason that you should be in a camp? Really, that makes you think.

I think that the whole war was a grab for territories. And the idea was to divide Mostar between Croats and Serbs with no Muslims. East Mostar for Serbs and West Mostar for Croats, and Muslims nowhere. But Muslim army defended the territory – not the Muslim army – the Bosnian army, they call it now, but it was all kind of religions there basically. So they were the ones defending the town and people in this army were mainly people from the town itself. Mixed religions. And that was the only reason why Mostar survived like this now. Serbs didn't manage to keep the East side. Some people say that the East side was sold long ago to Serbs for I don't know how much money.

Muslims were supposed to stay in Sarajevo and nowhere else. That was it. Sarajevo and that's as far as it goes. It was obvious. They were trying to make big Croatia or big Serbia. But luckily they didn't succeed in their aims. I don't really follow politics much, I think Dayton Agreement is good as far as I'm concerned just because it stopped the shooting and it's making people live again together. But in Dayton, some people lose, some people win, usually. Depends who's losing or who's winning, which side you get.

I have the feeling that there is a lot more to say, a lot more anger.

I spend the afternoon cycling round the island amid the oaks and oleanders and cypresses. I find the Roman ruins and they are impressive, a temple and large residential complex rising up a gentle slope overlooking a bay. The Romans had an eye for the best locations for their real estate. But now it's decidedly past repair, just a few columns and walls. The view is perfect though, turquoise water slinking round the curve of the bay, and cypresses lining the far shore.

A quick swim and then back to observe a rehearsal of the *Medea* music. Birlyant is not comfortable with her songs and again cannot find a way of communicating with the others. I try to help but things don't come together. Afterwards she smiles at me and insists on teaching me a Chechnyan song which I write down in my little book.

Supper is chips only.

Vocabulary learned today
barcalla – thank you (Chechnyan)
dikdu – good (Chechnyan)

Saturday

I go to the beach this morning with Asya – swim, snorkel and sunbathe – bliss. She's so sweet, always translating at mealtimes for her mother, though she does have sudden moments of frustration, turning away her head abruptly. But mainly she's patient and sociable – and she's only eleven. She has a little keyboard that someone here has given her, and she begs me to write down the Moonlight Sonata for her. A tall order, but I do write down the first few lines; I've never studied it so I hope it's accurately stored in my brain from somewhere. She wants to play it immediately.

'OK, put your fingers over the chord, then it's easier,' I say.

She hesitates before each new chord, looking up at the music and then down at her hands. She is playing her new piece.

This afternoon, I coach some Schubert Quartettsatz. The topic today seems to be rhythmic flexibility. Which is necessary in this work since there's a startling interplay of terror and lyricism. Being able to jump from one to the other is not easy.

'If you each try to feel the music metronomically, you won't be together and most likely it won't sound musical even if you are together. The question is, what kind of pulse is inherent in the music? in this section? at this moment? Is it bouncy? lazy? sultry? driven? nervous?

'What other kind of quality could it have? Does it linger at ends of phrases? at significant harmonies? Or does it stumble on breathlessly?

'And then when you're agreed on what kind of rhythm you want, how do you feel it together? at the same instant? to the same degree? as one?'

The usual questions. The usual issues. So hard to achieve, but so wonderful when everyone's internal pulse and ebb and flow are synchronized. It's like dancing, ballroom dancing, where two partners listen with their bodies to the music and to each other.

I sit in on another rehearsal of the *Medea* music then take the boat over to Mali Brijuni, where they are rehearsing the play. It's a dynamic production. Medea's voice is so deep that it sounds like a man's when she sings. Jason arrives on a motorcycle, and Birlyant speaks and sings in Chechnyan. Ancient Greece seems to be able to absorb all this. Someone gives me a copy of the play in both English and Croatian. Chaos is hovering close to my brain.

Dinner is at 10 p.m.: green beans and potatoes.

Tonight Aidan wears a broad smile: he has just received a fax showing the official registration for the orchestra. 'So now the Mostar Sinfonietta officially exists!'

Vocabulary learned today
so skripachk yu – I am a violinist (Chechnyan)
(That is close to Russian – *ja skripachka*. Sounds a bit like a screeching beginner.)

July 2002

Sunday

I go early to Fazana to buy yet more batteries, and bananas. It's good to sit and drink coffee on the quay. Then I wander round the tiny village which feels built-up and bustling compared with Brijuni. The streets are narrow and higgledy-piggledy, the houses painted in pretty pastels. I go into a souvenir shop and see one shelf of books; among them are Shakespeare's sonnets, the *Diary of Anne Frank*, and *Star Wars*. An eclectic choice. For a souvenir shop.

After another coaching on Schubert and Joplin, I practise for the first time here. It is so hot that perspiration drips down my face. Bach C major solo Sonata. The fugue is a puzzle, as well as being a finger-twister. I've been working at it for years, but today I feel inspired and try some new dynamics and rhythmic group-ings. Much better, but I get cramp in my left-hand fingers. Terrifying.

Dinner is *dobro* – chicken, mash, carrots. While we relax after eating, Birlyant sings some Ukrainian songs for us all. She's loosening up now. When I tell her that my grandfather came from the Ukraine, she tells me that Ukrainian women are very beautiful and that they sing all the time. What an astonishing thought – that there is a land of singers and that I am descended from them . . .

Medea is with us too and says she's unsure if she wants to continue living in Los Angeles, where she put down roots after escaping the war. 'Maybe LA isn't right for me. I don't feel a sense of community.'

Of course I've heard this before about LA, but I say, 'Do you think that playing Medea, who is an exile and doesn't feel at all at home, is possibly influencing your mood?'

She laughs.

'Yes, it's possible. I guess I won't be making any decisions while I'm here.'

I'm introduced to a therapist who works with refugees in the Netherlands. She is visiting here because she knows some of the actors. I ask her about *Medea* and the issue of revenge, and she says that the play illustrates well how the accumulation of trauma, including exile, can lead to loss of control. And how, once the idea of revenge has been conceived, it can become an obsession.

'For instance, one of my clients who was from here actually, wanted to take revenge for what had happened to himself and his family. It's very common, it's part of the culture. After I worked with him for some time, it turned out that he wanted revenge firstly because he thought that his family wanted it, and secondly because he couldn't feel like a man if he didn't take revenge. I suggested that he talk to his family, and when he did, he found out that they did *not* want revenge. That was the first thing.

'Then I asked him if he could think of a situation where revenge was not necessary, in other words, could he give himself permission not to revenge. Yes, he said, if he were working and not thinking about it all the time. So I got him a job and he threw himself into it, really threw himself into it, and he got promoted, and the vengeful feelings dissipated.'

She goes on to suggest that the tendency towards revenge in this region might also be the consequence of enmities from the Second World War not having been fully processed.

'You know, the stories that parents tell their children are very important. They grow up with certain beliefs. And here the stories make them vulnerable to racist propaganda when they become adults. So war becomes more of a possibility. Children need to learn to trust. Not blindly, but with discrimination.'

I mention that the horrific climax of *Medea*, challenging our basic beliefs – and needs – regarding motherhood, enacts something that must also happen in real life.

'Yes, mothers do kill their children – it happens more than you think – and they do it when they lose all hope, when they feel helpless. Medea has lost her home, she's a foreigner in a foreign country, with no friends, no emotional support, no hope of a future. And when her husband leaves her, it's the last straw.'

There's a huge lightning storm. Five minutes of heavy rain. Blue lightning bugs appear on the path. The air is already feeling fresher.

July 2002

Monday

This morning I coach Joplin and Schubert. I bring up the issue of tone colour and how to match sounds. 'There are many ways of changing tone colour – for instance, bow speed. If you move the bow faster, the sound becomes less concentrated, more airy or excited. And if you play near the bridge, it becomes more brilliant; away from the bridge, it is warmer. It can be helpful to look at the others to see how they are using their bows so that you can match the sound. And of course the vibrato affects the sound too – it can be narrow or wide, fast or slow, or none at all.'

Again the basics. Matching rhythms, matching sounds, finding ways to blend, to become as one instrument. Occasionally the music does demand that one voice stands out from the rest, but that's not usually difficult to achieve: we all have our individual way of producing sound, plus each instrument has its individual sound, so the challenge is rather the other way round, the blend, the adjusting, the sensitivity to our colleagues' sound. Listening not only with our ears, but with our eyes.

Lunch, then sleep, then back to Mali Brijuni for a complete run-through of *Medea*. It's a powerful play, not simply about a 'mad' woman who kills her children, but a complex portrait of a person under intolerable stress. The issue of exile is illustrated brilliantly by having Birlyant speaking in Chechnyan, a language that sounds very strange. Her language separates her from the other actors, as well as from the spectators. She's the foreigner in the community, the outsider, and Birlyant *is* a refugee, she *does* find it hard to make herself understood. But the songs she sings convey her heartache and homesickness and make us feel for her.

This is my last boat ride. It's a very dark night. Apart from the wake, the water is black.

I don't want to leave. It's good to be out of doors for so many hours in the day, to be on the water, and in the water, to feel the heaviness of the air. To be with so many fascinating people from so many different countries. And to be in touch with great theatre, powerful issues, lives lived intensely.

After supper, at about midnight, the quartet performs the

Schubert and Joplin outside on the terrace. They play better than they have ever done. When the music starts, the tiredness of the theatre company seems to lift and a balm seems to settle on the air. Schubert under the night sky. Sublime.

Joplin, bouncy and relaxed. Light relief from the torture of the plays.

The actors love it. Jason comes up to me and gives me a big kiss. 'Why didn't you play for us every night?'

I chuckle. 'If only you knew how much preparation *this* took!'

It's good to feel that I have contributed something, not only to the musicians but to the community as a whole. Aidan tells me that he's glad that I was able to 'feel the pulse of the situation and have fitted in well, not something all our visitors have been able to do'. I am beginning to understand that 'fitting in' does not necessarily feel comfortable, and is not necessarily obvious when it's happening.

An outsider seeking the pulse, listening, watching, blending.

Tuesday

My last morning on Brijuni. I feel a calm sadness.

After breakfast, we have fun reading the Stamitz clarinet quartet. I insist on everyone cueing and moving and phrasing – I'm not going to let them get away with their old habits just because it's my last day! I also sit in on another rehearsal of the *Medea* music and manage a little yoga too.

At lunch, heavy rain soaks the tables (and some of us), so we all move indoors. I finally find Mira and she tells me her story.

Mira

'Medea' has a special resonance definitely, and there are special reasons to do it right here in this place where hatreds were so great, and hatred couldn't be transcended, and hatred and fight is continuing over the dead bodies, which is exactly what happens in

Medea. *Their struggle continues even after the whole catastrophe
happens. It's a play about humans not being able to transcend
their hatred and that's exactly when wars happen, and that's
what happened in our country.*

*You know also it's a play about the positive energy of love being
transformed into this incredibly dangerous, negative energy of
destruction, which is again something that happened here. We all
kind of 'loved' each other – you know there was this slogan of
brotherhood and unity and so on. We were the happiest place on
earth, that's what we were taught in schools. And then all at once
there was unbelievable bloodshed and incredible violence and
horrible hatred all over the place. Which, you know, you can see in*
Medea. *It's not only a man-woman relationship kind of play
but also a metaphor for wars, and this inability to transcend
opposition and struggle and hatred and so on.*

*For me on many levels it's incredibly interesting and it's a very
important experience, I think, in my life to be back and to play in
my own language, which I haven't used on stage, in TV or on film
in . . . I haven't used it in eleven years! So just to be able to speak
that language is . . . an experience. I don't want to say 'wonderful'
or this or that, I don't want to label it, but it's a very deep and
important experience. And to be here, and to work with people who
I haven't seen in such a long time and so on.*

*Also it's a particularly strong, female play which I enjoy so
much because the position of women in this society – I mean all
over the world, in every society more or less, but specially in this
society – is so despicable I would say. Yeah, absolutely despicable.
And in a way my whole story of being exiled and being blacklisted
and so on and so on, at the beginning of the war, could never
happen in that particular form to a man. It could only happen to
a woman. To a woman actor, you know, whose morals are always
questioned. So the insult was very very . . . it had a very, how
would I say . . . sexual content. Which was particularly hurtful.
And that's why, in a way, 'Medea' is a play about revenge, so in a
way, in a* good *sense, it's* my *revenge, you know?! . . . ha ha ha . . .
but via theatre, through theatre, and I think that's . . . through
strength, you know?*

Before I went to Los Angeles, I lived in Zagreb, and then I lived

*between Zagreb and Belgrade, which as you can imagine created
big big big problems when the war started, because I'm married
. . . I happened to fall in love with a person who is actually from
Zagreb, but he's of Serbian descent. He's a director, and he went to
study in Belgrade, and his whole work was in Belgrade. So my life
was between those two cities. Also I happened to be a, you know, a
Yugoslav actress, just because I worked so much in film and TV
and theatre all over the country which was called former Yugoslavia. And that idea of being able to cross borders and to live in
all the places and to work there, when the war began, had to be
exterminated, had to be . . . annihilated. And people like me and
Rade were annihilated along with that idea.*

*The work didn't just dry up, no no no, it was much more
dramatic than that. There was a media campaign, of big proportions, where every single paper was throwing stones at us. I mean
writing about our private lives, analysing the nationality of our
high-school boyfriends, since kindergarten to all the relationships
in your whole life. It was all analysed through the prism of
nationalism and, I would say, there was definitely an element of
fascism in the whole thing.*

*Then it all resulted in death threats that were coming to me,
something like a hundred a day, I'm not exaggerating. So it was
really about my life, I mean it was my safety which was an issue.
And I realized that I cannot be an actor any more, that I became a
symbol, I was transformed into an idea. And you know an idea
cannot act on stage, because people either applaud, or they throw
stones at you, but all for wrong reasons, it has nothing to do
with your work. That's when my husband and I decided to leave.
And we left and went to New York, which was always my
favourite city.*

*There were no soldiers with bayonets and so on, but it was very
difficult to leave, I mean emotionally and psychologically because
you were leaving your whole life. Everything that you've achieved.
Everything. I mean property and your friends, and your status
and your career and your network, let's say, that you built
throughout your life and that's been all erased.*

*So we really truly had to start from zero and that's what we did.
And then you know, I got a job in Los Angeles on a TV series called*

Babylon Five, *and I did it for five years and that moved me to LA where I live now. And this is my first time that I came back after eleven years, to play this thing.*

It's great to be here you know, but I was very, very afraid. And I had many, many doubts. But I'm happy that I did it. Although of course, you have to compromise. And compromise is an everyday occurrence, in terms of the pressure to do interviews with people who were kind of the same people that attacked me eleven years ago and so on. So I'm . . . there are no . . . there's no . . . there are no clean stories. I mean, this idea of purity and staying clean is just unachievable. And you have to kind of . . . and that's the package, you know, you kind of accept the whole package, you know? These politicians that you don't agree with all at once are sitting at your table and you are shaking hands with them and you feel what am I doing? why did I even go away? why did I pack my suitcase and leave everything behind? It all gets to be very messy. But apart from that we are doing this beautiful play . . .

We both go into the bathroom and while she puts on her make-up, Mira tells me that she is really nervous about meeting the journalist who is waiting for her. There is fear in her eyes.

I pack hurriedly and run down to the waterfront to say goodbye to everyone before the boat takes them away to rehearse. It appears that the rehearsal is delayed because the boat has been commandeered by the President who arrived yesterday.

The goodbyes are sweet. We've agreed that I will come to Mostar in December for a couple of concerts, so I will see them soon.

Aidan and Asya walk with me to the Italian ferry and help with my luggage. I give Asya my yellow cotton sunhat which she's admired several times. I'd bought it on tour in San Diego, a quick purchase in the 1980s becoming a gift to a Chechnyan refugee in 2002 – the unexpected journey of a hat.

I embark and find a seat next to a window. As the large ferry pulls out and the green island starts floating into the distance, the last twelve days begin to toss inside my head, as if caught in the broad white wake of the boat – the people, the music, *Lear*, *Medea*, Brijuni, rehearsals, conversations, the big party . . .

And I feel more and more astonished at how my work as a musician has led me into such a rich, unexpected world.

And this is only the first chapter.

Next stop, Mostar.

December 2002

A violin bow for Rada.

I hadn't forgotten her request. A decent bow could make quite a difference to her playing, would give her more of a chance to produce an even sound, crisp articulation, springy spiccato. But a good bow with a strong, flexible stick can cost several thousand pounds, probably more than she can afford.

I picked up the phone. 'Aleth? Do you think you could help me find a bow for the leader of the Mostar Sinfonietta?'

Aleth Michel is a rare bird – a young female violin-maker, French, living in Bristol. A few years ago she made me a 'second' violin, one for taking to countries where the customs officials – shall we say – make me nervous, or the weather is extreme, or where things are just too unpredictable. (Bosnia would fit at least two of these categories.) And Aleth knows about bows since many come her way for re-hairing.

Not only could she help, she thought we could raise enough money to buy a bow for Rada. The idea galvanized us both. If we succeeded, I would present the bow to the Sinfonietta, for the use of Rada. We had only four months though, if I was to take it with me to Mostar in December.

Aleth's enthusiasm propelled us into a frenzy of fund-raising. I wrote out a notice on my computer which I sent to music and instrument shops to put in their windows, appealing not only for donations, but also for letters of support and encouragement to the musicians of Mostar. Aleth organized cake sales during rehearsals of the amateur orchestras in which she plays. We both talked about the 'Mostar bow' everywhere we went.

The response was tremendous. People seemed grateful to be able to make a concrete contribution that was specific and personal, a small way of tipping the balance against all those helpless, hopeless moments in the face of faraway disasters. Many wrote touching letters – those who had been to Mostar before the war, amateur musicians who knew the value of playing music, ordinary people who wanted to send a word of encouragement directly to those who had suffered.

One man passing by a music shop was so intrigued by the notice in the window that he not only gave a donation but found himself eventually travelling to Mostar and meeting Rada, and writing a booklet of poems about the 'Mostar Bow'.

Meanwhile I started to spread the word to audiences at my concerts, suggesting that they give a contribution in proportion to how much they enjoy the second encore. (Yes, it could have been embarrassing . . .) On one occasion, I gilded the lily by walking out for said encore in a rather fetching 1920s hat which was lying in a stash of theatrical costumes backstage. I also balanced a large top hat upon the head of my pianist, allowing him to tower over me to an even greater extent than usual. Hatted thus, we played our Elgar encore, then threw the hats towards the door and listened as the banknotes and cheques silently filled them up.

Meanwhile, Aleth and I found two bow dealers who very generously each lent a bow for me to take to Rada, from which she could choose one that would suit her style of playing and her violin. When it was time to leave for Mostar, I was able to pack two bows, a scrapbook full of letters for the Sinfonietta, and bags of donated strings, resin, music and CDs.

I also brought the orchestral music for the concerts. I'd decided to start the programme by playing the beautiful Adagio and two Rondos by Mozart for solo violin and orchestra, to be followed by Haydn's Symphony No. 88 and the Joplin Rags that the quartet had explored on Brijuni.

Reconstruction of Stari Most

Preparatory works for the crane electricity power supply.
Crane mounted on concreted platform.
Iron anchors 2 metres long nailed down into rocks on both banks, and foundations concreted for the centering (bridge scaffolding).
Pontoon built spanning the river, communication deck laid.
Steel trusses and girders placed across river. Heavy scaffolding erected following arch of bridge.
Eight temporary geotechnical anchors 15 metres long fixed in concrete pillars to withstand concentrated force of arch stones during construction.
Archaeological excavation continued on both banks.

Tuesday

It is snowing and the snow is making everything beautiful.

The plane was on time, but Aidan is nowhere to be seen. Sarajevo Airport reminds me of many a nondescript East European airport – a long, low building with one booth for changing money, one for organizing hire cars, and one that sells third-rate postcards. I finally sit on a bench and stare out at the snow steadily veiling the cars in the car park.

I'm looking forward to seeing the musicians again, and excited about conducting two concerts with them, but I'm also aware of a little knot of anxiety which I try to ignore. After an hour, in comes Aidan, apologetic about traffic and snow and schedules, and soon we are driving into town. I don't see much of our surroundings, or is it that the outskirts of Sarajevo are drab and uninteresting? I think I'm too focused on what Aidan is saying: that we're on our way to have supper with a Swedish oboist – ah yes, there are no oboists in Bosnia – he's called Daniel and he's the teacher of the two fledgling oboists (still in school) who will play the concerts; and tomorrow Aidan will take me to the Sarajevo School for the Blind where some of the Mostar musicians teach; and he'll find somewhere to photocopy the orchestra music that I've brought with me; and there's very little work here; and the music scene in Sarajevo is run by two men who can't stand the sight of each other and the poor musicians are caught in the middle. And tomorrow's rehearsal won't be happening because not enough players are available, so he'll drive us to Mostar tomorrow evening.

I think I'm exhausted already.

Wednesday

The handful of musicians working at the School for the Blind in Sarajevo are all in their twenties, very enthusiastic, lovely people, and they use music to develop many skills – listening, memorizing, spatial memory, counting – as well as teaching songs. When I enter Aidan's first class, I see about fifteen children, aged around seven to ten, sitting round a large wooden table with a couple of teachers among them. I'm introduced as an English visitor, which seems to be the cue for the *Dobrodošli* song – *Welcome* song – which has numerous verses and has obviously been sung many times before. I notice that it has seven beats in the bar but nobody here seems to have any trouble with it, which certainly wouldn't be the case in England. Then the teachers empty a sackful of percussion instruments onto the table and proceed with a game in which the children try to identify the sounds of rattles, tambourines, and all kinds of drums. Everyone gets to touch and play the instruments and there's a fair degree of excitement. In the next class the children sing and bounce on big rubber balls and there's lots of giggling. The atmosphere is really lovely.

In between classes, some of the music team tell me that they all need to support their parents as well as themselves because there's so little work. So they are constantly looking for more income.

When we leave, I remind Aidan that we need to get some of the orchestra parts copied for the rehearsal tomorrow. The first copy-shop we find runs out of paper, but the second place is very efficient. It's a thriving business – some customers seem to be copying whole books, which would explain why the copy-shops run out of paper. 'Yes, it's cheaper than buying them,' Aidan says. 'In any case, you can't get books easily here.'

We have tea in a café nearby. Two middle-aged women recognize Aidan and join our table. They speak English well and offer to drive us into town. During the ride, one tells me a little of how it was to live through the siege of Sarajevo. How maddening it was to have to stay indoors with no human contact – no telephone – for a year, how people went crazy and ran outside without thinking and were killed. How, when it was safer, just going to the next street was an event. That all she ate was bread, oil and rice. That she never eats rice now.

This evening is a special occasion for the students of the Blind School. They live at the School and go out only two or three times a year, but tonight they are giving a music and dance performance for the International Women's Club in a small art gallery. Aidan and I arrive at the venue just as a van is disgorging the students. They are chatting excitedly and I'm touched to see how the partially sighted children help those who are totally blind.

After a short rehearsal, the room fills up with about fifty women, and the children come out and do their stuff. Two brilliant drummers, one of them a Roma, raise a storm with fantastically complex rhythms, more children emerge and sing a medley of songs, and then half a dozen of the older girls, aged between fourteen and sixteen, do a dance routine. It's hard to imagine how they are able to move and position themselves so accurately, never mind remember the irregular Balkan rhythms. But they all throw themselves into the music and their bodies find the beat and their faces shine with the thrill of it.

It's ten o'clock and finally time for Aidan and me to leave for Mostar. It will be a two-hour drive so there's plenty of time for easy conversation. The road is winding and the dark countryside rolls past, hiding its secrets. Occasionally the headlights catch an abandoned farmhouse, roofless, windowless, shattered. The talk gradually turns to the war, a tendency that seems to be inevitable.

'What they did, it's unbelievable. These bands of militias, if you want to call them that, sometimes Serbs, sometimes Croats, they'd come into a village and grab the first person they'd see and demand to be told who the Muslims were. If the person told, all the Muslims were killed – if he didn't, *he* was killed. Then things got more nasty, because sometimes, people would rather die than tell. So then they'd grab a child and say, "We'll kill the child if you don't point out the Muslims." That was an impossible choice. The person who told, or didn't tell, either way, he had blood on his hands. He was broken. And many Muslims were betrayed.'

Now I'm beginning to understand the nuts and bolts of how a village can be split, how neighbours can become enemies, how people can be broken, how a society can be torn apart.

It's so easy. It would work anywhere. You only need a handful of killers, let out of prison for the purpose, to start the ball rolling. It would gather speed of its own accord.

You don't need a violent society.

Or a backward society.

You just need someone to set the ball rolling.

And how would I react? How could I watch a child being shot? or hear my neighbours being shot?

How could I live without a consuming hate for those who did this to them? how could I live with the guilt and the hatred and the memory?

How could I live at all?

'It's understandable that there's so much ill feeling,' Aidan says.

How can any of them live together now?

❦

We drive into Mostar well after midnight. The destruction here was worse than in any other city caught up in the war, but it is very dark and I can see only ordinary square buildings. Occasionally we pass a roofless shell, left like a wounded beast. There are no people about. We drive over the river, over a modern bridge that has a few paltry Christmas lights on it.

And then we come to the road that was the front line. A long street of finely proportioned buildings completely abandoned. Three or four storeys with gouged-out windows, pock-marked with shrapnel, fire-damaged, roofless, huge black oblong holes.

The car speeds up.

We cross the river again into the East side, and pull up outside the Pavarotti Centre, once a large school built in the days of the Kaiser, bombed to bits during the recent war, and rebuilt as a music school with funds raised by Pavarotti. Next to it is a building, roofless and windowless, that has a sign on the front saying 'Attention: Dangerous Ruin' in Bosnian and English.

The Pavarotti Centre has two apartments and I'm staying in one of them. The outside is in the old style but the inside is modern – well, 1960s modern, though it was built only a few years ago.

I say goodbye to Aidan. I'm shivering – it's very cold and there doesn't seem to be any heat.

Vocabulary learned today
dobrodošli – welcome
drago mi je – pleased to meet you

Thursday

It is freezing in this apartment. I do manage to have a good hot shower, but there's no shower curtain so the water spills all over the floor. The flat is characterless and efficient like many another all over the West – open-plan kitchen/dining/living room, Formica and wood, two small bedrooms (bed, night-table, wardrobe), and two bathrooms. A narrow balcony looks out over some non-descript buildings that climb the hills in the back.

I'm just starting to practise when one of the Blind School team calls from downstairs. '*Dobar dan*, it's Toni, how are you?'

'*Dobro*, thanks.'

'I can show you some Mostar, if you like to come.'

I can't resist. Practising will have to wait. In a few minutes I step out into the sunshine onto Ulica Marsala Tita (Marshal Tito Street), a sad street with the odd shop and bar scattered among ruined buildings. Toni is fairly short, like me, and walks with an easy gait.

'Mostar is small town, built in valley of River Neretva. Next to river is old part, most built by Turks, maybe four hundred years ago.'

Soon we are walking on a white cobbled street, lined with little white houses with white stone roofs. It is very beautiful. White stone is used for everything. There are steps leading down to the river and they go at oblique angles with little cafés dotted around. The river itself is an astonishing emerald green and it moves fast. As we walk on, Toni identifies buildings: 'That used to be big hotel, that used to be Turkish baths and that was one of Tito's palaces.' They are huge pock-marked shells.

The main goal of the walk is of course the famous Old Bridge, the Stari Most, or rather what remains of it. You can see the beginnings of the span on both banks, like stumps, high above the river. Stones that haven't been exposed since they were placed there in the 1500s are now open to the air, and to our eyes.

A temporary wooden bridge has been slung over to allow pedestrians to cross while Stari Most is being rebuilt. There's a beehive of activity. Many of its stones have been recovered from the river and are piled high on a big platform, and there's a very large crane and scores of workers putting up scaffolding around the ruined towers. It will be rebuilt exactly as it was, and with the same techniques, and a small version – like a maquette – has been constructed spanning a tributary nearby. This is breathtakingly beautiful, a distinctive arch, pristine white. A sign announces the opening of Stari Most in January 2004. That's little more than a year. I'm eager to see it when it opens.

It was 1983 when I became enamoured of bridges. That was the centenary of the Brooklyn Bridge, and like most New Yorkers (I'd lived there fifteen years by then, so counted myself as one of them), I'd grown to think of it as my favourite bridge. I loved its patterns of cables, its height, its strong stone towers. The centenary spawned many articles about its history and construction and I remember taking books out of the library as I became more and more puzzled as to how the caissons could possibly be sunk and how the span could possibly be raised and how the whole thing could possibly fit together. The moment of joining the two halves of the span, as they crept towards each other from the banks of Brooklyn and Manhattan, was in fact frustrated by the unseasonable weather, which prevented them from meeting in the middle. The temperature and humidity had to be perfect for the material to be neither expanded nor contracted. More than 150,000 people walked across the Brooklyn Bridge on the day it opened. Later, it was acknowledged that the diagonal cables that were added to brace the structure and that make it unique were not necessary. Bridges have fascinated me ever since.

Toni tells me that during the war, all nine bridges in Mostar were bombed, so people could cross the river only by boat or makeshift pedestrian spans. The front line, the street that I saw last night, is a little way into the West side. 'It was very important we hold front line, important we are not pushed to river. Otherwise . . .' He pauses.

'Is it always this colour?'

'The strange green colour yes, is mineral deposits. The current is usually very strong. It's possible to swimming but not easy. You must be very strong swimmer.'

At one point, we come to a place where there used to be another bridge. The road simply stops at the top of the cliff without any safety barrier. I look over and there's a rusting car smashed up on a pile of rubble far below. 'People say somebody was probably drunk and forgot bridge wasn't there, and just drove off edge.'

Amid all the rebuilding and beautiful stone, there are the ghosts of buildings, hollowed-out death-traps, with or without the 'Attention: Dangerous Ruin' signs. 'Big big stones fall off these buildings sometimes so better not walk close.'

'So that means we have to walk on the road?'

'Yeah, it's either stone or car.' Toni smiles.

Although badly damaged these ghosts look sturdy, Austrian-Empire style with ornate plasterwork occasionally visible between the shrapnel marks; but they feel like black holes, ready to swallow you up. In one, a kitchen table still stands in the ruins and I imagine how the domesticity of that kitchen must have been shattered by the moment of impact of the shell. Some buildings have sprouted saplings that grow through the upper floors, rooted in some crevice in the wall, reaching for the sky.

And I think how the people living here can't avoid these reminders of the war. Right in the middle of town we pass a new cemetery with startlingly white headstones. Some have photographs of those buried – young, fresh faces mostly; almost all were in their twenties when they died. Most died in '93 or '94.

Toni runs into a friend of his who, after we're introduced, explains that the narrow valley and steep hills on either side of the Neretva made the town vulnerable to shelling. 'See, the Serbs shell us from that hill and Croats shell us from this hill.'

He says, 'Here, on this street, on this corner, was where all Mostarians were together against enemy, Mostarian Muslims, Serbs, Croats, we were together, stood together here and fought. Because we are all Mostarians.'

Toni tells me he was caught up in Sarajevo during the siege, and before that, when he was about fourteen or fifteen years old, he was in a Serbian work camp and 'was very badly treated'. I can see scars on his forehead. Perhaps his easy gait is more of a swagger, and I can understand this as a kind of defiance. I ask him how he adjusted to life after the war and he says, 'By forgetting it all. It's only way you can live, just forget it.'

Toni and his friend leave and I pick up a greasy pastry filled with potatoes, before going back to the flat to practise and mark the orchestra music. I'd like to pencil all my personal interpretation marks – phrasing and dynamics and tempo changes – into everyone's parts, and it takes a great deal of time. I want to avoid the situation that I've witnessed many a time when the conductor is simply repeating what he'd said in a previous rehearsal. Not to mention many a concert where the players struggle to remember what they've rehearsed. Nobody's memory is infallible but there are always players who are unwilling to mark their parts. Even if they've remembered to bring a pencil. (I've brought with me twenty pencils, oversized tourist-from-London pencils, to hand out as little gifts and big hints.) In any case, my putting in the marks now precludes misunderstandings. It's interesting that the best orchestral players do mark their parts and it shows. You can hear if everyone is shaping the music in the same way.

Finally the first rehearsal. Aidan arrives at about 6 p.m. bringing music stands. We are rehearsing in the flat since very few musicians can come. He explains that it's a scheduling nightmare. Selma, the first flute, is available only on Friday and Sunday, and the principal second violin has to miss two important rehearsals. We consider having somebody else lead the seconds, but the only other possible candidate has to miss three rehearsals. It's a jigsaw and I need to think carefully how to organize the rehearsals so that everybody gets enough time with each piece.

Suzana, the violist wife of Ivica the bass player, is the next to arrive. We hadn't spoken much on Brijuni – she doesn't have much English – but it's nice to see a familiar face and hers is kind and maternal. I'm then introduced to an older violinist, Miro, who, Aidan tells me, hasn't played much violin since his schooldays, but is conscientious in his preparation. *'Drago mi je.'*

'Drago mi je.'

He smiles and nods in the way people do when there is no common language.

So we start with a three-player sectional, Aidan translating, and we do some good quality work. After an hour, Rada arrives and we greet each other like old friends.

'Dobro veče! Kako ste? Wie geht's?'

Two more players arrive, so we – almost – have a quorum. One of the schools' music team who plays the clarinet obliges by playing the cello part, as there's no cellist in Mostar (Aidan is importing one from Sarajevo). I decide that the best thing is to read through most of the programme so that's what we do. Now they know what's in store. And so do I.

By the time we finish, it's 9.30 p.m. and I haven't eaten a proper meal for two days. So Aidan takes me to a restaurant by the river where we have trout and Swiss chard and potatoes and it's very good. And after that he takes me to a bar where he is to play some Bosnian folk music with a singer friend. The bar is noisy and smoky and lively with chatter, drinking, laughter – and singing.

Teo is the most amazing singer of the most amazing music I've heard for a long while. He is young and well built with a chubby face, and while accompanying himself on the guitar he sings in a voice that is smooth, dark and has the most enormous wobble. What's utterly unexpected is that the wobbly vibrato is what's exciting – it gives the long notes colour and warmth and exoticism. The music itself is Balkan and is called sevdah, which Aidan describes as 'soul' or 'love'. It sounds like a meld of gypsy, Greek, Turkish, Romanian . . . I'm entranced. Then Toni walks in with his little drum, and joins Teo and Aidan who is now improvising on violin. The evening lifts off, taking me with it.

My first day in Mostar. From one extreme to the other.

Vocabulary learned today
proba – rehearsal
divno – wonderful

Friday

Another freezing night. I seem to put on almost as many layers of clothing to go to bed as I do when I get up.

Suzana phones early this morning: '*Molim*, students – lesson – come please.' She wants me to hear her students. There are two floors of small teaching studios and classrooms in the Pavarotti Centre – fortunately the sound doesn't seem to travel up to my apartment – so she's just downstairs. I go immediately and listen to two young girls who have recently started lessons. Suzana asks if I can show them anything so I teach them how to be 'sirens' (the fire-engine kind) and they love it. It's a good exercise for stretching the left hand and for flexibility of the finger joints. Suzana has brought a loaf of home-made bread, something between bread and a crumpet, and she gives it to me with a jar of home-made jam. I'm very touched.

The rest of the day I spend practising and marking parts, apart from being summoned to help with two more of Suzana's students, boys this time. I go out for some fresh air and see that there are many little posters on the buildings, with simple type, bordered in green or black, and some of them have a photograph. I realize that they're death notices, announcing recent deaths. And I remember walking the streets of New York soon after September 11th and seeing all the hastily made posters of the missing plastered on every surface, the agony of the wait so clear, the snap-shots of the missing taken at parties or on the beach, smiling, sometimes with a glass in their hand.

I find a little café near the Stari Most. The waitress is young, in her twenties perhaps, and gentle. As she sets down my food, she blurts out (in German):

Waitress

My brother died during the war. But not in the fighting – he was killed in a road accident. And everyone else was dying fighting, or being killed as a result of the war. His death was kind of ignored – it wasn't the same as the others. Nobody paid much attention. It was terrible for me. I couldn't mourn, during the whole war, I couldn't mourn.

A sister's loss diminished. Unnatural and violent, but a common road accident nonetheless. This is a waste of a death, a young life lost unnecessarily – it should have been a shell at least, or enemy fire on the front line.

In time of war, an ordinary death is not possible.

❧

Evening rehearsal. It's nice to see Ivica, dragging in his bass.

'*Kako ste?* How's life?' I ask him.

'OK, but I'm afraid.'

'What has happened?'

'*Ne*, nothing, but I expect violence, danger. All the time. This is Mostar.'

Then Selma arrives.

'I'm looking forward to this,' she says, taking out her flute.

There are seven players now, including two flutes, so the music is beginning to sound slightly less skeletal. These early rehearsals are basically to enable the players to get acquainted with their parts and to hear how the lines fit together.

During the break, I ask Selma, 'What will the audience be like? Will people come?'

'Hard to say. Mostar is a place with a great history of culture in many ways,' she says, 'not just music, but art and everything you mention basically. It was really centre of culture of ex-Yugoslavia. But the problem with Mostar now is all these people who were used to coming to these shows or exhibitions or whatever, they have gone and didn't return since the war. So now you have all these people from surrounding villages who came to Mostar during the war, and they are not the kind of audience that has been educated in that way. So it's very hard. Every time we have a concert it's a struggle. You never know. For example if we say that we are going to play sevdah, which is a folk music, you'll have a full hall. But if it's any kind of classical things, it's usually ten people in the audience.'

'Oh dear,' I say, 'if there are only ten people, then there'll be more of us musicians than people in the audience. I remember when I was in the US, we used to say that if there were more people on stage than in the audience, we wouldn't play. Of course, not if we were a huge orchestra . . .'

'What Vassili said, in Russia, it's a strange custom, you know, if during the Communism period, if you had to play concert in some place where there isn't many people, if there is nine people they wouldn't keep a concert, if there is ten they would have a concert. So that was the breaking number. If there's ten or more you have a concert, if there's less than ten you don't have a concert.'

I don't relish the prospect of the Sinfonietta performing for ten people. Or fewer. Not after all the work they are going to put in. And surely there are people here who would love to have the opportunity to hear classical music. I put it out of my mind and resume the rehearsal.

When we finish, I know that this is the right time to present the gifts I've brought from England, including, of course, The Bow. I call Aidan to translate and begin by saying that I've talked a lot about the Sinfonietta in England, and that people there have responded very generously. I hand out the resin and the strings and show them the pile of music and CDs. 'Choose whatever you would like.' Ivica immediately riffles through the CDs.

'But I have one very special gift,' and I bring out the two bows. Rada, astonished, comes up to me and whispers, '*Hvala, hvala,* you remembered,' and hugs me and we both have tears in our eyes.

'*Sie helfen mich ein wählen?*'

'Yes, I'll help you choose one,' and I hear that everyone in the room is applauding.

'And one more thing,' I say. And I bring out the book that I've prepared with all the letters and poems, and everybody crowds round while Aidan tries to translate them.

'Dear members of the Mostar Sinfonietta, I believe the work you are doing is very important in rebuilding cross-community ties and I have great admiration for your determination and commitment. Please accept this donation as a small gesture of solidarity from musicians of Bristol.'

'. . . music can generate a sense of identity and belonging within a community. It is my hope for you all that your love of music and for one another will continue to grow . . .'

'. . . I feel very lucky that I can live and work in peace and freedom. I think the work you are doing in Mostar is wonderful – I believe music can be healing. I hope that some of the music and recordings I have collected are useful for the Sinfonietta . . .'

'I am eleven years old. Take some money – you need it more than me at the moment . . .'

'. . . may your music transcend all barriers and build bridges . . .'

This moment marks the end of the project. There were many times when I thought we wouldn't succeed and I'm still amazed we managed it, Aleth and I, managed to raise the money and find the bows and prepare the book, and to do it all in time. Now I'm thrilled and relieved to see a huddle of bodies exclaiming and pointing . . . In the end, it's not so much the gifts themselves, but the connecting with strangers, anonymous friends, whose words and generosity show that the Bosnians are not forgotten, not isolated like they felt they were when the world watched as they endured war.

When everyone has left, I make myself a cup of tea and try to relax. But I'm feeling quite anxious. Only two weeks ago, I'd found a new, more 'authentic' edition of the Mozart pieces for violin and orchestra, which differs in many places from the edition I was using before. There are even different notes so I have to relearn some passages. And I'm also anxious about the conducting, whether my beat is clear enough. And about the Sinfonietta, whether I can get them to respond to the music, to cohere and to sound like a little orchestra. More players are coming from the Sarajevo Academy and I've been told they're not experienced. Some have never even played in an orchestra before. And whether there'll be any audience at all . . .

Vocabulary learned today
sviramo – we play
ponovo – again (as in 'again please', *ponovo molim*, essential for rehearsals)

Saturday

This morning while I'm working on my scores, there's a knock at the door and two white-coated women wordlessly bring in five sponge mattresses and lay them side by side on the floor of the main room. Each is then neatly made up with crisp white sheets, a blanket and a couple of towels, making 'my' living room resemble a makeshift dorm, or an emergency rescue centre. Which I suppose it is, as the Sarajevo half of the orchestra are coming in for the weekend and this is their billet. The spare bedroom is also prepared for one of the cellists, who is pregnant.

The invasion takes place at around noon, six young women with instruments and backpacks, so after saying a quick hello, I leave them to settle in and go out for a brief lunch. When I return, the CD player is blaring jazz and, now joined by three young male musicians who are staying in the other apartment, they are all smoking and having a great time. This is going to be an interesting weekend.

So, our first full rehearsal, nineteen players in all. We are now downstairs in a small hall where the concert will actually take place. I've scheduled to start at 3 p.m. and work until about 7.15 p.m. with a forty-five minute break. I've planned a careful timetable for the weekend's rehearsals, estimating the amount of time needed for every movement of each piece, making sure that each movement gets rehearsed twice so that the work we do is reinforced; and scheduling a complete run of the Haydn Symphony at the end of tomorrow's rehearsal to give the players a feel of the work as a whole, and to identify any places that are still insecure. The Sarajevo contingent will leave tomorrow evening and come back only on Wednesday, the day of the concert, so I'm hoping I've been realistic with the planning. But it's difficult to make decisions when I've no idea how the new players actually play. And I've no idea how well or how quickly everyone can gel. It can be a disaster if a timetable isn't meticulously organized and adhered to. I seem to remember performing a Brahms symphony in New York soon after my student days, and upon reaching the last movement, looking at pages of notes that I'd never seen before! There was equal horror on everyone's faces.

I've also scheduled in the rehearsal breaks, though I sense that musicians here don't expect regular breaks. Unlike in New York, where the union will come down hard and fast on any cavalier conductor. I think breaks are needed for many reasons – for good concentration, to allow everyone to get up and stretch and make phone calls and drink coffee, to give the muscles a rest, to allow some emergency practising of unexpectedly difficult passages, and not least to show respect to the players. I tell them when the breaks will be so that they can pace themselves, and I try to organize things so that the movements which don't have the full complement of winds are rehearsed at the beginning or the end. There's nothing more likely to annoy a wind player than being told they are not needed for fifteen minutes just when they've struggled to arrive on time, or have rushed their coffee break. On the other hand, I can't avoid some hanging around because, for instance, the

Mozart Adagio uses flutes but not oboes, whereas the other two Mozart pieces are scored for oboes but not flutes.

We get off to a bad start. Some of the music is missing, and there aren't enough stands, necessitating an improvised conductor's desk with the aid of a chair. And though the hall is a nice space with a wooden floor, large windows and good acoustics, the lighting is inadequate and it's cold. We lose about fifteen minutes at the beginning of the rehearsal trying to solve these problems, but no heating ever materializes, which is hard on everyone's intonation, not to mention fingers and toes.

It also means that I don't get enough work on the Haydn first movement, which makes me immediately nervous and I hope that I've built in enough time tomorrow for it. The orchestra sounds rather raw and rough-edged – G sharps jostling with G naturals, quavers masquerading as crotchets – as though most of the players don't know their parts and don't sight-read well. And because they're struggling with the notes themselves, they're in their own world and not able to pay much attention to anyone else, and certainly not to what I'm doing with the stick. So I have to stop and verbalize much more frequently than I would like. On the other hand, I'm heartened by their young, eager faces, and miraculously, once I explain, or sing a passage, they are able to respond. In the end, they make some very promising sounds.

However, the two teenage oboists are very shy. It seems that this is a new experience for them and they are reluctant to play their entrances. I don't think the second oboist plays a note during the whole rehearsal, even though Daniel, her Swedish teacher whom I'd met in Sarajevo, has come and is sitting with her and cueing and playing her part. It's a pity that he can't play the concerts himself but evidently he has to go back to Stockholm.

Rada is also having difficulties, not only repeatedly miscounting, but seemingly unable to give effective cues and cut-offs. All this is gobbling up the rehearsal time and I'm already behind schedule.

During a break, I try to calm myself by sitting on my bed with a cup of tea. But within one minute, the CD player is blaring jazz again so I march into the living room and say, '*Molim*, no music.'

How can they want loud music when our ears have just been exercised for the past two hours? The other day someone was saying that a consequence of the war seems to be that people can't bear their own thoughts and feelings and so need to fill any silence with television or music. I can understand, but for these ten minutes, I desperately need silence. My brain is churning with Haydn and Mozart and can't take in any more.

Because of a scheduling problem with the hall, the last two hours of the rehearsal have to be in the apartment. Which seems impossible considering the mattresses and luggage as well as its normal furniture. With great difficulty, we somehow manage to squeeze in the chairs and stands, and we go through the last movement of the Haydn slowly so that everyone can play comfortably and accurately. This feels good. It's a relief to hear clean playing, even if greatly under tempo, and I feel that everyone is regaining a sense of control. I've found that if I alternate between taxing the players and making life easy for them, they tend to stay alert and produce good results. When we get to the end of the movement, I tell them what the real tempo will be – I want it to go like the wind – and they all look shocked and say, '*Ne ne, ne može.*'

I grin at them. 'We'll see . . .'

I finish off the rehearsal by reading through the Joplin, though some of the parts I've marked so carefully are inexplicably missing. The syncopated style of the Joplin is foreign to them, as it was to me when I first encountered it in the US, which is why I've taken so much trouble to pencil in all the articulation and accents. I can't understand how the music could have disappeared . . .

During the day, I manage to exchange a few words with only two of the Sarajevo musicians – the others either don't speak English or are too shy to try. Edo, the energetic bassoonist, tells me he's still studying at the Academy.

'The Sinfonietta it's really nice. To see how I'm playing, it's getting my ears wide open, you know? It's really nice, it's a small chamber orchestra and I'm hearing myself – I don't like big orchestra when you must play and the sound is not yours, you know?'

'How much performing do you get to do?' I ask.

'I don't have opportunity to play a lot of bassoon but I try.

Sometimes I play in cafés, bars, I play piano, jazz, ethno, ethno-jazz. And this is how I earn money. But with bassoon this is more, I have to say, love, nothing else. Yes, you cannot live here from bassoon. In this time. It's very hard situation. A lot of people don't listen classical music, and we don't have a lot of musician, that will be also a problem. Because a lot of guys went to foreign countries.'

'So there are not many orchestras,' I say.

'No. But I don't want to live anywhere, only here, because I'm used to, I like that kind of life. Music is not a job, it's more a love you know, it's friendship and getting . . . like jazz, like jazz, for example, it's not only to play music, it's just a way of thinking. When I look my friend, we don't have to speak. He's just playing what I am thinking about. It's kind of interesting.'

I leave the 'kids' to party in the apartment, and go out with Daniel, Aidan and his girlfriend (who heads the music therapy team), and a young American music therapist who arrived a few days ago. The old streets are almost deserted and they look beautiful in the moonlight. The river races by maniacally, swirling with eddies. We eat in the other good restaurant (Aidan says there are two in Mostar); I have shark, and the talk is of music therapy and US politics, and thankfully, not music. I get back around midnight expecting to have to act as matron, and find everybody tucked up in bed with the lights off.

Vocabulary learned today
gdje – where
note – printed music
ne razumijem – I don't understand
nema problema – no problem (most often heard when there definitely is a problem)
ne može – not possible, can't be done (most often heard when things can, and must, be done)

Sunday

This is our big rehearsal day, six hours in all. We can get a lot done, and we need to because very few players are available tomorrow or Tuesday; and Wednesday is concert day. On Thursday there will be a second performance in Sarajevo, so we get two chances.

When I come down to the hall, I'm astonished to find the cellos and bass and bassoon already tuned up and rehearsing the bass line together. Very impressive! Then Daniel tells me that he can after all stay for Wednesday's concert and will play along with the second oboist. Things are looking up.

Today's scheduling works fine, there is good concentration, and we get through everything as planned. It's a relief to have a day which goes smoothly. Everyone seems to be settling into the ensemble and real progress is made. Now it sounds more co-ordinated, more musical, more characterful. I've learned some particular rehearsal words in Bosnian, but most of the time I speak in Italian musical terms – *piu forte molim, meno presto molim* – and for the more complicated comments, Aidan translates from English. It is a disadvantage having a translator, because it takes time and slows the pace, besides not being conducive to light remarks or funny asides, useful ingredients in the rehearsal process. I must try to study Bosnian . . . at some point . . .

I spend some time on the opening of the Haydn. I grew to love this symphony as a child, its humour and liveliness. We had a recording of Bruno Walter rehearsing it, quite a rare opportunity to hear a great musician at work. And I remember how he became increasingly frustrated about those opening chords, singing them in a kind of intonationless way to convey what he wanted. I'd like them to sound declamatory without being pompous, or gruff, or staid. The rhythmic gesture is particularly hard to catch, and all the silences need to hold an expectant tension.

Perhaps the Mostar Sinfonietta has not often been exposed to this kind of musical grappling, but they are intrigued by it. There is a very good working atmosphere and before long they're playing with a nice bouncy energy where it's needed. As for the Haydn last movement, they surprise themselves by being able to play it really fast, and everyone is exhilarated. '*Divno, divno!*'

Yesterday Aidan had told me that the orchestra is suspicious of conductors, and that their previous foreign visitors had played within the orchestra as section leaders. I think it's much better that they lead themselves since it will give them the experience as well as the confidence to know that they can do it when there isn't a guest. As for the suspicion, that's normal – every orchestra considers a conductor guilty until proven innocent. It's up to me to earn their confidence, and when some of them now tell me how much they're enjoying the playing and how much they're learning from it, I think I've passed the first hurdle. I've even cancelled the proposed rehearsals for tomorrow and Tuesday evenings, because I don't think there's any point in rehearsing with less than half the orchestra, and the most benefit will come from individual practice. On the other hand I've arranged a two-and-a-half-hour rehearsal on the day of the concert to refresh everyone's memory. This is certainly not the ideal way to organize rehearsals: the two-day gap can scupper all the cohesiveness we've just achieved.

So now I can focus on practising myself. My own practising always seems to come last, but I prefer to feel that everyone else is prepared and that it's just up to me to pull the rabbit out of the hat. Tomorrow I'll get in a good practice. I'd also like to walk round Mostar at a slow pace and take photographs and try to get more of a feel of the town.

During one of the breaks, I see Teo, the singer with the wonderful wobbly voice, sitting at one of the tables in the lobby.

'*Dobar dan*, we met the other night in the bar. I was with Aidan.'

'*Dobar dan*, yes, I remember. Do you want to sit?' and he gestures to the chair next to him.

'*Hvala.*' I ask him if he's waiting for Aidan, and he says no, he often hangs out at the Pavarotti Centre. He's a member of the Schools Music Team.

'Once a week we go to each child because we have many schools, from like fifty . . . sixty kilometres, something like that, so we work in like, I'm not sure, but at least in twenty schools.

'Music keeps kids away from drugs. I think this Pavarotti Centre is the right place for that. But unfortunately I think there's still too much drugs in town so, I don't know what happens in future . . . For me, in fact, because I like music, I'm here every day. I used to drink a lot, but . . . I'm still drinking but now I have something to do, before I didn't have, I was unemployed. A lot of the young people are unemployed, that's why many young people are going to foreign country, western country. My all friends, they are all now America, England, Germany. Well this job still keeps me, I had luck because I'm here since beginning. I have not so good salary but I can live, you know, it's OK. When I see some other people it's very bad. If I lose job I will have to go somewhere, I don't know where but definitely I will go. But I don't know how long this job will be going.'

Teo says he will be putting up posters tomorrow for the concert, so I say I'll help him.

'You come with me?' he asks disbelievingly.

'*Naravno*. Why not?'

We arrange to meet tomorrow.

Ivica and Suzana have invited me to their home for supper. They live in a small block of flats with a concrete stairwell that reminds me of similar blocks in St Petersburg. There is no light so I climb up in the dark and enter a room that contains a sofa and two chairs, a coffee table, a cabinet with some books and ornaments, and a television which is turned on and remains on for the whole evening. There is a tiny kitchen at one end, and Suzana has set out some food on the coffee table. They have three young children whom I'd met on Brijuni, so we eat *en famille* and make small talk. Soon Ivica wants to watch an inspirational talk on television, so Suzana shows me a photograph album of pictures taken on Brijuni and at birthdays. After a while, I make a move to go, but Ivica says firmly, 'No, you must stay, thank you for coming, you stay,' and turns back to the television. He is obviously delighted that I'm here, but . . . I begin to realize that watching television all together is exactly what they expect and I suppose it's a compliment to be treated as family.

When I finally persuade Ivica that I really must be getting back,' he drives me in his old car, speeding along the 'front line' just as Aidan did when I arrived. 'You know, the Americans, yes, the Americans started war here. Yes yes.' There has been no mention of the war up till this point, but it seems unavoidable.

The Sarajevo players have left a terrible mess in 'my' apartment – food, dirty pans and dishes, full ashtrays, overflowing rubbish bins . . . I spend an hour tidying it all up and here I am staring at five unmade beds squashed together on the floor.

Vocabulary learned today
slušajte – listen (as in *violini slušajte flauta* – never mind the grammar)
bolje – better
puno – very (as in *puno hvala*, thank you very much)
idemo – let's go (literally, as well as in the sense of 'let's get on with it')

Monday

The two white-coated women come in this morning and remove the mattresses, returning the flat to normal. It's great to know that I have a full day ahead to focus quietly on the work, and I'm soon engrossed in the Mozart violin pieces, three delightful movements composed on separate occasions. The B flat Rondo is rarely played – I've never heard it performed; it sparkles with good humour and radiance as if all's right with the world. Not an obvious state of mind to dredge up in a place like Mostar. Of course Mozart himself knew the real state of the world, but it's a dream worth dreaming. Especially in a place like Mostar.

It's Rada's turn to ask me to hear her students, so I go down to impart what wisdom I can. And after that, I bundle up and walk around town putting up posters for the concert with Teo. I ask him whether displaying posters two days before a concert is not too late.

'*Ne*, two days before is fine. No-one think about tomorrow, just think about today.'

The posters have been provided by the British Council in Sarajevo. They are a generic design and can be used for all the Sinfonietta concerts with just the addition of a strip stating the date, time, place and programme of the next performance.

We put them up on both sides of town, and I comment on the ruins surrounding us.

'I'm used to seeing bombed buildings here,' Teo says. 'I was here during the war, I was in the army, I was fighting for three years. So for me now it's normal. It was strange also in the beginning, but you're used on that, you have to.'

When I get back to the flat, I'm met by Selma, the flautist in the Sinfonietta who was on Brijuni. I'd invited her to visit, to tell me about the Sinfonietta and music life in general in Mostar. We cradle cups of tea to warm our hands and she tells me about the difficulties of working here. But soon she reminisces about other things.

Selma

When the war started, you know, there was Serbs on one side, fighting against Croats and Muslims. In that period, East and West Mostar were still open to leave to Croatia – through West Mostar and then onwards to Croatia. Until May '93. So whoever wanted to leave had all this period to leave and to go. And then in '93 no one could get out. No Muslims could get out, at all.

And Serbs, they are living in West Mostar before the war, and I lived across the street from a building where mainly military people were living, Serbian military men with their families. As if they know when the war is going to start, they were moving out of Mostar at two o'clock in the morning. So we all knew that something is going to happen. They were leaving their places with furniture and stuff, all these long lorries with all the furniture. They were moving their families out. My mum was standing on a window all night through, saying something really bad is gonna happen you know, I feel it, I see this, it's not really good thing to see.

And the war started in April, I believe in April, end of March

*beginning of April '92. So since then until 9th of May '93, you had
all this period to leave. I left in this period, my family stayed on.
My brother was married, his wife was pregnant, he was living
together with her family in the same house. And my mum and dad
were staying in a flat. I left in September, so I did experience a bit
of war, but only shelling, not the horrible things of people being
taken away and stuff like that. And then the hell started in May
'93 because then there was a breakout between Croats and
Muslims, and for my family particularly, they suffered a lot.*

*Because our neighbourhood was really horrible to them during
the war, they really suffered a lot from my neighbours. Except for
one family who were protecting my mum and dad, Croat family,
they were protecting my mum and dad all the time. My dad
basically went into hands of Croats by his own decision. He
didn't want to hide. He said, I'm going where my people is going,
I'm not going to stay here. And this particular family, the
husband, the head of the household, said to the soldiers who came
to pick my dad first time, he said, 'Look, you have to kill me first,
before you take my neighbour away.'*

*And I'll never forget that. These are things, in this kind of
situation, you never ever forget. It's something really to remember
for ever, it took a lot of courage, for sure. When everybody was hiding or even saying horrible things, just to make themselves look
really important and big, to, excuse my language, suck up to the
people who came to take away anyone, he basically stood out
between all ten houses in the neighbourhood and said that.*

*He died of a heart attack, died really peacefully on Christmas
Day, couple of years ago. He went to bed in the evening and
didn't wake up, he was a very old man, so he died of age I think.
At least he managed to see everybody being happy again. It's a
very nice family. I go and visit on a regular basis, because his wife
is still alive but she had a stroke and she's not mobile any more,
and she's perfect with her head and her brain. She's an old
woman, really nice old woman, so I go and visit.*

*My dad was in a concentration camp from May '93 until March
'94. So almost for a year. Ten months or something. My mum
stayed on. She's a very brave and very strong woman. She'd been
sorting out papers, false documents of course, for my brother and*

his wife to leave Mostar. In the meanwhile my sister gave birth to a child which was dead. So they were going through a rough period as well. And my brother escaped because he was wanted for 500 Deutschmark, which in pounds in those days means about £150. So he was wanted for 500 Deutschmark because he was working in security, but they thought he was a bodyguard for one of the important people of the army, which wasn't true, they just made up the story. So they had to run away in one small village in the middle of a Croat area. I have family there and they were sleeping in the gardens for some days. Then my mum found someone and paid somebody to get them out, to Split, from Split to Zagreb, and my uncle who was living in Sweden since the '60s sent them air ticket and visas and they left to Sweden, to Stockholm.

And my dad was in the camp already, in a concentration camp. The camp was in Herzegovina, just outside of Mostar. There were three different camps and he changed to all three of them. So he was in all three of them.

Twenty days after my mum got my brother out she was basically made to leave her house and run across the front line – you've seen what it looks like, and now it's beautiful comparing to what it looked like during the war – and she says the only thing in mind that she had is, if the bullet has to hit me, I wish I was dead. 'Cause she says if I'm wounded, the dogs will come and eat me alive, because no one could help anyone who was there. And every day that was happening in streets of Mostar. Muslim people were made to cross to East Mostar, over the front line, with bullets shooting from everywhere. And luckily, nothing happened to her.

So, she's got a sister who lives in East Mostar, and has a house nearby here. She took her in her house, and basically eighteen of them lived in one room for very long period of time. And then when my dad got out – the war already stopped, that was the last exchange that was happening between Muslims and Croats – so my dad, thank to God, came out alive and lived with this family, my aunt, for more than a year, in a small apartment, and they were never brave enough to go back and live in West Mostar.

My parents are orphans, both of them, from the Second World War. They grew up in orphanages, both my mum and my dad, *both of them. So the way me and my brother was brought up was in a very Socialistic way, because that was the system. And it just makes you not understand how someone can have these really stupid ideas when for fifty years you've been studying in your history books what means to try and kill one nation. What it means to try and open camps, what are the camps like . . . what is it for a family, or for a member of a family they are taking away. And it's just horrible . . . horrible.*

I don't try and speak to people about the war because I don't have a right because I haven't been here. And I don't like talking about it. Even my dad doesn't talk about camps. Just a few things, but usually it's funny stuff he tells us. Something funny that happens. My mum, I think she suffered in a worse way than my father really. Because that kind of feeling that you don't know where you are, or you don't know when they're picking you up . . . and no we didn't know about Dad for four months. Because they'd been hiding my father from the Red Cross for four and a half months. He was one of the army people, and basically they thought they can change him for a lot of their soldiers. Exchange my father for many of their soldiers because he was one of the people in the army who was having some kind of position there, I'm not sure what it was.

But anyway, four and a half months later, I don't know how, but they've left him in the same cell together with everyone else – because he was spending time on his own for a very long time in cell by himself – a Red Cross team came in. They were the only connection with the outside world, they could write messages that would come three months later. But any kind of a written word, of handwriting from my dad would really make me happy. So four and half months later, a Croat lady who was working in a Red Cross team, recognized my father, he was her professor in school, in high school, and she came up and spoke to him. And he said, I don't know what's happening with my wife, because he heard all sort of stories that my mum is being raped and that she's making coffees for these Croat soldiers, that they beat her up, and all these horrible stories that can drive you out of your mind. And he said, try and look for her, try and find where she is and please tell her I'm fine, I'm alive.

So she found my mum and that was the first news that my mother had that my father was alive, she even crossed to East Mostar to find my mother. And my father can't even remember what's her name, which is very strange. He said I couldn't remember – because he worked in education for about forty years – so he said I just couldn't remember her name, because he wanted to thank her in a certain way, you know these things are . . .

So they were hiding from me about Dad for four and a half months, they didn't want to tell me, because I'm really close to my father, more than to my mother, which is very strange, but we have an unusually close relationship, my dad and I. So they thought I'd go probably crazy or something, being in England, not being able to do anything about it, so they didn't tell me for four and a half months. And then by accident I found out by somebody who thought I knew, and they said don't worry he's in Heliodrom, and that's the day when I started smoking. So . . . and that was it basically. And I knew . . . I thought he was dead, and that's why everybody was avoiding him as a subject. And when they actually told me he's in camp, I felt relieved because I knew he's alive. That gave me more energy to live my life again.

And there was always a little hope in me. I knew my dad, my dad has an unusually strong character, and I knew that people were going half crazy in these camps. And I always knew he will find a way to get out of this, that it will not affect him mentally, I always knew he's strong enough to go through anything. I really believed in him always. And there was always a little bit of hope that I'm going to hear him one day and see him one day. I never believed that anything bad is going to happen to him. Never, even for one moment. It's very strange, because that wasn't a very nice period of my life and I was very depressed person, and for one moment I never thought that something can happen to him. Somehow I always thought that he has some kind of angel to watch over him. And one morning the phone rang and it was him on the phone, and we couldn't speak for ten minutes, we were both crying, and he said, for the last ten months this was the moment I was waiting for, this is what kept me alive, all this time, just to hear your voice . . .

Selma breaks down and I put my arms around her. We are both crying.

'I'm sorry, I'm sorry,' she sobs, 'it's the first time I've spoken about this since the war.'

The first time. I'm very moved.

I'm also devastated. It was so hard to hear her story, to keep eye contact, to keep listening.

Now the nightmare of her mother's experience stays with me.
And as for her father . . .

Memories of my own father come flooding back, because my experience was like a mirror image of hers. Unlike her, I always feared for my father, though he was never in a concentration camp. Except for the one in his mind, and he did not survive it.

I walk slowly along the streets. It's just stopped raining and the sky is still overcast. I feel oppressed. This town doesn't feel at all normal. It's not the people, who on the whole look like people anywhere. Yes, there are a few older men and women who look exceedingly worn, weather-beaten, shrivelled, war-beaten. But the younger ones wear blue jeans, they walk confidently, they sit in the cafés drinking coffee, they smoke. They *all* smoke. But I don't see any men in their thirties or forties. A whole generation is missing.

And perhaps it's what Toni had said the other day – the way to survive now is to forget. I feel the forgetting. People may look normal but it's an effort to be normal.

I feel the trying.

And you have to try hard in this town, surrounded by the ubiquitous ruins, overbearing, beckoning like enormous black holes that might suck you in as you walk past. And breathing the air, with the dust of the explosions unable to finally settle but being disturbed by the slightest breeze, and mixing with the water vapour that is constantly thrown up by the Neretva as it hurls itself along its course.

And there's something else. A silent screaming in the air. Terrified faces, just out of sight. And pain, unspeakable, steady pain, days . . . months . . . years of it.

I don't believe in ghosts, but they are here. Everywhere, in the air itself, which I have to breathe.

I remember visiting Dachau and feeling the legacy of cruelty and violence, but it felt more at rest there, and no-one was drinking coffee and pretending to be normal.

I suddenly remember what Aidan had said about visiting Mostar – that 'internationals' collapse in some way on their fourth day here. I suppose it was a warning. I take refuge in a café I've grown to like, an Austrian pâtisserie, and try to soothe myself by writing in my diary and eating sweet things. The coffee takes some of the chill away.

The one person who knows about these matters is Nigel Osborne and luckily enough, he arrives this evening. He travelled repeatedly to Bosnia during the war and instigated the founding of the Mostar Sinfonietta as a way of helping to pick up the pieces. Over dinner he listens to me talking about the ghosts of Mostar, and his verdict on them is 'repressed grief'. First the grief. Then its repression.

A double burden. Twinned black clouds sitting over the town.

It's reassuring to see a friendly face and Nigel is nothing if not generous, kind, and grounded. He's idealistic but his head is not up in the clouds. He tells me he's looking forward to hearing the concert and thanks me for coming to work here. I keep forgetting that I'm volunteering for all this.

Tuesday

Another cold morning and I'm out looking for little presents. I choose some woven table mats decorated with leaves and trees, birds and animals, and that bear a close resemblance to gifts that I've bought in Peru and Mexico. I'm intrigued. Was there a migration across half the world? Or is there a more prosaic reason, like the way the stitching restrains the style? 'Bosniak, *da, stari* Bosnia,' I'm assured by the shopkeeper.

I've arranged to be picked up by Selma and driven to a primary school where the Schools Music Team teaches, and soon we are on our way to a nearby village. The road winds through rolling countryside, sometimes wooded, sometimes open. There's not much traffic but we do pass some SFOR (NATO Stabilization Force) army vehicles parked by the road and a number of soldiers working on the verge.

'What are they doing?'

'Oh, they'll be clearing mines.'

Selma fills me in on the school. 'The children come from villages around. You'll see it's very basic, for instance, there's nowhere for the children to play, just a small area in front where teachers park the cars. Also it's on a bad corner, and a few weeks ago, one child ran into the road and was killed. We are still shocked. The cars go too fast here. At least now, they put a sign saying "School".'

As soon as we turn into the entrance, a small, low, oblong block comes into view. It is fronted by a muddy patch of ground, where a gaggle of young children in multicoloured coats are racing around some parked cars. The appearance of a stranger with camera slung over shoulder prompts a mad dash in my direction, with shouts of '*Foto! Foto!*' And they form a raggle-taggle group of grinning, jostling kids all wanting to be centre-frame. This has evidently happened before. 'Yes, we do get international visitors. They are curious about us. And the kids are curious about them.'

There are four classrooms comprising old wooden desks, chairs, and blackboard; and a tiny staff room. I sit through four classes, and marvel at how the young teachers can create such a wonderful atmosphere – laughing, singing, drumming, playing musical games

– when the classrooms are so cold that everyone keeps on their winter coats, and still the cold penetrates to the bone. But this is education through entertainment and the kids are eager to participate in the fun. The liveliness of the teachers vanishes as soon as they sit down for a cigarette and coffee in their break. Half an eye is kept on the television that's hanging on a wall: it's showing the War Crimes Tribunal in The Hague. One of the teachers mutters something at the screen. Colourful children's paintings line the walls.

This afternoon, I practise and then mark up my scores with strong blue pencil. I need to be able to see the wind entrances and major dynamic changes in an instant, so that I can give cues and keep the ship in order whatever the excitement, or catastrophe, of the moment.

And in the evening I go to Rada's home for supper. It's so nice to be able to see the musicians at home, to get a glimpse of how they live. A huge wooden door gives onto a small courtyard and I duck under a tree and climb an outside staircase into what looks like a newly renovated flat. (I suppose most houses here are newly renovated – out of a pile of rubble.) It's clean and ordered, and I'm offered slippers as I enter. Rada greets me with her usual graciousness and calls her children to say hello. Anna, who's about five, gets out her violin and plays me a little tune, and her younger brother David plays me a CD, and then they both sing songs into my tape recorder. As the evening progresses, they become rather rambunctious, but Rada remains exceedingly patient with them.

She tells me how everyone loves Anna and David but that sometimes, when their names are mentioned, she senses disapproval, because these are not Muslim names. She says, 'If my children are badly treated or shunned, we'll pack up and leave. I don't know where we'll go.' The ferocity of a lioness lurks in those eyes.

Her husband Pedja arrives from work, fair-haired and handsome (what a beautiful couple they make), and then Aidan and his girlfriend come in, and we all sit round the table, together with Rada's mother who is visiting from her country home and looks just like Rada. It's a lovely meal, seafood, topped off with a deliciously fresh goat's cheese that her mother has just made herself. They call it 'new cheese'.

We chatter in various languages, allowing ourselves to be constantly interrupted by the children. I can't understand everything, but it doesn't matter.

I'm breathing again and I feel warm.

As I walk back to the Pavarotti Centre, a mangy dog approaches me. There are quite a number of cats on the streets, all very thin and wild-looking. Not so many dogs. This one gives a little jump and nips me on the hand. No blood is drawn, but I'm startled and utterly horrified, thinking back to Selma's story of her mother and the front line and the dogs.

Wednesday

Concert day. I'm savouring the quiet before the Sarajevo crowd descends. Though they won't be staying overnight, this flat will nevertheless be their changing room and warming-up room and resting room and who-knows-what-else room . . . I don't suppose I'll get much concentration time once they're here.

The phone rings early. It's Aidan who tells me that a professional violinist who was to fly in from Germany to play the concert has come down with flu, and although she was packed and had her ticket, she'd called to say she can't come. So we are one violinist short but this is not a bad thing, I think, since she's missed all the rehearsals and we are used to the balance as it is.

After a quick breakfast, I go through the scores and try to plan the afternoon's rehearsal. I need to cover everything, tighten things up, remind everyone how to listen and watch and breathe together, to phrase together, feel together, to give themselves to the music. Another six hours of rehearsal would be nice. As things stand, I'll have to be selective, and choose issues that I can explain easily, and that Aidan can translate easily. For instance, the humour in the Haydn. It's difficult to have a twinkle in your eye when you're trying to dig out every bit of concentration and determination and will-power to give a good performance. It's one of the paradoxes of performing – to be ferociously confident so that the fingers hit their mark and the bowing/blowing technique is reliable, and at the same time to express emotions like innocence or fear or fragility. Or humour. One often hears players conveying seriousness of purpose as a kind of default setting, instead of conveying the music itself. It gives classical music a bad name, not to mention ruining the music . . .

Today I'm ruled by the clock. I practise until 1 p.m., and then go for lunch with Nigel, Daniel and the clarinettist, who has a bad cold. Thank goodness the food comes in time for us to actually eat it, as opposed to the big rehearsal day last Sunday, when it took forty minutes for the order to arrive, leaving us five minutes to get it wrapped and dashing back to rehearse without eating a morsel. Now there's even time for me to cash a travellers' cheque, but after several banks respond with the usual '*ne može*', I give up.

The rehearsal is planned from 3 p.m. to 5.30 p.m., leaving an hour and a half for everyone to recover, relax, have a cup of tea and do whatever pre-concert ritual we need. The concert's at seven.

Rehearsal. The hall is freezing again. Nothing is set up. Where's Aidan? I push the piano aside and set up the chairs and stands myself. With Aidan still missing, I start the rehearsal, and get through most of what I've planned. Aidan arrives about an hour late, explaining that there'd been a crisis with the posters for tomorrow's concert in Sarajevo; and that he couldn't contact anyone because his phone had suddenly been cut off. He says this with amazing good humour. Despite being obviously over-burdened, he's a delight, all the time.

We finish rehearsing at ten to six. I manage to make a cup of tea and to rest for twenty minutes, and then I run down to make sure that the seating for the audience is arranged correctly. But the hall is locked and I race around trying to find Aidan. My blood pressure is rising.

Finally the doors are opened and I set out the chairs into rows, hoping that some of them at least will be occupied by the time the concert begins. Then I run upstairs again to change into my concert clothes. It's about fifteen minutes to concert time. As I enter the flat, I see Daniel standing motionless as a statue and with a most pathetic expression on his face. I also see that he is holding on to the waistband of his trousers which look to be a few sizes too big.

'You wouldn't have a belt I could use, would you?'

Since he hadn't been expecting to perform, he hadn't brought any black concert clothes with him from Stockholm. So he'd borrowed these trousers from Aidan and they are decidedly too big for him.

'I've brought one belt with me and I hope it's not too small for you,' I say as I rummage through my case. 'But maybe it's too wide to go through the loops.'

I hand him a grey belt and luckily it fits, and I think we are both very relieved that the guest oboist doesn't have to go on stage holding his trousers up. Or worse, that he might forget to hold them up . . .

At about one minute to seven, I join the orchestra who have assembled in a tiny room at the back of the hall. Everyone looks fresh and shiny, and they've all remembered their black shoes. Ivica is inexplicably wearing a cloth cap and evidently intends to keep it on. Too late to deal with that now.

They tune carefully and then after one last smile all round – good luck, this is it, let's go, *idemo* – we walk out into the hall, to be greeted by an overflowing audience, the door at the back crowded by people straining to get in. I feel a surge of exhilaration, and when I turn to face the orchestra, I sense their excitement and eagerness to play, to get down to work, to give the most that they can. The audience quietens down, and into the silence that is bursting with expectation, the first E major chords of the Mozart float, warm and generous.

It is a good concert. There are inevitably some rocky moments, including one disastrously wrong entrance in the Haydn last movement that throws half the orchestra. Yes, Haydn is toying with unexpected entrances but it's one thing for the listener to get wrong-footed, quite another thing for the orchestra . . . Somehow I manage to get them back on track and the coda races at a tremendous speed to the end. I think the players are as surprised as

I am at their sudden virtuosity, and the smiles of the audience are matched by the smiles of the musicians.

I have decided to introduce the Joplin as I suppose his music is not much heard here. '*Dobro veče. Ne govorim bosanski.*' Wild applause. Aidan translates as I say in English that it's my first time in Mostar and I'm glad to be here, and as I briefly describe the swing of ragtime, my mind strays onto its own track, imagining itself into the minds of the people I'm addressing – Selma's parents are here, people driven out of their villages are here, people who survived the Mostar siege and the camps and the mayhem are here – all these enthusiastic faces relishing these sixty minutes of music, sixty minutes of release from their nightmares and their struggle to be normal, from their bitter selves, their fragmented selves, sixty minutes in a world of order and beauty and love and hope and light-heartedness and all the feelings we wish were with us always. And I'm struck by their willingness and courage to confront these feelings that remind them of better times, and that pose a terrible question for the future.

I think I have finished talking about Joplin, so I turn round and, struggling to control a rogue tear that has crept into my eye, I bring in the first riff of the Joplin. The clarinettist with the bad cold does wonders with her solo, and the concert ends with an almighty round of applause.

The tiny room backstage bubbles with pride and relief and glee as everyone packs up their instruments. It's hugs all round, and then they go out to rejoice with their friends and family in the audience. There's such a feeling of general happiness that I suppose I shouldn't have been surprised, when I come down to the lobby after changing into 'civilian clothes', to find it packed with musicians and friends, drinking and smoking and . . . making music! Toni has his drum, Aidan his violin, Teo his guitar, Nigel is blowing into a beer bottle, and everyone is singing their favourite sevdah tunes. Even I'm beginning to recognize some of them, and soon I'm holding hands with Rada and Suzana as we dance in a line, arms raised, feet going back – forwards – sideways – back – back. I dance until I'm exhausted and still the music doesn't stop.

And then at 11 p.m., a crowd of us go out to eat a slap-up

supper at the old theatre restaurant. Every few minutes someone thinks of another toast – to Mostar! –

pour another glass – to the Sinfonietta! –

another glass – to music! –

to Haydn! –

to sevdah! –

to life! –

živjeli!

It's very late when I walk home (home!) to the Pavarotti Centre, and I still have to pack. Because tomorrow we're leaving, we're going to Sarajevo.

Vocabulary learned today
ne govorim bosanski – I don't speak Bosnian
živjeli – cheers! to life!

Thursday

The sun is hanging over the land this morning and the air feels fresh. I've come out early to take photographs and to say goodbye to the old town, particularly to the absent bridge. As I walk up to the east bank of the Neretva, I can see that the stonemasons have already filled in much of the gaping hole in one of the side towers, and now they're chiselling away at the white stones and fitting them in. And for the first time I can look past the destruction and devastation of Mostar and see the rebuilding. And I'm wondering if it's just a result of the sunshine or if it simply takes this long for the shock of being here to recede.

At about 9 a.m., Aidan and I set off for Sarajevo. The drive is beautiful, the hills and trees shimmering under a light scattering of snow. But after only a few minutes, my attention is yoked back to the details of the day, as Aidan tells me that Selma is ill and won't be coming. This poses quite a problem as both the Mozart Adagio and the Haydn feature prominent flute lines. We discuss whether to search for another flute player in Sarajevo who can possibly play the concert on one rehearsal; or whether it might be better to ask a violinist to play the flute part. We are still debating what to do when we see Suzana standing by her car at the side of the road, flagging us down. Aidan slams on the brakes, gets out of the car and runs over to her. A flat tyre? No petrol? No, it is good news – she says that Selma has just phoned her on her mobile (Aidan's mobile still being inoperable) to say that she's feeling better and will be coming after all, so we don't need to find a replacement. Problem solved! 'I think she might be pregnant,' Aidan says.

We get back into the car with relief and wave to Ivica and Suzana as they drive off ahead of us. It's then that we notice that Suzana has left her handbag lying on the boot of their car. Ivica is no timid driver and soon Aidan is standing on the accelerator in order to catch up with them. The road to Sarajevo twists and turns and goes in and out of tunnels, and many times we lose sight of the car and I keep my eyes focused onto the side of the road to see whether the bag has fallen off and is hidden in the grass. After about ten miles, they must have noticed the bag is missing, for they stop the car, retrieve the bag from its resting place on top of the boot, and Aidan and I continue at a more reasonable pace. I think I've already had enough excitement for one day and it's not even ten o'clock.

We talk a little about last night's concert and how well it went and how wonderful it was that the hall was full. 'Yes, and you know,' says Aidan, 'evidently all the posters that you put up on the West side of town were torn down within twenty-four hours.'

'What?' I exclaim.

'Yeah well, the nationalists on the West side don't like the Sinfonietta because of what we represent, you know, all inclusive.'

I'm shocked.

One reassuring piece of news is that Daniel can, after all, stay for tonight's concert. I don't trouble my brain with how a musician can suddenly discover two unexpectedly free days in his schedule . . .

The concert will take place at the Sarajevo Music Academy and it has been arranged that I will give a master class there before the rehearsal. We arrive with only five minutes to spare, enabling me to grab half a cup of tea and two bites of a cheese sandwich before entering the grey Habsburg-era building. It must have looked quite distinguished once, but now it is shabby and neglected. The concert hall is a perfect oblong with a nice stage and good acoustics. One wall has a large hole where a shell had struck. The negative shape of the shell, together with the damage it caused as it tore through the brickwork, is encased in glass, like an exhibit, a preservation of a violent intrusion into a room dedicated to music. If architecture is 'frozen music', what is this?

There are about fifteen people in the hall, mainly students. The first to play for me is very young, perhaps eleven years old. But he is a real talent and an extremely natural player. What a delight. He plays the Bach A minor Concerto and we work on vitality and phrasing and how to listen to the accompanying orchestral part which I play on the piano. The other students are good too, though at first they are shy and don't want to play. At one point I encourage them all to come to the front and teach them how to dance the Sarabande. And after that they all want to play for me and of course now there isn't time, so they ask me to come back tomorrow. I'll come back tomorrow.

Most of the students are studying with a teacher called Marina, young and beautiful and serene, who translates for me. She has copious black hair, a radiant smile, and a wonderfully kind face. It's the same kind of serenity that I see in Rada. If angels exist, they will look like that. And during the break, she talks about angels, how the Sanskrit word for musician means a being who conveys the eternal, the divine, to the people here on earth.

She also tells me about not being able to play the violin during the siege.

Marina

I decided to stay in Sarajevo. Every person from Academy, not every, but ninety-five per cent of students from Sarajevo, went somewhere. Just took their instruments and left. And I decided to stay because I realized that it's impossible for me to leave and to think about what's happening here. No, I'm not brave, it's not that. I just didn't want to live somewhere else – I couldn't fight, I couldn't do anything – I just wanted if it's possible to do anything by staying, by getting killed, anything to help . . . I don't know. In some cosmic relations . . . I don't know, I just wanted to stay.

After it went on and on, long time, and during that time, I couldn't bear to play the violin. You know, I would go to my violin, open my violin case and look at the violin, I only looked at it but I couldn't pick it up while people were being killed outside . . . outside the window. I could hear . . . how can I play music? I couldn't even touch it.

I met my husband at that time. We were working for the Children's Embassy helping to bring food, lots of things. And we fell in love, you know, and we were married. And I had a baby. During the siege. Yes, it is crazy! We didn't want to have children in war, during war, in violence. Nobody wanted to have children then. But it was long time, the siege, and I began to feel that I want to live, to live life. How to explain, I did not want war to prevent me having a baby. Maybe I would not survive, but if I survive, it is God's will. And so I thought, I want to live how I want to live. And if I have a child and we survive, it is God's will. I thought, maybe people will be angry with me for being pregnant – is it selfish? – but people were happy. Even women I didn't know, when they saw I was pregnant, they came up to me and they said they were glad. And they gave me food, food for the baby, they said. A new life, it was hope, a sign of hope. So many people were dying and here was a new life.

I am weary. Marina's story, and the master class, and the car ride . . . and it's hot in the building and I'm very hungry and thirsty, and I must practise . . . and there's just forty minutes before the rehearsal. The most useful thing I can do is to lie down and rest, so I stretch out on the carpet and close my eyes.

When it is time to rehearse, I can't imagine how I can summon enough energy to wave the stick around, never mind play the violin and conduct a concert. I'm sure I must look pale and depleted, so when I face the orchestra, I reassure them that, although I might look exhausted now, I will be fine for the concert.

I don't fully believe my words, and so it comes as a surprise that, when the first sounds of the rehearsal pulse through my body, it's as if a magic current wakes up my cells and pours a stream of energy into me. The music is like a magnet, drawing to itself the wish to be alive, fully awake, engaged and alert. It pulls me into it – how can I not respond to its beauty and liveliness and change-ability? to the life in every note? the flow of every phrase? the intensity and unpredictability of the musical journey?

It's a wonderful lesson. To know that music can wake me, that in an instant I'm up and away and in my element. So even though there is no time to eat and no time to practise and that I'm running on empty, I know it's going to be a good concert. I tell the players that I don't want to hear any of the mistakes that they made in last night's concert. Ivica interrupts with 'yes of course we'll probably make new mistakes,' and I say 'that's OK, I don't mind new mistakes, I just don't want to hear old ones'. I also tell them that not only the mistakes should be different, but that I want the music to be different, to be fresh. And that I'm going to take the last movement of the Haydn even faster.

And the concert *is* fresh, and the Haydn *is* faster. And the mistakes *are* new . . . and sometimes hilarious. Rada gets lost in the first movement of the Haydn and I resort to singing the first violin part to help the section find their way back. The worst moment comes in the second movement, when the two oboes fail to play their crucial solo bar that comes straight after a vehement fortissimo of the whole orchestra. I give them their usual cue, but this time there is total silence. They only have two crotchets to play, and strangely enough, they *look* like they are playing. Only there's no sound at all coming from their instruments. Daniel is sitting right behind them, and with an expression of absolute panic, he is waving his oboe from side to side, not knowing which oboe part to play, and not playing either. The sudden silence seems to last for ever, my heart misses a beat, and I try not to catch the eye of anyone in the orchestra for a few minutes – everyone's head is down as we struggle to keep the concentration and not to dissolve into laughter. There'll be plenty of time for that after-wards.

And there is indeed general merriment after the concert, as everyone seems to accept that they have achieved far more than anyone expected at the start of the venture. Even the young oboists are riding high despite their empty bar, telling me that 'it has been wonderful to play, that music is our life now'. And I feel that the music has carried everyone in its arms, has taken them away from their everyday lives, into a rarefied place that is, at the same time, more true to their lives. And mine.

It is suddenly time to say goodbye to the orchestra as the bus to Mostar is leaving immediately, and the Sarajevo musicians prepare to celebrate with family and friends. It feels too abrupt and everything is slightly spinning. There's a heady atmosphere and we try, unsuccessfully, to say what needs time to say. Rada finally chooses her bow and we give each other a warm hug. I say goodbye to Aidan and thank him for all his dedication, to which he replies with a grin that I am 'a real conductor' – quite a compliment coming from him.

When everyone has gone, I pack up my things and go with Daniel to have a meal, the first of the day. Since Daniel comes here regularly from Stockholm to teach, he knows the restaurants of Sarajevo well and soon we are seated in a quiet, surprisingly plush space with tablecloths on the tables. I think it's one of the few times that I am able to order a balanced meal, this trip being notable for neither haute cuisine nor healthy eating. After a glass of good red wine, the adrenalin starts to abate and my muscles begin to relax. I can't quite believe that the concerts are over. Is there really no more planning to do? no more music or time-tables or words or people or readiness? I know there's something tomorrow but I can't remember what it is. I know it's not a concert.

We're both staying in the same hotel, and as we walk there Daniel tells me the sequel to the trousers story. For tonight's concert, he'd borrowed a pair of trousers from his landlord who's much smaller than him, and though he'd managed to pull them on, the flies wouldn't close, so he'd had to pin them together, which can be rather worrying for an oboist who has to take constant deep breaths. He'd also borrowed shoes from the same landlord, but since they were at least one size too small, the only way he could walk was on the sides of his feet. And he proceeds to give a little demonstration of walking on stage, as dignified as possible, in his tight trousers and pinching shoes, taking tiny steps with his knees glued together, and I collapse into uncontrollable giggles. And then I remember his panicked expression during the oboe-less silence and his oboe wafting from side to side in horrified indecision, and I laugh even harder. Yes, the whole week has been an intense emotional ride and this is surely a release, but these images of sweet, earnest Daniel coping with unruly trousers and oboes make me double up with laughter all the way to the hotel . . .

And then when we finally arrive, there's this crazy business with the room keys. My room number is 600 and Daniel's is 800, and the woman in the reception says to go up in the lift. But this is not a large hotel and there are only four floors, so we wander around the quiet corridors searching for our rooms, even though it seems obvious that there can't be rooms with such high numbers.

'Maybe my room is number 6,' I say, but that turns out to be a cleaning cupboard. A cleaning cupboard with a room number?

Number 5 is the toilet. They put a room number on the toilet?! We look at each other in disbelief.

Suddenly Daniel says brightly, 'Maybe we are both holding our key tags upside down.'

'What?' I gasp.

We turn the tags round. Now mine reads 009, and Daniel's reads 008. We realize simultaneously that these two numbers are the only ones that are reversible, setting us off into another fit of giggles. I feel I've fallen into a faintly surreal world, and as I enter my room (number 9), I glance over my shoulder to check whether a familiar charmer in evening suit is not perhaps emerging from room 007.

Friday

My last full day here. When I'm on tour, I try to add an extra day or two at the end so that I can get a leisurely feel of where I am. Otherwise I'm hopping from one town to the next, repeating the stop-clock ritual of practising-rehearsing-eating-resting-performing, with little sense of place. I sometimes have to ask myself which town I'm in, even which country I'm in . . . And an extra day provides time to follow up on meetings and libraries and music shops. And art galleries. And zoos. Today there's the master class at the Academy, and a meeting with the Director of the British Council.

But first I wait for Edo the bassoonist, who wants to take me to meet his mother who has a shop in the old part of town. When I've waited long past the appointed hour, I decide to find my own way into the centre of Sarajevo, hoping that I might stumble across him or his mother's shop. Though I don't know what kind of shop I'm looking for, nor what his mother looks like.

Soon I'm wandering around the cobblestoned Turkish streets lined with little shops selling jewellery and wedding dresses, hats and slippers, paintings and metal coffee sets, books and rugs and souvenirs and coffee and nuts and plumbing supplies. The low houses and criss-crossed streets, teeming with people strolling and chattering, give way abruptly as I step across an intersection and a few centuries, and find myself in a completely different city with wide boulevards and tall, elegantly plastered buildings. This is the Austro-Hungarian part of Sarajevo. And this is where all the Viennese pâtisseries are.

I remember that I still have my Eurocheque to cash, but it turns out that I need not only the receipt but my passport, which is of course held by the hotel. So I change some British pounds into euros, which most people prefer to receive anyway rather than the official currency KM (Konvertible Marks). After the war, the currency became German Deutschmarks, but Germany doesn't use Deutschmarks any longer whereas Bosnia still does. Another muddle of time and place . . .

It's soon time to meet up with the lady from the British Council. 'I know a really nice café somewhere near here in the old town. Let's see if I can find it and we can have a spot of lunch.'

We wander up and down the narrow streets until finally she phones her office to get the address. And while she is on the phone, my eye is caught by some unusual fabrics draped over a mannequin outside a clothes shop. I walk over to take a closer look and am astonished to see a large poster of the Mostar Sinfonietta in the window. I'm staring at it when the door is flung open and a plump, beaming woman exclaims, 'I know you!'

I'm startled as I don't think I've ever seen her before, and she continues breathlessly, 'You are violinist, you played concert! I am mother of Edo!'

So I've found the shop after all!

'Oh! *Super! Drago mi je.* Is Edo here?'

'*Ne*, I don't know where. Come, come, *molim.*'

'*Hvala*, I can't, no time. Can I come tomorrow?'

'*Da, da*. I tell Edo. *Ciao!*'

The Director of the British Council tells me that she is retiring in a few months so we talk generally about the music situation in Bosnia. I offer to help in any way that I can, but the conversation is inconclusive.

Then I go to the Academy again and meet the Dean, who is a violinist. His English is good and we chat about instruments and teachers and the difficulty of getting printed music there, particularly music for their orchestra. 'We don't have winds here. Partly because there are no wind teachers. So it's string orchestra. Can you please send me music from England?' I say I will.

When I enter the hall, I see most of the students from yesterday's master class are tuned up and ready to play, and Marina greets me warmly. We work hard for a few hours on both basic technique and musicality. Marina says she knows most of the exercises I show the students, so she must have had good teaching herself, or has had contact with good teachers. As for musicality, the students play dutifully rather than expressively. Which is most often the case wherever I teach master classes. But I think that every student, whether apparently 'musical' or not, can be encouraged – actually taught – to find the feelings in the music they are playing and to play with emotion. And colour. And shape. And there are many ways of approaching the task, of finding a way in to the student's emotional life. Today, one of the younger students is inspired by imagining *where* the music is sounding, what the landscape might be. Another imagines he's in a film. There are lots of smiles as vistas open up.

After the class, Marina is going to a choir rehearsal and I ask if I can come with her and listen for a while.

'*Naravno!*' So we walk along the broad streets and she tells me that her husband is a lawyer.

Marina

My husband is trying to find war criminals. You know, many are still free, it's terrible to see them walking in the streets. There is much work, we must take them on trial.

You know about the rapes? Yes, during the war, there were camps where women were raped, every day, by many men. It was part of war. And you know, when I was in hospital to have my baby, there was a woman next to me, in the near bed, and she had a baby from the rape. She ask me please, feed my baby, I don't want to feed it, I can't look at it, I don't even want it, please take it from me. It was very difficult, but after some days, she knew that this baby was innocent, and she decided take it home to be with her other children, she had own family. Even though, when she looked in baby's eyes, she said she saw the rapist each time.

She took baby home. You know, she was a real mother, that is a real mother.

The choir rehearsal is in preparation for a Christmas concert in conjunction with the Sarajevo Philharmonic. It's a large choir but I count only about fourteen in the orchestra, one wind player and the rest strings. I don't know if that is the full complement, but even if it isn't, it must feel terrible to everybody in the city to see their orchestra so depleted.

At the sound of the voices filling the space, I sit back and sigh involuntarily. The singing feels like a gift. Not directed at me, but a gift in general, for the heavens, for everyone. It's immensely touching that people can have this gift to give, even if they have little else.

This evening I seat myself in the tiny restaurant in the hotel with my diary and the expectation of time for myself. Although I am the only person here, it appears that there is very little food available.

'OK, *nema problema*, bring anything, whatever you have, *hvala*.'
What they have is a tin of chicken soup and some bread and
cheese.

The waiter speaks about five words of English and the same
amount of German, but it doesn't stop him from telling me his war
experience, as so many others have, without invitation. Through a
combination of sign language and the odd word, I understand that
he was a policeman during the siege and often took the wounded
to hospital. That he and his wife and child survived in a basement
for four years. That he took in his sister-in-law and her two small
children when their father was killed. And he told me how he had
to go out to get water for them all, which was very risky because
of the snipers killing people who were going out simply to get
water. He said that Bosnian people were always nice, that they had
always been living together, that they intermarried, and that there
were never any ethnic problems. And that it was Karadžić and the
outsiders who came in and started all the shooting.

I nod and make sure he knows that I understand him and feel for
him. It's very hard to be a receptacle for all these stories, very hard
to remain emotionally open to all this pain. But I can't run away.
And in some sense, I'm privileged to hear them, first-hand. To be
the object of a connection, however anonymous. I don't assume
there is anything special about me that so many want to tell me
their experience. I have the impression that it's precisely because
I'm an outsider, an international, and that they want the story to
go outside their world, to lift their inner siege.

Saturday

I have a few hours before going to the airport, so I try to find a
shop that sells Bosnian wood for making violins. It is reputed to be
an excellent wood and I'd love to get some for Aleth in Bristol.
But the shop that I've been directed to sells only instruments and
accessories.

Disappointed, I make my way to the old town and Edo's
mother's shop. A cluster of soldiers, peacekeepers from Italy, are

strolling along the streets like everyone else. They don't seem to be on duty, but I suppose it's impossible to know. I feel reassured by their presence. In Mostar I've seen groups of soldiers too, from France and other NATO countries, and their presence is equally unobtrusive and reassuring. Some of the musicians have mentioned that they don't want the soldiers to leave, at least not just yet.

Today Edo's mother is dressed in layers of colourful clothing, bohemian yet fashionable, and the shop itself is bursting with colourful fabrics draped everywhere. Little metal cups of sweet Turkish coffee are brought in and we sit round a tiny, low, circular table, chatting. I'm reminded of my grandfather with his thick Russian accent, serving tea to all and sundry who dropped in to his little shop in Leeds. There was always a pot brewing and gossip to share.

I give Edo's mother some gifts and then try on some clothes, eventually buying a black evening top which will be ideal for concerts. She adds a black velvet cloche which I can't imagine wearing, although it does look chic. Edo walks in after about an hour and we chat and drink more coffee.

Edo

For me music is, how to say, manage to stay calm in my head. Because of everything, of the war. And you know, I were in an occupied territory. I were in Banja Luka for all war, and there was a very big nationality problems. You cannot be a Catholic or Muslim there, I was only Muslim in my school . . . it's a bad story. Everyone is talking about it . . . blah blah blah . . . and it's passed, you know, and I don't want to go back, don't talk about it, just go on. My day is ruined when I'm talking about it.

I come to this part of Bosnia, it was really interesting, really, because I didn't know . . . I didn't have a picture of this. They were saying on the television all kind of things, but . . . I were in Zenica, for example, it was normal. I didn't believe my eyes and ears, it was real nice situation, and Muslims and Catholics and Orthodox living together.

When Swan Lake Comes to Sarajevo

I've seen a lot of things and bad and nice, and I now know what will be, it will be. I don't expect too much, from anything, I'm just cruising, and what will be will be. The future it's . . . I'm a believer. I were several times in bad situation and I didn't do anything and I just pass it, like someone carries me. Someone looking after me, yeah my . . . some guy in the sky, I think. Because I'm just a regular guy, you know? I don't want to be rich. I don't need it. If I must some terrible things to do, I don't want it. I just want to have a normal life, to play, to musician, this is my life. And to travel, I love to travel.

And the music, and this is a main thing for me. I didn't know I will be a musician or this kind of thing. I know that I have some talent, before the war, but when the war came, I got music and like a flower, you know? go . . . bloom. Yes.

Music – like water in the desert of war. Edo's eyes glisten with determined optimism. He has already seen too much in his young life, too much to make sense of.

It's time for me to go. I ask him to recommend some CDs of sevdah and he says that most of the sevdah recorded these days has a modern flavour and a 'pop' kind of beat.

'I'd really like to find the original style,' I say.

'All music is get like pop music you know, young people want only pop music. Hard to find real sevdah now, but I try.'

We go across the street to a CD shop where he chooses a couple of discs, and I am thrilled to know that I'll be able to hear an authentic Bosnian wobbly voice in my own living room.

I get myself to the airport in good time and settle in front of the huge glass window in the waiting area. My mind is racing with impressions of the visit – all the distressing things I've heard and seen, and all the moments of elation, a profusion of voices and images and . . . I'll think about it all later.

Everyone was asking when I'm coming back. I don't know. But I will come back.

It's time to leave.

My heart's in my mouth.

Do vidjenja,
do vidjenja Sarajevo.

Coda

There was a lot to absorb.

And I found myself remembering things I hadn't written in the diary, for instance the regular call to prayers from the mosques. Far from being a beautiful male voice, it was a tinny electronic sound, probably pre-recorded, and this, I felt, was somehow fraudulent: if they were going to wake everyone up early, it should be a real person using his own natural voice. At least the calls could have been synchronized, instead of hearing each mosque starting half a minute after the last one, an atonal fugue in surround-sound. I also remembered the enormous cross set upon the highest hill behind Mostar, floodlit at night, so that every time you looked up at the stars, you couldn't avoid seeing it. What an exquisite intrusion, to be reminded of the death and destruction poured onto the besieged city from that very hill, just at the moment when you wish to escape from this earth, with all its earthly business, by gazing away at the stars.

Now I was feeling anger, an anger directed at the symbols of religion that, in this place and context, seemed to be overlaid with hostility and challenge. I was told that foreign money had built the mosques and churches, and that each one became successively taller. 'The height of the spires in relation to the scale of the buildings is absurd, and simply provocative,' someone had said.

At the same time, I felt enormous admiration for everyone's resilience. Each person I passed on the street had survived the nightmare, and was taking their scars into a brave new future. Through forgetting, through walking tall, through pretending to be normal, through telling their stories, by any means they could, they were somehow managing to live on. I wondered at how they could do it. Of course, not everyone could. I was told that every week there was news of an unexpected death, strange accidents – it was an accident-prone city.

But the strongest feelings arose from hearing the tales of war, and these continued to distress me for months. To be suddenly confronted with a personal cry to hear, to bear witness to the telling of what needs to be heard and told; to look into the eyes of the person telling and see their anguish; to hear their simple words and the quality of their voices marking their utter incredulity at what had happened to them; to not close up but keep listening, keep looking, keep the contact – all this was extremely challenging. All this carried its own pain for me. No, I didn't experience what they experienced, but not being a participant entails a strange relationship to their reality, a call to be passive fighting against an instinct to be desperately active. Bearing witness is all they wanted from me, but bearing witness, though physically passive, is a demanding activity in itself. And not without consequences.

The torrents that had been poured into my ears became part of my emotional luggage. The worst was Selma's story and the visions that it struck in my imagination. They tormented me and they wouldn't leave. I didn't want to encumber any of my friends with the same visions, but I realized that I needed a witness for myself. I went to the Medical Foundation for the Victims of Torture in London and spoke to someone there who had listened to such stories for years, and it soon became clear that bearing witness has risks that are well known. It was a relief to discuss this and to be told that the listener must take steps in order to survive the stories, that sometimes the listener must withdraw, and of course, that the process of passing on the story is the process of drawing its sting.

This first visit to Bosnia left me with many strong memories. The location itself, with its bullet-riddled walls and collapsed buildings, was a new experience for me. As was making music in such surroundings. Music goes anywhere, but here it was in its element, touching raw emotion, going straight to the heart. I have played the same Mozart Adagio in the Hermitage in St Petersburg, a splendid palace with room after room of magnificent works of art.

These two places stand at opposite poles of human activity, and the music filled the space in different ways. But I felt the same connectedness to the Russian people, setting aside their daily lives for the moment to come together in Mozart, as I did in Bosnia, we who were playing, and those who were listening, brought together into a temporary community, the sounds vibrating through us all simultaneously.

October 2003

Here the chaos of Bosnia enters my writing. There were three visits between 2003 and 2005 during which my diary-keeping became more and more sketchy. I was overtaken by the constant unexpectedness of life there, and ordering my thoughts at the end of the day was more than I could contemplate. Contemplation itself seemed to have spread its wings and fled.

In Bosnia, planning doesn't often happen. Things get done, if they do get done, at the last possible moment. The struggle to work at anywhere near normal efficiency eventually led me to loosen my grip and become more 'Bosnian' myself. A general unfocused and lackadaisical attitude can be infectious; though one could say I was just being flexible. One casualty was my diary-writing. So what I remember are disjointed events and impressions, much like my experience of being there.

Whatever corners became frayed, I kept my concentration on the musicians, on raising their game, boosting their confidence, encouraging their pride in being professional, pride in their increased ability to play, to feel, to listen, to perform and to enjoy the process of making music. I suppose I hoped that as they appreciated their own achievements, their more focused attitude would spill over into other areas of their lives. The glow on everyone's faces after those first concerts seemed to beckon an expanded future, and I was going to do my best to keep it expanding.

❧

It was for a different purpose that I returned to Bosnia the following year. Not to work with the Mostar Sinfonietta, but to attend a conference in Sarajevo of Musicians Without Borders, a young organization based in the Netherlands. I emailed Marina to say that I would be available to teach for a few days, and I took my violin with me. It would be interesting to see what my impressions of Sarajevo would be without the stress of preparing a concert. I wondered if it would feel as intense and chaotic; or if it would feel more ordinary.

Ordinary? How could that thought have entered my mind? The extraordinary popped up like showers in April, just when the sky seems to be an endless expanse of blue.

Reconstruction of Stari Most

Six wooden half-circled planks lifted by crane and placed on steel centering, wooden covering added.
Portal crane built to order and positioned on centering.
Bridge stones chiselled off-site, each stone exactly as in original bridge. Blocks chiselled by row (2–5 blocks per row), holes for dowels and cramps chiselled into blocks, molten lead poured into dowels.
Blocks transported to bridge site.
Stone-wetting pool built to immerse each stone-row for 24 hours to enable optimal contact between stone and mortar.
First stone of arch placed on upstream east side.

❧❦❧

On the flight, I sit on the last row and chat to a comfortably plump Englishwoman who is a tour representative for Saga. She tells me that the money she earns enables her to spend two to three months every winter at a school for destitute children in Romania. She is like a grandmother to them, giving presents, playing games, helping with homework . . . an amazing woman. There are so many people doing unexpectedly generous things with their lives.

There is no snow this time as the plane touches down in Sarajevo. Yes, I do remember the airport, just as featureless as before. This time I am met by Ermin, a jolly fellow with a ready smile who is helping the conference (and the Mostar Sinfonietta) in practical ways, like driving people to and fro in his large battered car.

'How is everyone?' I ask.

'*Dobro, dobro*,' he nods. 'Selma has baby. Everyone fine.'

Ah, so she *was* pregnant . . .

❧❦❧

'This afternoon we are meeting in front of the main cathedral.'
'Oh?'
'We're going to be a samba band.'

About thirty of the conferees gather in front of the cathedral, where a pile of percussion instruments has materialized.

'Choose an instrument,' yells a large young Dutch-Caribbean who seems to be in charge of the proceedings.

There are huge drums, medium-sized drums, small drums, triangles, rattles – I take a side drum. We group ourselves according to our instruments and form a semicircle. Then the maître d' assigns each percussion section a short rhythmic pattern which we quickly memorize.

'All together now!' and hey presto we sound like a Brazilian samba band! A few variations follow; for instance, when he blows a whistle, one section will play a two-bar riff, then boom boom on the bass drums and we are all to join in again. And then we're ready.

We have been in Sarajevo for only a few hours and here we are, a motley group of foreigners and Bosnians, processing down the main street, tapping out our rhythms as loudly as possible and jiggling our hips in response to the huge Latin noise we are making! Fifteen children caper ahead of us, dancing and waving scarves above their heads. In five minutes we are in the old town and everyone comes out of the shops, looking astonished; then they smile and jiggle along with us. I notice a few of the old women putting their hands over their ears, but their discomfort doesn't seem to mar their glee at seeing such a rowdy, rhythmic, joyous band of players bouncing down their narrow street. It must feel so alien to them, and to the memories of these stones, but if it's possible to drown out the bad memories with our rhythm, we are determinedly trying. Sometimes we stop and play in place; sometimes we play softly and neatly, only to explode in a riot of sound again. A policeman accompanies us, looking embarrassed, as if we are definitely mad and besides, this is an assignment he has not been trained for. But here we come, a samba band in old Sarajevo, a celebration, of energy, of togetherness, a togetherness of strangers.

The evening is taken up with a choral concert at Dom Armje, a large concert hall that must have been grandly elegant in its time. The choir is of the highest standard, singing with sensitive phrasing, greatly varied dynamics and emotional commitment. The Pontanima Choir is multi-ethnic in a country where this is the exception. It originated in a church whose choir had been decimated by the war, prompting the priest to take the step of inviting singers from other churches, and even other religions, to bolster its numbers. The Pontanima, meaning 'spiritual bridge', now has about sixty members from all religious communities in Bosnia, and is often invited to sing abroad as a 'witness to peaceful co-existence'.

What is even more unusual is that they build their programmes from combinations of Hebrew, Christian Orthodox, Catholic, Protestant and Islamic songs. As the programme notes explain, this means that at any given moment, some of the singers are singing 'the songs of their enemies'.

I try to imagine what it must be like for them.

How can they take these melodies into their throat? And so soon after the war.

To sing songs of the enemy is a way to enter into another's world, to destroy the divide.

This is real courage.

The voices, the music, the unforced simplicity of such courage, moves me to tears. As it does every one of us in the audience.

I'm staying in a private house, perched on the edge of a hill above the city. It is newly built and belongs to a woman called Asa, who earns some money by renting out a few rooms. She leads me upstairs to a tiny attic in which are squeezed four beds. Four beds only, no other furniture, not even a chair. I see I'll have to live out of my suitcase. Three women from the conference are sitting on three of the beds, and I'm introduced to Anastasia and Periman from Macedonia, and Valdete from Kosovo who is the youngest.

Valdete speaks English well, Anastasia has only a few words, and Periman doesn't seem to speak any English at all.

The room next door also has four women. I'm told there is one bathroom. For eight women. This is feeling a bit too much like a youth hostel, except that we are no longer youth, and I'm not sure I'm up to it.

Periman is painting on nail polish when I enter the room and the fumes are overpowering. So the first thing I do is to ask if we can please have the tiny skylight open. It's freezing outside, and they look at me as if I'm mad, or maybe just a typical Englishwoman.

I realize that I've forgotten to explain.

'Just for a few minutes until the fumes are gone,' I say. Valdete translates. They humour me with reluctance. It's been a long day.

✧

An older man stops me on the stairs of the Academy. 'You're Ruth, aren't you? You played here last year.' He must have come to the concert. He tells me he's a violin teacher and asks if I want to come for Shabbat service tonight. Normally I would decline, but in Sarajevo I say yes to things like this.

I ask Shura, a singer from the Netherlands who's attending the conference, if she wants to come with me, and she takes it upon herself to invite Laura (Argentina), Ofer (Israel), Nabil (Israel) and Marjolein (Netherlands). Nabil is an Arab Christian from Nazareth and he wears a large cross on top of his white tunic. He also brings his oud, but no-one seems to mind. And Ofer brings his guitar. David the violin teacher and his wife lead us to the synagogue. We walk across the river, but this is a tame river compared with the Neretva. Today the Miljacka is a dull brown colour and, with no steep cliffs, it flows more like an urban, well-behaved river.

It is too cold in the synagogue itself to hold the service, but I peer inside and notice that it is beautifully decorated in a Persian style, with what looks like Islamic tiles, though it is actually paint. A handful of people are waiting in the entrance and we all go downstairs to a basement with a low ceiling and pillars, a serving bar, a long table set for dinner, and a few rows of straight-backed chairs. We seat ourselves on these chairs and David starts singing the familiar chants of the Friday night service. It has been years since I've heard these sounds, but they bring deep memories of my childhood, nothing particular, just a sound-memory, a smell-memory, the feel of being among warm people breathing comfortably. And in this foreign place, in this company of scattered people, I sense this Friday night in other places and other countries where there are Jews, the same sounds floating into the air, as they do each Friday night, as they have done in countless basements and synagogues for centuries, space and time condensing . . .

The service over, we all settle ourselves round the dinner table. Our hosts are mainly elderly, small in stature, dressed in their dark Sabbath suits, but their faces are lit with excitement at this unexpected influx of foreign guests. The old man next to me grins and shuffles in his chair, saying in Yiddish that it's a pleasure to sit with a beautiful woman. This causes general merriment and shouted comments by the others, which eventually get translated for my benefit as, 'Water that has gone past the mill can't grind the grain!'

In between the laughter, blessings are said, wine and bread are passed round, and we all relish a small square of cheese, a slice of potato and a boiled egg, though this meagre fare causes me acute embarrassment, since it is because of me that the food has to be stretched in this way. No miracles of fishes tonight! But our presence seems to more than compensate: conversation is plentiful, in whatever languages we can muster, and there's a sense of great pride in being offered this opportunity to host such a gathering.

And then, music is heard. A wonderfully deep, strong voice emerges from Shura, as she turns towards David at the head of the table and sings in Yiddish. Her singing is expressive, her hand gestures urging the music along, her face reflecting the emotion of the song. Everyone is astonished and utterly delighted, and more music follows as Ofer's guitar and Nabil's oud are brought into play. The Israeli Jew and the Israeli Arab Christian improvise together, concentrating on the other's sounds, taking up the other's pulse and rhythm, smiling at each other when a phrase lifts and takes wing; or they accompany Shura as she launches into more and more Yiddish, then Ladino, songs, and the company seems dazed at all this joy.

The evening wears on and nobody is tired. Spontaneous magic.

Getting home is another story. I find a taxi and Laura from Argentina says, 'Just say you want Asa's house and the driver will know,' as she closes the door and waves goodbye.

The driver sets off in the opposite direction from what I expect. He speaks no English at all. Or German. Evidently there must be more than one Asa who has a guesthouse. And nobody seems to bother with addresses here. It's hopeless trying to remember how to get there – I've been there only once, after all – but then it suddenly comes back to me how last night, Laura had directed the driver to go to the Hotel Saraj, then go further, and whenever there was a fork in the road, she looked one way and then the other before saying 'turn right', until we arrived at house No. 4. At least I think that's what happened. It's worth a try.

'*Molim*, Hotel Saraj,' I say.

The driver turns the car round and starts driving back to where we have come. A promising start. When we reach the hotel, I gesture for him to go further up the hill, and each time we are confronted with an intersection, my hand points to the right. I'm not sure I recognize anything. Soon we are at the top of the hill and we round a bend and house No. 4 comes into view. *My* house No. 4.

'*Da, da, OK, hvala.*'

Yesterday I wouldn't have guessed that I'd be so happy to see my 'dorm' again. And how remarkable that my normally less-than-reliable memory is able to come to the rescue in an emergency.

The conference has been a good opportunity to meet many different kinds of musicians, and to exchange notes on how we are trying to bring music to troubled places. Future collaborations are in the air, and the final event suggests an example of how this can be done. It is to be a concert performed by the conferees, the first half to consist of short pieces from each of us in our normal style; the second half to consist of pieces created by 'crossing borders', where we play with others from a different country and in an unfamiliar style.

A tall order as far as I am concerned: I haven't touched the violin for three days; there is no pianist with whom to play, leaving me with no choice of repertoire but unaccompanied Bach or a Paganini Caprice – no contest, though Bach on less-than-top form is an unsavoury gamble too; I have only my 'Bosnia violin' with me which will not sound at all well in Bach; as for collaborating with my fellow musicians here, I have no idea what other kind of music I can play, and with whom; and on top of it all, I have nothing suitable to wear! And with only a few hours in which to arrange it all, this comes perilously close to the typical 'musician's nightmare', in which one is about to walk out onto the stage of Carnegie Hall with no idea of what the repertoire is, and no concert clothes – and sometimes even holding an instrument you've never played before! It doesn't take a professional to understand this dream, but I'd hoped it would always know its place – as a dream.

In the event, I borrow a long black skirt from my dorm-mate Periman; I find a space in the corridor to practise the Bach Andante from the 2nd solo Sonata for twenty minutes; I'm corralled by a Scottish violinist and a Sarajevan accordionist to play some Scottish ceilidh ('OK just D major, eight bars repeated, then the middle sixteen – shall we repeat that? – mainly double-stops with a few riffs'); and heavens above! the music for two Bosnian sevdah tunes materializes and, at the appearance of Nigel Osborne with his guitar, our little group rehearses for ten minutes. Sevdah in ten minutes? And I'm supposed to play it in front of a local audience in Sarajevo? I imagine rotten tomatoes hurtling in my direction (and rightly so).

I gulp down a slice of pizza and a banana and it's time to begin. An amazing array of performances gets under way, including an excellent pop group, a Dutch choir, Nabil playing the oud,

Periman singing Macedonian songs with great power, a rather wobbly rendition of Bernstein's 'Somewhere', a moving piece for accordion written by the accordionist, and Shura singing a Sarajevan prayer for children, that they can grow up in peace, that they can grow up. And me: the violin sounds dreadful, the acoustics dead as a doornail. This is not my finest hour. Never mind – wait for the second half . . .

After the interval, the players combine to romp through a set of Brazilian songs with drums, then African songs with drums and dance, and then it's time for us. The ceilidh sounds fine, and I think my riffs fit in well enough with the Scottish fiddler. Now for the sevdah, and as soon as I start playing the melody, a surge of energy races round the hall, the audience rise from their seats and sing and sway with raised arms. *Moj Dilbere* – it's their song and they love it. I love it too, ever since the first time I heard it last year. Maybe now it's also one of my songs . . . and here I am, playing it, together with terrific musicians, the audience yelling and screaming as we come to the end! The noise and elation are overwhelming. I feel I've entered a new musical world, one that is centuries old, and part and parcel of this geographic region like the trees on the hills.

Of course, there is a party afterwards, and of course no one knows exactly where it is, so some of us wander round Sarajevo ('I think it's up the hill a bit, maybe it's to the right, no the left'), eventually coming across a noisy bar that seems to be our destination ('I knew it was somewhere round here'). All the conferees are there, drinking and celebrating.

'Do you have your violin?'

It's Nigel. I should have guessed.

'May I?' And he launches into Bosnian tunes, starting another energetic three hours of music and dancing.

When I can't stay awake any longer, I retrieve my violin and order a taxi. I'm confident this time in my ability to find 'Asa's house', and in any case, I'm not alone as Anastasia and Periman are with me. The driver follows my gestured instructions and we arrive without difficulty at No. 4. But the front door is locked, and no-one has a key. We ring the bell continuously and knock on all the windows and call out. It is 2.30 a.m. We look at each other helplessly.

We are stranded in a narrow, dark street, and dogs are gathering. Normally I like dogs, but these are wild-looking. I remember that they ate anything during the war. Anything. I remember how one bit my hand in Mostar. I'm feeling the beginning of panic. The dogs are circling us.

Suddenly, two people walk out of the darkness. They turn out to be conferees and are also staying at Asa's house. I am reassured by this increase in our numbers and also grateful that they speak English. Luckily one of them has a mobile phone. Plus Asa's phone number. Things are looking up. The phone call is made and the door opens to a very apologetic Asa, rubbing the sleep from her eyes.

This is our last night and the women in my room are all more relaxed. It almost feels like a friendly student dorm now; even Periman shows that she does have some English after all. As Anastasia brushes out her long hair, she starts to sing a lullaby and the evening ends with each of us singing in the dark a lullaby in our own language. Sleep arrives to the gentle lilt of a song from Macedonia.

❧

On the day following the end of the conference, I'm invited by Marina, the young violin teacher from the Music Academy, to her home for lunch. I'm glad to see those large, trusting eyes again. Her flat reminds me of a Russian apartment. The plastic, Formica '50s look. Drab. No colour.

We sit in the kitchen and chat while she prepares lunch: cauliflower soup (cauliflower, milk, garlic, butter, oil, flour), vegetable patties, spinach (with milk and garlic), cornbread, chard salad. Then sweet rice with honey and fruit and yoghurt. As we sit down to eat, she tells me her story, starting with her parents and grandparents and how they dealt with their own war, the Second World War.

Marina

My mother had a very strong need to talk about that every day again, with all details. And in one way it was easier for her but it was very difficult for me. She told how all of children, they took them in front of house and then they tortured him and then they killed him. This is my grandfather, my mother's father. And many other bad things happened. That's Serb Nationalist Paramilitary Formation. My mother was seven. And of course my grandmother miscarried, she lost the baby. Two older sons were Communists, they were in Partisans, and those were killed by other extremists, Croat extremists and nationalists, in Croatia.

And then when they killed her father, they took all food from house. They were pretty rich, they had big land and people working on that land for her. They took all food out of house and they put the guards on the wall outside the house, so nobody could come and bring them food. They left them to die of hunger. Two women and nine children. And then one Serb woman, neighbour, every night, very late at night, she came on some mysterious way on other side when there weren't guards and she was feeding them. And it was like mother for all of them. And she was Serb as well, like those who killed my grandfather.

And my grandmother, she was illiterate, but she was raised – and that's the Bosnian spirit – that all people are good if they are not bad, if you don't have reason to believe that they are not good. And after the war when my uncles were in the school, somebody told them (they were so young they couldn't remember), her father killed your father, you have to beat them. And when my grandmother heard about that, she of course she beated her sons at home and told them, you are the first who have to help them if they have any problems. They are not guilty for their parent's sins.

And so my mother when she was twenty-five years or something, went to that . . . in our language it's 'working action' you know, everybody wanted to go, like place to work in the country. Of course for her mother, it was very difficult to let her go, she was a widow and to leave daughter to go somewhere alone with young men . . . but she let her. And then my father fell in love with her. And of course she was raised in such an old-fashioned way because, you know, she don't have father, and her mother was very rigid, so she didn't pay attention of any young men.

Then she heard that my father is playing violin and then she fell in love. And he's a Serb, from Serbia. Of course, for my grandmother, it was really not a problem. And you know I just wanted to tell this story for you because in Bosnia it's normal – if you are not nationalist – it's normal if somebody kill your father and he's a Serb, that you don't have any kind of idea that you have to hate all Serbs. And it's normal to get married to Serbs, or anybody, or to have children or anything. And I'm so happy that I have parents like that. Because I don't have any kind of possibility to be a nationalist, you know, or racist or something. Because it's completely normal for me that if my daughter come with a . . . I don't know . . . Indian, or black guy, or of course a Croat . . . because it's so difficult to find the right person, especially today when everybody are you know, computers, TV, pornography on every corner, it's very difficult to find the match soul. And I'm raising my children as well, and I hope that they will be good people.

You know first day of Bosnian war, 6 April 1992. We are counting first day of war when first victims fell here. And I was there, on the same place where those two women were killed. Because they put the barricades in the middle of town. Because month before they tried to start a war, those Serb extremists. And they put barricades and people came out on the streets for one day. You know people just came out of houses and barricades were there and everybody went home. And then one day people realized that they have to do something, and everybody came out, and just walked through the barricades and the Serbs ran away.

Next time, those nationalists from Serbia realized that it's impossible to do that with Serbs from Sarajevo, and then they released the killers from the prisons, junkies, and all kinds of problems. They gave them weapons and they put them on the barricades. And then we tried again to walk through the barricades and on that bridge, they were like just eyes, all black like criminals, they were criminals, and they were shooting on us. I was like . . . I couldn't believe that this is happening. And I know that that guy is talking the same language. I know that he is not, I don't know, from Australia or other planet, he's from my country.

And then when I saw blood, I was in shock. It was really miracle that I wasn't killed then.

So that's the way war started. And then all of that from my conscious and subconscious, all those stories that it is possible to survive that your brother is killing, you're trying to kill your . . .

Sometimes, I'm walking in the street, several times, and I feel a bullet is coming to me. And suddenly time goes very slowly, it stretches, I can hear the trigger and the bullet going through the barrel, I can hear the bullet in the air, it's going slowly, I just move my head some centimetres and it goes through my hair. And there's time to think, while the bullet comes for me, please I hope I will be with God, please forgive me God.

You know, because of working for Children's Embassy, we – my husband and I – met many different kinds of people, you know, all possible . . . bad people, and to stay alive . . . OK we had some sort of immunity from them, some sort of protection, Children's Embassy, the United Nations and everything, many papers, and we weren't unknown, you know, so you can't just disappear. But the only way of communication with these bad people is that you pretend that they are normal, and it's not true that all of them were unnormal.

Some Jehovah's Witness gave me a bible book, little bible book, and I was taking that sort of for luck, because those women were so positive, you know, and full of love. I felt some positive energy in that book. And I was always carrying that. And then I realized that the best way to avoid some unpleasant conversation with extremists, you know Serbs and Croats, because all of them started to be great Christians suddenly, you know with crosses and everything, and in the same time killing people because of that cross – I have cross and you are not Christian, I will kill you, you are guilty because you're not Christian – you know that crazy things. And then I started to talk with them about Jesus and love and you know, they started to act, to . . . I don't know, to be better, not to be so aggressive. So it was very helpful, talking about bible in some situations.

And then of course we had several captures – is that the right word? – when you are not free. First by Croats then by Serbs, and then the last one was when I was in six months of pregnancy with my first pregnancy. And we survived everything. Really it's impossible not to believe in God after everything. He looked after me during the whole time, I'm sure.

And the main idea what helped me to stay normal, not to get crazy or to have some breakdown was, 'Everything will pass and one day I will realize that the worst situation can be the best, now I feel horribly in some situation and one day I will realize that it was good for some reason.' And it was like mantra for me, you know, I was telling to myself all time, all time, all time, that thing. And the other one was, 'One day when everything is finished, I will have my children, and I will tell them while we are walking through the city, "Oh this was destroyed completely, there was a huge hole, you know, of grenade," and they will think that it's funny because there isn't any holes and any destroyed buildings.' And then, you know, it was very comforting for me.

And of course love, of course, on the first place, you know when you are in love you can take war like it's not your life, it's like . . . like a film you are playing some role in it. I was in jail, with my husband, he was in one part and I was in another part in one jail, and you know, I didn't hate the people who keeping us there. I felt pity for them, even love for them. And all the time I love my husband. I could survive because of love for my husband. And believing that God is protecting me because of my love and there is a meaning for all this.

She continues by saying that after the war, she became depressed and dissatisfied with her life. So she has intensified her belief, not in any particular religion, just her own personal belief in God. She is sure there must be a meaning for everything. But it seems that her husband is alienated by her religiousness and this is straining their relationship.

Her husband is away at the moment, but she introduces me to her two young children, aged nine and eight. They are sweet and playful. When I leave, her little girl walks with me to the bus stop and says she wants to come with me to England.

Over the next two days, I teach master classes at the Academy. They are mostly Marina's students, but every now and then, a new student shyly opens the door asking if it's possible to play for me. We go through the Bach E major Concerto, Bach C major solo Andante, Bach G minor solo Sonata, Kreisler Praeludium and Allegro, Schubert The Bee (a lovely little piece by a different Schubert!), Mendelssohn Concerto, and Bruch Concerto. The standard is varied. The boy with the outstanding talent from last year is here, but some of the older students are not as advanced as him. One older girl is nervous and not at all well prepared. As we talk about this, she suddenly says that she is hungry. I give her a packet of almonds that I happen to have. Surprised, she says, 'You're very nice.' I wonder when anyone last offered her food.

There is a lot of Bach. I probably shrink a little every time the reply to my question 'so what would you like to play for me?' is, 'Bach.' I steel myself for a reading that wallows in a warm rich sound, a declamatory style, and a wayward sense of rhythm, all punctuated by loud, ungainly chords. I long for intelligent phrasing, harmonic awareness, shaping and moulding and pacing, drama and intimacy. I long for a full range of emotions. Students all over the world often sound disappointingly the same, whatever the repertoire, as if they, or their teachers, are following a set of unvarying instructions, even to the extent of committing the same counting errors. It can be quite depressing.

'Why are you playing the opening loudly?' I want to ask, when yet another stentorian Bach G minor Adagio is offered. Bach rarely marks any dynamics so it's up to us to ferret out the dynamic shape of each movement. A question like this can fluster students as they don't often know why they are playing as they do. And they don't expect the question anyway, normally being in the passive position of receiving suggestions (or instructions) as to how to play. So usually I refrain, but occasionally I do ask it, and if an answer is forthcoming, a discussion can ensue, a dialogue not so much between the student and myself as between the student and the music. I love it when this happens. A student who uses his mind, who knows that emotions without intellect lead down blind alleys, that before you can respond emotionally to something, you have to know what that 'something' is. And know it intimately. Love at first sight is only the prelude.

More often than not, I'll ask them to choose the section they like best, and to tell me why they like it, and to play it again with more conviction. And then we'll explore what other ingredients are present, and before long, we're off and running, straight into the heart of the music, noticing what's really there, taking apart and pulling it all together into a whole that might, in the end, transform or even obliterate the aspect originally liked.

The work is slow. Half an hour can pass and we've explored only a phrase or two. But hopefully the class is absorbing more than just a couple of phrases. I'm encouraging the students to see that Bach's world is much more abundant than they thought, more touching and robust, more human, more divine, infinite. I'm trying to show them how to question the score, how to take responsibility for their decisions, how to start on their own personal journey to become mature musicians. I'm trying to eliminate their need for a teacher.

One day I visit Edo the bassoonist in his mother's shop. I am glad to see him. He tells me that he is going to Slovenia to study for four years. Probably a good move, though we will miss him in the Sinfonietta. A friend comes in and talks about the politics in the Music Academy, how the teachers are possessive of their students, how they are strict, and how they don't really teach 'the music', complaints I've heard many times in many places. 'The other students don't care – they just want to graduate so they can get a teaching job.'

There is a rather decrepit upright piano at the front of the shop. Edo's sister is studying the piano and says she practises on it for five hours a day. She plays me some Bach and Rachmaninov and she plays well. She says it draws people into the shop. I'm not surprised. When was the last time I heard Rachmaninov emanating live from a little London dress shop?

I have now moved to a *pension* at the edge of the old town. It has a small lobby and breakfast area, the bedroom has no heating, and everything smells of cigarettes. After two days, a heater appears in my room. As for eating, I don't seem to be able to find any particularly enticing or healthy fare. And in the evening a woman alone becomes the target of many a glance. One day I go out for some soup; there is a cockroach in the bread-basket. The saving grace is the pastries. Austrian in origin, they exude nuts, cinnamon, meringue, chocolate, cream. Sometimes I end up indulging myself more than once a day . . .

'Let me take you to the best place for *burek*.' Everyone seems to know where to get 'the best *burek* in town', and leads me to it with pride. Marina is no different. Only this time, I think she is right. It is a tiny café mainly for take-away, with only one table. There are three large cylindrical hobs onto which the bakers continually pile red-hot coke in layers, like a big dirty wedding cake, and the *burek* cooks underneath. The cylinders are suspended by big iron hooks in a pulley system which raises them off the pie pans when the *burek* are ready. It is very hot work.

Our spinach *burek* consists of a light pastry with a tasty filling, and for the first time, they are not at all greasy. The shop is busy with a constant stream of people coming in and taking away *burek*. Marina and I sit at the table. She says she has often thought about me since last year. It crosses my mind that, for good or ill, she can't avoid thinking of me, because in the entrance to the Academy, my name is stuck onto a huge noticeboard that is otherwise empty. It's a remnant of the Mostar Sinfonietta poster from last year's concert – the only bit of the poster left.

An old man has been sitting at our table and now he leans over and asks Marina a question. She laughs. He has heard us speaking a foreign language but we both look Bosnian, so which of us is Bosnian?

He thinks I look Bosnian. Maybe I am.

When it's time to leave, the café owner says he is so honoured to serve a foreigner that he doesn't let me pay for my *burek*. Marina says I must accept his generosity, so I take some photos of him and his Albanian female chef and I'll send some prints from England.

Today Sarajevo is shutting down for a state funeral. The Muslim Bosnian President has died and his photo graces every shop window. (There's a rotating presidency between a Serb, a Croat and a Muslim.) I've been told that all city roads will be closed from 10 a.m. and I need to find a way to get to the airport for my afternoon flight back to London. So I've made an arrangement with the father of the talented student who played for me at the Academy the other day. Irfan will take me to his home slightly outside Sarajevo, I will teach his son, and then after lunch, he'll drive me to the airport without going through the city. I think I have the best part of this deal. My only task is to get to the central bus station where we are to meet at ten o'clock.

The hotel receptionist starts phoning for a taxi while I drink my coffee and continues for half an hour without being able to get through. 'All lines are engaged. I keep trying.' At 9.45 a.m. I can see that she is not getting anywhere, and that 10 a.m. will no doubt arrive with 'sorry, *ne može*' and a shrug. So I dash onto the street with my luggage and miraculously hail a taxi as it races round the bend away from the river.

'All roads closing,' the driver says as he jerks the car into motion.

'I know,' I say, holding on to the back of the front seat. We seem to bounce over each crossroad just as the police move the barriers into place. Sometimes we have to double-back as we see a barrier ahead of us. We are finally stopped by one as we near the bus station, but I am close enough to see Irfan waiting for me.

His home is on a hill and the surrounding houses are in various states of completion. 'This is near where front line was. We built our house with our hands.'

He shows me in. It's spotless, and tastefully decorated.

'We have just finish the stairs,' he says with pride. His wife is Polish and a real beauty. She plays the cello in the Philharmonic. She gives us coffee, and then I start the lesson, first going through some detailed exercises and afterwards working on Corelli's La Folia. It's a pleasure to teach someone with a solid technique and excellent concentration.

Lunch is spaghetti and Irfan asks if he can turn on the television to watch the funeral. It is raining and the crowds have raised a roof of black umbrellas under the dark-grey clouds. There are a great number of people, silent except for the occasional chant. The cortège seems disorganized, people being unsure of where to go and what to do, as if they haven't rehearsed enough. The TV cameras are fairly static and minutes pass in silence between the sporadic commentary. The High Representative for Bosnia, Paddy Ashdown, approaches the microphones in a black raincoat. He looks much older than I remember, craggier, drawn. The effect of working in Bosnia. 'It's appropriate that the heavens are weeping,' he says. I look over to Irfan.

'Very rare that it rains all day,' he explains. 'Never happens.'

We take a long, circular route to the airport and arrive without a problem. I sleep all the way to London. It has been a tiring week, with poor food and constant smoke. An unforgettable week too, with wonderfully kind people and uplifting moments, of music fulfilling its promise of inspiration and unity, of new friends and connections. But underlying it all, I feel Sarajevo, seething in turmoil.

April 2004

Sviramo we play *iz početka* from the beginning *ponovo* again.

Essential vocabulary.

For a conductor in rehearsal.

My young Bosnian teacher in London was more accustomed to the language of the business world, so she greeted my request with amusement and interest.

'Make a list of words and phrases you want to learn, and I'll teach you them next time.' I did.

What time is the rehearsal?
Where is the music?
Please listen to the cellos.
It's not together.
Just the winds, please.
Much better.

Etcetera. Plus of course, numbers. Though it would probably be quicker to say the bar number in English and have it translated, than for me to work it out accurately in Bosnian. In any case, I considered it well worth the effort to write rehearsal letters into each orchestral part; so that instead of asking the players to 'begin at bar 128', I'd just say 'five bars before letter D', placing the letters at tricky spots that looked likely to invite trouble. I just made sure I had my numbers one to ten fluently; being able to say in Bosnian 'ten-minute cigarette break' would be much appreciated.

I took only four lessons but that was enough for the rehearsal basics, plus the usual 'My name is Ruth. What is your name?' and more usefully, 'What is his name?' I couldn't address the 2nd horn as Mr Secondo Corno for ever.

⌘

The programme was ambitious. There were no oboists in Bosnia now, since the scheme that enabled Daniel from Sweden to teach was no longer operating. 'But we have a clarinet, and two horns, and though Edo has gone, maybe we can find a bassoon. And of course two flutes.' Not exactly a full-size wind and brass section, but wouldn't it be wonderful if the Sinfonietta could play something large in scope and unabashedly romantic? It would have to be a work that could be scaled down without losing essential lines or harmonies, a work that had lots of doublings (many instruments playing the same notes, albeit in different octaves), that would not suffer greatly from lack of sonority. Something fairly simple, full of verve and grand sweeps . . .

During my early days in New York, I was asked to play for some performances of *Raymonda*, a full-length ballet by Alexander Glazounov. The principal male lead was to be Rudolf Nureyev. I didn't know the ballet at all, this being its first US performance, but as soon as rehearsals began, I fell in love with the rich, colourful, intensely Russian music. However, it was the presence of Nureyev that lifted the experience onto a transcendent plane. It was thrilling to be so close to him, to feel his rhythm and grace, his supreme muscular efforts always clad in effortlessness. I memorized as much of my part as I could so that I could play while keeping my eyes on him; he seemed the embodiment of romanticism, exuding dignity and radiance. And ardour. From that time onwards, *Raymonda* has glowed in my memory.

The big *pas de deux* is set to a beautiful violin solo that begins in a soft, honeyed D major, full of the promise of love. To perform this Grand Adagio in Bosnia . . . I wondered if, through a feat of alchemy, some of Nureyev's radiance could pass to the people of Mostar . . .

I took myself to the British Library to look at the score. As expected, it's written for a huge orchestra, including piccolo, oboes, trumpets, trombones, tuba, harp and percussion, none of which we had. It asks for four horns – we had only two; three clarinets – we had only one. But in the Adagio itself, the main orchestral lines are for clarinet and horn, and the harp would be missed in only a few places.

I looked more closely. The trumpets, trombones, tuba and tympani play only five bars – two in the middle and a crescendo at the very end, so we could manage without them. I could give the 2nd clarinet entrance to horn 2, and the oboe entrance to horn 1; two later bars of oboe solo can go to the 2nd flute whose notes can be played by horn 1; further on, flute 2 can take the 2nd clarinet line underneath clarinet 1. The lines juggled in my mind as I tried to cover the missing instruments while retaining as much colour as I could. Would the balance be better with the horn above the clarinet, or vice versa? I got down to work.

Re-orchestration was not something I had done before, or if I had, it was long buried in my student days. But I found it a fascinating activity, a puzzle that played in my inner ear for weeks. Once embarked on the project, I was inspired to programme some more movements from the ballet, so I eagerly trawled through the score only to find that in one piece the harp was essential, in another the trumpets, and in another, the violins had too many tricky passages that would in all likelihood not be well negotiated. One movement after another bit the dust.

But then I came across the beautifully simple Romanesca, an elegant flute solo; and two exotic dances from Act Two which, although scored for full forces, could probably be scaled down without being mauled too badly. And they were real virtuoso pieces that would show off the orchestra and allow the players to make a grand noise and let off steam. There was only the small matter of the tambourine, an essential rhythmic colour in the *Danse des Garçons Arabs* and the *Entrée des Sarrazins*. But surely there would be someone in Mostar, a student perhaps, who could take that part.

Once I had come to grips with the orchestration, the task of writing out the parts began – and lasted far longer than I anticipated. The activity of transposing horns in F to clarinets in A provided uncommon stimulation for my brain cells and burned much midnight oil, but the end result was a sheaf of orchestral parts, written specifically for the Mostar Sinfonietta, of a work that was exciting, passionate and rarely heard. It might even be a premiere in Bosnia . . .

To fill out the programme, I chose Tchaikovsky's Scherzo for violin in an orchestration by Glazounov, an interesting juxtaposition; and to provide a contrast, Haydn's Symphony No. 52, mainly because I thought that the oboe parts, having little or no independence, could be played by the flutes. I took the decision reluctantly – I don't like to alter Haydn in any way and flutes will sound rather weaker than oboes – but there is very little choice of repertoire for strings and winds without oboes. And the classical style is fundamental. All ensembles need to immerse themselves in it, to learn its language and customs, to walk its paths in comfort.

Reconstruction of Stari Most

Mortar made using natural components (gravel, lime and powdered bricks) exactly matching original mortar.

One row on each side of the bridge assembled each day and placed on wooden arch.

6mm layer of mortar placed on top of each row (dowel holes protected by wooden caps) before next row of stones laid, dowels inserted into holes of previous block, cramps added.

Drying of channels in blocks leading to dowels to eliminate water and impurities, providing ten minutes only for the pouring of molten lead into them and around the dowels. Pouring must be done at a particular and even tempo to prevent unequal disposition or premature cooling.

ᔕᔕᔕ

My first evening in Mostar is beautifully mild. People are sitting out at tables drinking, or strolling up and down the narrow streets. A few kids are tearing around on bicycles. I sit in a little square and there's a fountain playing in front of me, occasionally some music wafting in from somewhere. The square is manicured with white stone pathways and rows of young trees. But on two sides, there are the shells of large buildings, roofless, pock-marked, the night peeping through the hollow window frames.

I'm happy to be back. Yesterday, I was apprehensive about seeing the destruction again, of hearing disturbing stories, of feeling the pervasive tension and sorrow. There has also been news of sporadic violence in the north. But now that I'm here, I'm able to focus on why I have come and I'm feeling a rising excitement.

The flat in the Pavarotti Centre is not available, so Ermin, whom I'd met briefly last year and who is now the manager of the Sinfonietta, has found me a room in a private house. An extra room in a home means income, so many people offer rooms to visitors. From my point of view, it feels better to help the local economy in this way rather than to stay in a hotel that may belong to an absent or foreign owner. And I prefer the personal experience of being in someone's home and meeting a local family. As long as I have privacy and can practise.

The street is narrow and winding and there is no pavement. The houses give directly onto the road and most are being repaired or rebuilt and there is a white dust everywhere. Next to 'my' house is a tiny shop selling onions, potatoes, apples, bananas, tins of food, cigarettes, drinks; whenever I come by, two or three old men are sitting outside, drinking and passing the time of day. They look at me suspiciously the first time they see me, but after a few days, they ignore me. The house where I'm staying is not visible from the street. There is just a door in the high wall that leads to a concrete passageway covered with corrugated iron. Next to it is a space where the owner parks his car.

He is a middle-aged, serious, slightly nervous man who teaches at the university. Upon entering the house itself, he hands me an enormous pair of hard slippers, indicating that shoes are not to be worn indoors. I leave mine alongside the other pairs of shoes that line the little hallway. I have a choice of three rooms, two of which are next to the front door. I go for the one at the very top of the house, which has its own bathroom and feels somewhat cosy. All the furniture has seen better days and carries a strange smell, but it's a fair-sized attic with two single beds pushed together, two sofas, a coffee table, television, wardrobe, and a small formica table with two chairs. Plenty of room to spread out, and after only a few hours, all available surfaces are covered with orchestral parts, scores, phrasebooks, rehearsal schedules, lists of phone numbers. Feels almost like home.

My host asks if I would like breakfast downstairs and I say yes. The next morning, I go down to the little dining room and he makes me an omelette. His English is hesitant, but he obviously feels that he should stay and make conversation.

'Do you want sugar?' he asks as he pours my tea.

'*Ne hvala.*'

'Saccharin?'

'No, no *hvala.*'

'Me saccharin.'

'Oh,' I say.

'Diabetic,' or some word that sounds very similar.

'Uhuh.' I'm not sure how to respond.

'Ten years diabetic. Stress. Because stress.'

'Oh, yes,' I say sympathetically, calculating back ten years to the middle of the war.

'My brother died, six of my family died in war.'

I shake my head. 'I'm very sorry.'

'In 1993 this house bombed, Croats. We build it now ourself. Here, watch video, video of bomb, I show you *da*?'

I'm aghast that an innocent question about sugar has led to this. Sugar to bombs in six easy steps.

I didn't want this visit to Bosnia to be like previous times, with me being a receptacle for so many people's pain. I had been determined to protect myself, to ration the stories, to appear less available. But here I am, less than twenty-four hours after arriving in Bosnia and I'm being offered a chance to see the aftermath of this very house being bombed. I have not invited this, have not encouraged the conversation in any way. But how can I remain silent when my host says he's lost six members of his family and here's the video?

I steel myself and say, '*Naravno, da.*' The walls of the room are already crumbling.

The video itself is not distressing. In black and white, it shows a few people wandering through the ruins of the house, pointing to timbers, shattered walls, gesturing and speaking in silence. It feels ghostly and in the past. But I can sense something complex working within my host: not the wish to relive the event, for he looks at the screen dispassionately; more to have it pass before his eyes without emotion, to deaden its power. And I feel his urgency to air it once more in the presence of a stranger – for this is surely not the first time – that I can know what he has lived through, can know that this is an essential part of his identity. Perhaps it is a way of wearing his suffering with pride. To make his invisible scars visible.

The subject is not raised again during my stay here, but from now on I take breakfast in my room.

Like many secular Jews, I have a soft spot for Seder night, the family meal that celebrates the onset of Passover. Actually two Seders normally take place over the first two evenings of the Holiday, incidentally solving the problem of how to squeeze all the aunts and uncles and cousins, not to mention the in-laws and all the children, round one table, or even round two tables as we did at home. As it is, each side of the family can have their day, and many families arrange things so that one night is for doing the cooking and the other for doing the visiting.

This year Passover falls during my time here, and I'm curious to see if I can be part of a Bosnian Seder. Sometimes the synagogues arrange a meal for those who have no family or who cannot (or prefer not) to cook. And there is a tradition for families to invite a stranger to their home for Seder. Maybe I'll be lucky.

As it turns out, I'm lucky three times over.

The day after I arrive, I visit Ermin and his wife, Alma, who is a lovely woman of great warmth. They live in the centre of Mostar, in a small apartment building above the post office. I climb an indoor staircase that feels like an outdoor staircase with its cold concrete walls and steps, but the flat itself is cosy and light. We sit in the main room which combines a seating area, dining area and kitchen, and drink good, strong coffee.

They are both comfortable people and have the knack of making me feel instantly at home. Ermin has grey hair and I take him to be at least fifty, but later he tells me that he's in his early forties. The war must have taken its toll.

I venture to ask if there is a Jewish community in Mostar. 'Because it's Passover tonight,' I say. They look a little blank.

'On the first night, there is a special meal, and I just wonder if there is anything organized here.'

Alma gets up. 'I know someone in Jewish community. She will tell me,' and she picks up the phone and makes a call.

'There is no something tonight, but there will be meal in five days,' she reports. 'She say you please come. She say she is very honoured. I will take you.' Then she adds, 'She say also, she is very sorry, but please, she ask for . . . money, some donation, it's for community, they need money, and she say your name is put in official paper, to thank you. Just some money. She's very sorry.'

'It's fine,' I assure her, 'that's really good. Thank you.'

It is very surprising that the Seder is postponed – a bit like celebrating Easter Sunday on the following Thursday – so I ask Alma if she knows the reason.

'She say they need a special bread and a special wine, and there is not in Mostar, and she can't go to Sarajevo getting it until Wednesday, so they wait.'

Ah yes, *matzoh*, the unleavened bread, and the Passover wine. I muse over all the preparations that must be going on elsewhere for this evening's meal.

Suddenly Alma says, 'I make you meal tonight. We do it here, *da*?'

The idea seems ludicrously absurd, here, in a Muslim household, without any of the correct foods and no Haggadah (Passover book) to read from and me the only Jew.

Yes! I race round the town, buying ordinary crackers to substitute for *matzoh*, ordinary wine, apples and walnuts for the *charoset*, parsley and eggs. Alma has a chicken leg and she insists on making soup, and at about seven o'clock, Ermin, Alma, their teenage son Jasmin, and I gather round the table for our improvised Seder.

One of the reasons why Passover is so appealing to me lies in the passing on of the story of the exodus from Egypt. Instead of being intoned by a rabbi in a synagogue, it is read out in the home, by the head of the family, mainly for the benefit of the children. Every year, the story is retold; the symbolic foods are eaten – for instance, bitter herbs to remind us of the bitterness of the Jews' lives, *charoset* to remind us of the mortar with which they built the pyramids, *matzoh* to remind us of the haste in which they left; the youngest child asks the Four Questions; the ten plagues are enumerated, four glasses of wine are drunk, blessings are given, the door is opened for the prophet Elijah, songs are sung. And then there is the game in which a piece of *matzoh* is hidden until after the meal is finished, at which point the children search for it, the one who finds it receiving a little present – a clever way of enticing the children to stay awake until the end.

I remember the excitement as a little girl of being allowed to set the table, and as the years passed, of experimenting with more and more elaborate serviette-foldings. There was the aroma of chicken soup, the buying in of *matzoh*, the chopping of apples and walnuts for the *charoset*, and the sickly-sweet Passover wine. The table would be extended to its largest size and later there'd be added another little table for the children. My grandfather would lead the service, first saying the blessing of the wine and *matzoh*; then he'd unfailingly forget his brother-in-law when it came time to go round in descending order of seniority – 'Uncle Abe!' we'd all yell, 'you forgot Uncle Abe!'; the youngest child would ask (in Hebrew) the Four Questions – I had only a few years of this, thank goodness, before my younger brother took my place; then the ten plagues – 'all together now!'; Grandad's mumbling of the story at a rapidly accelerating speed as stomachs began to rumble; the first glass of red wine accidentally spilling onto the white tablecloth ('put salt, put salt'); the inevitable discussion about the texture of the *kneid-lach* (soup dumplings) – Grandma insisting that 'they should be solid and substantial, I don't like them too light' and one of my aunts rebutting 'but they shouldn't be as hard as a rock'; filling the glass of wine for Elijah and opening the front door for him to enter ('close the door already, it's cold') – he never showed up anyway . . .

The ritual, though formally presented, allows – encourages – informality. Questions are welcomed, and not only from the children; interruptions abound; someone has to go out every so often to check that nothing is burning in the oven.

And in a strange way, this Seder in Mostar follows the same pattern. The story is told, though admittedly in a rather garbled and greatly truncated fashion because I can't remember it all; there are many questions, which I do my best to answer; I hide the *matzoh* for Jasmin to find later; the wine is drunk and the meal is enjoyed. What's novel is the presence of people who are new to the ritual, who don't know the symbolism or the details of the story. So this is not so much a retelling as a first telling.

The essence of Seder.

Which keeps memory alive, never to forget the slavery nor the salvation. To be watchful and to be grateful.

Jasmin seems curious in an amused way; Ermin and Alma seem curious and exhilarated at the same time; I am exhilarated.

The following day, I am invited to a Seder in Sarajevo, and it couldn't be more different. It takes place at the home of a US aid official whom I'd met briefly last year. This is a detached house with Western soft furnishings and carpets, a quiet home, comfortable and ordered. The dining room is quite formal and a large table is set for twenty, bearing an array of vegetarian food, a combination of Middle Eastern and Western dishes. The company consists of Americans and Bosnians, with a handful of 'others'.

To my surprise, our hostess leads the service, reciting the initial paragraphs in Hebrew with obvious familiarity – so this is an enlightened approach . . . Each of us is handed a copy of the Haggadah, and each of us in turn reads a portion in our own language. Many sections are read twice, once in Hebrew, and once in Bosnian or English. The polyglot nature of the evening is dizzying, but the atmosphere is supremely cordial and friendly and gracious. And the food is plentiful and delicious.

And after a few days, my third Seder! Alma puts on a black jacket and red scarf and leads me to a little hut across the river. There is no synagogue in Mostar: the former building was turned into a puppet theatre. So this is it, a run-down 10 foot by 15 foot space with posters of Israel hanging on the walls. About a dozen people, all ostensibly over sixty years old, are here when we arrive and they greet me as an honoured guest. But no one seems to speak English so after a while, they go back to their conversations. The place is disordered: amid a scattering of boxes, there are one or two small tables but everyone sits on chairs that seem to have fallen at random around the room. Alma talks to her friend. I ask her to enquire whether this is the whole Jewish community and where are the young people? She translates the reply. 'Young people leave Mostar as soon as they can. No work here. Yes, this is most Jewish people in Mostar. The community probably dying now.'

No-one says the blessings or tells the story. I'm too embarrassed to ask if they have already gone through the service, which I doubt, as according to Alma we did not arrive late; perhaps after decades of living under Tito, they don't know how to do it. It's impossible to believe that they have lost interest. Food is being eaten already – boiled eggs, chicken, *matzoh*, and wine. There is no *charoset* or bitter herbs or any of the other symbolic foods. I don't feel any joy here, or warmth. Just the sense that the community hangs by a thread and everyone knows it.

After a while, people get up to leave and each is given a small box of *matzoh* and some wine. Perhaps my donation is to cover this. I say my goodbyes and walk outside with Alma, feeling dispirited and sad.

☙❧

The rehearsals are in the Pavarotti Centre, as last year. It is lovely to see everyone again, though some faces are missing. Selma is not playing this time as she is too taken up with the baby. And Aidan has left. He'd told me he'd felt it was time to leave, having over-stayed his original visit by some five years, and I understand that he was exhausted. I can't imagine living here for even one year. But things will feel very different without my UK colleague.

The organizing of the concerts has been taken over by a beauti-ful young cellist who lives in Sarajevo called Belma. She appears to be in her twenties, speaks good English and is utterly charming. She has augmented the violin sections with some of her friends recently graduated from the Sarajevo Academy, or in their last years there, raising the standard noticeably. The clarinet, which has such a prominent part in the Glazounov Adagio, will be played by one of the teachers there, though he's not available for our second concert. A student of his will perform that concert and will shadow him in all the rehearsals. I'm hoping this turns out well. The bassoonist is an older professor from Zenica, a city in the north where our first concert will be, and he cannot rehearse until the day of the concert, which Belma assures me will be fine.

The orchestra has a new cellist, from West Mostar. West Mostarians are in the minority in the ensemble, so she is a welcome addition. She's perhaps in her late fifties and she clearly loves playing. And we can communicate because she speaks French.

The first violinist to arrive is Vassili, the Russian violinist who has lived in Mostar for many years. He nods in my direction and seats himself in the leader's chair. Nobody says anything so I watch and wait. When Rada arrives, she hesitates. I step into the breach, perhaps unwisely, and say something to the effect that I expected Rada to be sitting there.

Vassili looks up sternly.

He hardly speaks English but he manages to say, 'I sit here.'

Rada looks surprised. I say that Rada has always sat there when I was conducting, and have they discussed it?

'I sit here. *Da*,' and Vassili shakes his head and waves his bow as if to dismiss any objections.

I sense an impossible battle ahead, and my glance towards Rada confirms it. It's all right, I'll sit next to him, I'd prefer no fuss, her eyes say as she moves over to the other chair. Not a democratic way to make decisions, but as I make eye contact with the rest of the orchestra and weigh Vassili's adamant position with Rada's clear preference to comply with the *fait accompli*, I decide to let this go.

Vassili is the better player. He has a facility that comes from having had an excellent training in Russia. His left-hand technique is solid, and he plays with a firm, warm sound that never wavers. I'm envious of that kind of reliable technique. When I was young, I did not put in the hours of practice needed to develop a virtuoso facility, and would not have known what to do in those hours had I attempted it. It meant a struggle to catch up much later. The system of violin teaching in the USSR was a thoroughly tried and tested model, which has produced many violinists with world-class techniques.

On the other hand, there are disadvantages in being trained specifically as a soloist, and as we start rehearsing I soon realize that work is needed in the areas of cueing, listening, and flexibility of phrasing. And there seems to be a tendency to ignore the ends of phrases, even to end them with a little bump. Vassili is by no means the only violinist in the Sinfonietta to fall into this habit, but he plays the bumps with more confidence than the others. After I've mentioned this to the section several times in several rehearsals over several days, and sung and gesticulated and tried to embody a graceful end of phrase at the appropriate moments to no avail, I shock them all by saying, 'The next time I hear anyone bumping the end of a phrase' – I think quickly – 'I'll bop them with the baton.' I'm sure they don't know what that means, but I'm also sure that they get the idea. I grin at them to let them know that this is all in good fun but I really do want to get results.

I start them off on the same passage for the umpteenth time, fully expecting Vassili to forget one of the numerous phrase endings, when I hear an enormous bump coming from the direction of Rada – meek and mild Rada, who looks up in astonishment at her own boldness! The whole orchestra is astonished too and everyone waits to see what I'll do. I keep to my word, and tap her lightly on the head, rather like giving a knighthood, and everyone laughs. From then on, the ends of phrases are considerably better.

⌒⊱❀⊰⌒

One day, I'm sitting with Ermin in his home. He's happy to be involved with the Sinfonietta, seeing to all the non-musical aspects like funding and transportation and posters. He likes music too and gestures to a few shelves of CDs. He speaks softly, smiling often.

Ermin

One of my hobby before war was music. I had huge big number of cassettes, music cassettes. And that's all disappeared in war. I think it's stole. Because in my place where I used to live is coming Serbs and push us the other side of river, and they took everything from our apartment. We all ran across the bridges because the people told us they're coming and killing. Neighbours, people – let's say one kilometre far from us – they're coming and saying they're in my house, please go, and you all leave, whoever stay they kill them. *Leave everything. We going on west side, West Mostar. That was 1992 that was starting.*

After a couple of months we go back because the Croats pushed them back, and we coming back. It was destroyed part of town, everything was destroyed, because they blow up all bridges, and bridge is very close to my place, Tito Bridge, and all the roof is gone. In the spring. And believe me, when I back in my apartment, you know what is the first thing I'm looking for? The pictures. That's the memories, what you cannot get back. That's something natural, I never thinking about this. Yes I find them all over the place. Some of the pictures is destroyed by water, they make a mess here, they try to find, I don't know what, or money or something, something valuable. And they put the pictures everywhere and I keep all these pictures. I didn't care about other things but I couldn't make another picture of myself or of my son when he was baby. That's good thing.

And I spent, I don't know, six months to repair my flat. With friends, help of friends, but in this period I really didn't have any money. And we dried the floor, floor was deep in water and I try to find some paint to painting. And there's no glasses on the window, we put plastic. Yes, to protect. And take me lot of time.

And it was on 1st May 1993 when I back in my flat, with my wife and my son. And we make one small celebration because we back here, we sleep in our flat. Even there's no electricity, no water, we decide to stay here. And 9th of May, start again, war with Croats. I was sleeping next to the window at five o'clock in the morning it start to shelling hard. We said what's going on now, we didn't know anything, and everywhere is fire round us on this front line. And we said let's go to sleep, they will stop, but they never stopped.

And then they destroyed apartment more than before. Yes we were here, all the shells come, in this room three shells coming. And it was funny things. In this period of course I was member of the army. And I'm coming home to sleep. And I slept overnight, we put this big cabinet in the window to protect us here in this corner. In the morning my wife told me why you didn't take all the bullets from your pockets?

I said what you talking about?

She said look, all these bullets are all around the room.

But that's coming from window, and we're sleeping! From the Gymnasium, machine gun bullets. We sleeping all night and we didn't know! My wife she thought I have in my pocket bullets from gun. And she start to collect these bullets from room and I say these are not my bullets and we find out there's hole in our cabinet. Put on the window to protect us. All night it's very loud, grenades and everything, so, so. But this is the kind of protection of body you going to sleep, you don't like the situation and you going to sleep and forget about everything.

Like in beginning of war, you never realize it's war. You always think, ah this is not true, and I don't know, some army or police guy or government will coming and keep this quiet. Another day, and another day is worse, then another day is worse and people is learning every day. It's worse and worse and after one month it's shelling everywhere, and people is killing, and you find out it's something bad. And it's very interesting what feeling I have during this period with shelling and killing and very dangering. I have feel I going sleep, I like sleep. This is very natural that's not controlled by my brain. My body and my brain like to go out of that, and what's the best thing you can do? Sleep. We all feel very tired, we try to go away from the situation, and we like to be in our dreams what is something really different.

And sometimes people from Mostar, in this enclave, we didn't have anything to eat. It was very difficult to supply this part of country. People is dying because of hunger. I have one cousin of my mother, we find her three days after she died, she didn't have food. It happens. Many people is find a way how to survive, but really survive. I don't like even to remember these times, it's really bad things. I like to put somewhere behind my brain, on the last place, not talk about this.

After years of this war we knew there's no any protection. And that's something we have to learn. And that's the reason because I like to speak about life, how is cheap life. We learned the value of the life is very important for us, each of us. You know maybe people are looking on the material things it's important. But it isn't, believe me. We had many more things before the war than what we have now, but I changed my feeling, because all these needs what we have now, it's not big value compared with life. The people should enjoy. We are human beings, and we can talk between ourselves. We can live together, we can smile together, we can be friends, and we don't need something like war, hate. It's interesting, I didn't have this feeling before the war, I didn't even thinking about this before the war.

Personally myself I was very obsessed about this of wartime. Day after day I thinking and I couldn't realize that's happened to us – it's real world – I thinking I'm dreaming. And many, many hours in the day I spent to try understand why is that. I couldn't find answer. I couldn't. I just ask why is that. And try to be in a body of the people who make a war, what they want from this war, because : . . . everybody's losing, there's no any winner. Who wants make killing other people? It's many families is killed of shrapnel, grenade, we don't need it. I didn't need it. I like . . . I love all people, I not hate anybody. Even I don't hate the people who make the war. I feel very sad because of them. I think they're not coming on the level of civilization.

Mostar in April is not exactly Paris in April, but my daily walk to and from the Pavarotti Centre is lightened by the sun and the blossoms on the trees. The tables outside the cafés are occupied by young people sipping their espressos and smoking their cigarettes, and the occasional group of tourists can be seen peering into the souvenir shops that have sprung up near the bridge. There are still the ruins of buildings, but the little saplings that have taken root inside them are about to come into leaf.

The bridge will be opened in the summer and there are plans for a huge ceremony and celebration. Although I feel the same ghosts in the air, the same struggle to be normal, the same tension between the present and past, there is now also a hint of optimism about. Once the bridge is opened, maybe things will be different, Mostar's symbol will once again be in place, the awful gap closed. Maybe having their Stari Most back will propel Mostarians to get on with the business of uniting their city. Because at the moment, it has two of everything: two police forces, two fire brigades, two education systems, two electric companies, two phone companies. Two budgets. And the EU's job of overseeing the running of the city is reported to be constantly hampered by the ministers of each department, one from each side of the city, who, instead of co-operating with each other, seem hell-bent on disagreeing about everything.

The good weather means barbecues, and Rada and her husband conjure up a wonderful meal of barbecued squid and sausages, mushrooms and courgettes. Ermin and Alma also invite me to a barbecue, at the home of Ermin's parents who live in the country. They have a little house in a row of little houses whose back gardens lead down to a river. Today the river is so swollen that the bottoms of the gardens are flooded. Nearby is a house that is in ruins. 'You can buy if you can find the owner,' Ermin jokes. Behind the houses is a large, stony field and behind that, rolling hills. The day is unusually sunny and unusually peaceful.

One evening I go with Alma to a performance of *Nabucco* which takes place in the cultural centre on the west side. This is a special event for Mostar and the hall is packed. The opera company and orchestra are from Sarajevo and it is strange to experience a third-rate production, with the singers largely stationary and the enormous cast placed into set tableaux, and yet be moved. The most touching moment comes when the slaves' chorus evokes a distinct humming from the audience. I recognize a woman from the Mostar Seder, humming along with the chorus of slaves.

Another evening, I have a meal with an American who's been working here for a couple of years. After comparing the usual notes on our impressions of Mostar, he changes the subject by saying that he had to pick up his car today after having it repaired. A banal comment, I think, until he adds that his brakes had suddenly stopped working. The electrical wiring was found to have been cut. He's glad to be leaving next week.

⤙❦⤚

I enjoy the company of Alma. She has an inner strength that makes her look to the future, but she is also able to talk about her war experiences without bitterness. I ask her what it was like at the beginning.

Alma

Before war started, I didn't know what is it. And many of us we didn't know, but we know that there's something in the air, and we look at the television, like footage from other areas in Croatia and Bosnia you know. But you always think it happens somebody else, you know. And it's far. And then you always think that your people are more intelligent than any other people, and you will manage somehow. But every day you feel it, something in the air. Even in the moment when you have that, you don't know that this is it. What I feel in this moment it's that it's not good . . . I can't breathe really good. It looks like something it's around very bad and you can't breathe with full of your lungs and everything. But you also don't like admit it to yourself, that this is such a bad . . . you always say no no no, tomorrow will be something else, tomor-row will be better. This is another crazy day, but this is last one, tomorrow will be better. You always always deny, and this is why people is such a crazy. If I was more intelligent, I can say this is enough, I can't contain any more this kind of bad feeling, come on, leave, and then I was thinking, if I leave, everything bad is gonna happen. I have to stay to help, that just positive vibration come again and help the good people to be a majority and win.

Sometimes it's like fairytale. Many times you ask yourself, am I dreaming or what? Because it was like a film, like a movie, like a book. You know, I was looking lot of films about Second World War, but you know what is funny, I say my God, this is not really war, look, my God they don't fighting like real war fighters! I was comparing all the time . . . and it was such a silly. And somewhere, you know how things going and growing growing growing after few months . . . and then you are in the middle of the tunnel. You can't see entry, you can't see exit, and you are there.

It's in your brain, what you think you don't know is there. Because coming a situation, what you just think about how to survive, in every situation. And even you know that it's war, and you can die now, in the next seconds, you just don't think about that, not because you don't like, not because of that, because it's something else you have to think: how to survive. And you have your targets, if it's pick up water, or if it's find your food, or just visit somebody, or to go to hospital, whatever you have to do, you're just thinking how to do this . . . you know, you're focusing on that.

And then, you're like animal, you can hear all sounds, you can smell it's dangerous, you can feel like animal. I feel like animal. I was like an animal actually. Oh this corner is not good, you don't know why, but it's not good.

And I was in my flat, not in my flat where I am now, because it was destroyed, another flat in my friend's one floor down. And then we had to sleep in one room. And this room actually not looking on a side where usually is shooting, you know, but somehow I not feel very safe. And I said, I'm not comfortable here, I don't like to be here, but my husband say OK, come on, why are you bothering other people, come on, sit here, don't move, this is just overnight. And one night, I don't know how, this shrapnel coming, like big piece of metal, it's like a piece of grenade, and coming across the window, we've been on the floor, sleeping, and I don't know how got through another wall, and another wall, and somewhere and all ceiling was damaged, and it looks like somebody just put flour on our heads and big noise wake us up and everything go down to cover us. I was really afraid. And it was actually answer, because days before I feel really uncomfortable in this room. And I wasn't only one with this feeling.

This is how in war you don't know how you can do it, many things that you don't know – how to provide food without food, how to provide water without water, how make fire – I never before make fire – but you learn, you know? It was really really interesting. You have pick up how in the middle of town to pick up wood, and just going visit ruins and take a pieces of floor or something. And back at home to make fire.

You have to learn which kind of herbs. I was in a situation with spring coming and I say it's enough beans, rice, flours, I have to find something but how? All town was surrounded and any humanitarian help who're coming they bring flours, yeast, oil, rice, macaroni, you know these kinds of things, and maybe some tins of meat, but it's dodgy things you don't like to eat, full of preservatives . . . I mean of course, this is only thing which you can transport and give people without fridges, of course, this is normal, they cannot give you say, fresh salad delivery, this is normal.

But then I say my God, why I'm never ever look in a book which kind of herbs I can eat? I listen a lot about these things. And I ask like older ladies which kind of, from fields, things I can pick up and make like a pie or some stew or something and they told me take this and take that, don't from this corner because people coming and I don't know, maybe lots of people coming and make something . . . you have to look another field where people usually not come. But you start to learn. You cannot go in the market and say OK give me spinach or this and that. And we look like we are modern human beings but we are actually so stupid we are not so capable to live, survive in the nature, in the middle of somewhere. And this is why they probably train armies, they just leave them down in the middle of the forest, and the jungle, with one knife and say OK for seven days, we will come to pick up who is survived. Yeah, this is actually, it was like that. And this is different kind, totally other brain that's sleeping all the time, wakes up and start work.

Man generally he was only to go in the front line, but woman in the same times, I was . . . look, I was a mother, I was nurse, I was helping wounded people. I'd visit them and one other friend made like a special cream from honey and herbs, because we haven't medicaments, you know, and she delivered to us and we visit people who have some wounded place or something and helped to healing them and of course give them the moral support and something, you know. And then I have make a food, I have to provide the wood, I have to clean my house, I have to cover and protect my son, I have to wait my husband, I had to do actually everything, you know. Many things. And think about everything . . . how to make a laundry without water, for God's sake, how to make without machine, it's a very big deal. But men just, they have to go to front line. This is always primary, but you know, this is not everything. Actually we were more fighters than them in the end, if you look. Because everything else and all the house was on *my shoulder – house, children, friends, him, everything, it was huge . . .*

I still think that we have this kind of energy because we are, I always say, we are masters of improvise. You know, we always improvise. Like in a war we likes to listen radios, you know, but we haven't electricity, we haven't batteries. And then there's some old cars, of course some batteries with acid inside. Still you can do it something, but how? My Ermin, and his cousin, they took some battery from car, and put on the bike, and on the bike they put dynamo, do you know what dynamo is? It's a kind of a little machine. And then they take one wheel out, and put one piece of wood that you can put this actual bicycle to standing here in a room. And then they put wires on the battery and they say OK if you like listen radio, evening, we have lot of friends in one flat living together, he said everyone has to driving bike in the room for two minutes, to fill up batteries, to fill up batteries and then later we can put radio on the batteries and you can listen half hour, maybe.

We improvised food, we improvised our lives. And I think that we are big improvisorists. We still improvise because now, you haven't job, and then you somehow try to keep water in a pot without bottom. This is very difficult. It's very difficult, it's sometimes our expression, you have two pots without bottoms and you try to keep water always, it's a very . . . it's like a Sisyphus.

When war was, I have lot of hope. I don't know if it was something what's coming from me or outside, but I can't control it. I just couldn't believe that we're gonna die, everyone. Because I always believe we will win, we will live, find a peace, we will survive, you know. And I always argued with my friends when they have kind of depression, we gathered together and then start talking and everybody have some news, somebody coming and tell me this, somebody coming and tell me that, and I say ah, come on, shut up, it's not true, it's such a crazy what you're talking about, it cannot be true, come on, let's think. And they say come on, you and your optimistic statement, come on, you're crazy, and we start to argue, and I say you will see, I don't know when but you will see. And this is when I start to talk, about October '93, and everything happened in April '94. First Washington Agreement, then Dayton.

And then you can see that you can manage, and why not more three years? Why not another three years like that, you know? And then we see we are such a small . . . people are such a small piece of what's being created on the earth.

When we have a dangerous situation, I'm very quiet and very concentrated, I can find the right way out of a situation. But usually after, I'm just collapsed – oh my God, what I do, I could have . . . this or that – and then I have a kind of panic and maybe broke, everything broke my nerves and maybe I start cry or something like that. Because you have time. In a moment when things happen you haven't time to think, just you know that you have your target there and you have to catch . . . somehow, you have to take it.

Of course I have my time now where I'm crying, but somehow I collect all these tears for some period, I just taking in my inside somewhere, and after few months I just explode and have all these tears from all these days. And then again I cheer up. Yes, my friend coming in my home and say, we just coming to have a little laugh, a look of your smiling face or something. And I don't know why I am like that, probably it's my nature. When you are squeezed, when you have a problem that is dangerous, I'm much stronger. But later I just start shaking. When I remember what can be, you know, how bad can be, later I'm thinking and analyse this, and then stress coming. So.

Alma smiles. 'You want another coffee?' she asks.

As she gets up to make it, I realize that I'm intensely curious about how everyone here survives now in their own way.

Alma says, 'I really like to talk about my feelings because I think that we have to share it. Maybe I was more lucky than other that my close family stay with me and nobody die, very lucky thanks God. But loads of people lose members of their family. And probably for them it's much difficult, more difficult to talk about that. I like to talk, I like to say people that they can do many, many things.'

I remember Toni's comments, and Edo's. This must be the first time I've heard anyone say that they like to talk about the war, that they talk not from an unconscious compulsion, but from a conscious desire.

I also recall what someone from the music therapy team had said on my first visit here: that those families that were able to talk about their feelings during and after the war suffered far less trauma than those that were not.

❧

The music therapy programme was established at the Pavarotti Centre at about the same time as the Sinfonietta, and there are therapists here from Canada and Denmark at the moment who are training the locals as well as doing the therapy. I'm new to the field of music therapy so I'm eager to accept their invitation to see a short promotional film that has just been made. I can hardly bear to watch the first part with its clips of the war, the wounded lying in a makeshift hospital, the fear on the faces of the adults and children. The abrupt editing and rough quality of the film make it all the more horrifying. The second part describes and shows the therapy itself.

The work is mainly with traumatized children, music therapy being ideal for those who can't find the words, or perhaps have lost the urge to speak at all. The music therapy room is a safe space where nothing need be spoken. Some children are referred because they are withdrawn, sometimes not even able to make eye contact; but they can hear the strings of a guitar or the tapping of a drum, and after a while they can make the sounds themselves and the therapist can play the same rhythm, a non-verbal empathy springing up that can open the door to other ways of connecting. Or sometimes children arrive with unmanageable rage and need to bang on a piano until they hear the therapist echoing the banging or singing along with it, suggesting a togetherness that might enable the child to begin to leave its emotional prison. The development and progress of the children is immense.

We talk about the film for a good while. Some of the therapists say that they wish more children could be treated. But many parents don't want to bring their children to therapy. Because of the stigma, or fear of the unknown . . . And then we talk about setting boundaries for ourselves, about protecting ourselves, about our own issues and why we are doing this work. About how to be genuinely helpful.

Someone suggests that I play Bach on the new Stari Most. And I wonder what it would be like to play there, or on the Spanish Square, where there was so much death and terror, and where, every year, there is now a huge pop concert. If only music could obliterate the bad memories, the bad energy! Maybe it does, temporarily. There is probably nowhere on earth where somebody has not suffered. I think of London with its plagues and fires and unspeakable violence over the centuries. But there the air seems to have settled. I don't feel residual pain when I walk its streets.

Here, suffering hangs over the town. Am I trying to drown it out, supersede it, overlay it? Is there a way to change the air? tilt its balance?

I realize that I'm afraid of the suffering of others. Especially when it is caused by violence. It is disturbing to be close to it and disturbing to accept. It can unbalance me, threaten my optimism, even my capacity for love.

I'm afraid it can destroy me.

Perhaps it is partly because of my fear, that I'm drawn to this place. Being in Bosnia forces me to confront my fear.

We all have complex motives for being here. Yet while we are here, it is a struggle to focus on issues like these. In Mostar, the world whizzes by and we can't fully experience it. So the days hover like a dream, unreal, not absorbed into the fabric of our memory.

And maybe this is somewhat like being traumatized, to have the past not put away properly, not put into the past where it belongs, but still it stays, an unstable layer of lava on which the continuous present builds.

Like trying to balance on a ball while living your life.

One day I have the idea of playing music on the streets of Mostar. After all, how many of the population come to our concerts? How many are familiar with classical music? If, as Selma remarked last time, Mostar received an influx of relatively uncultured people from the countryside during the war, how many of these have even seen a violin? Instead of hoping they will come to us, why not bring music to them, take classical music onto the streets of Mostar?

I approach our new young artistic director. A wave of surprise crosses Belma's face. 'I don't think anyone has done that before,' she says. 'We can try. It's OK.'

I suggest that four of us could play Haydn string quartets. 'Let's wear our long black concert clothes, to draw more attention. And let's play on both the east side and the west side. What do you think? And we can hand out leaflets for the concert. *Može?*'

It's agreed, and two of Belma's young colleagues volunteer to join us. We discuss where exactly we should set up. It needs to be where there are people, where it's busy, but where we would not block the road. And where we would not be in competition with a café or CD shop blaring out its own music.

The more I think about it, the more enthused I become. If playing on the streets is out of the ordinary, and playing on both sides of town certainly is, then perhaps the media should be informed. The Sinfonietta can do with some publicity. I invite several newspapers and TV stations to cover the 'event'. To my amazement, both Reuters and a local TV station accept.

A few days later, four musicians and two cameramen meet at the Pavarotti Centre, and we discuss our plan of action. 'We need to be somewhere we can get good shot of bridge, of course,' says the man from Reuters. The 'bridge' always means Stari Most, which is now almost completely rebuilt. When I arrived in Mostar this time, one of my first priorities was to see the bridge, and there it was, shrouded in a dense block of scaffolding, its unmistakable arch clearly discernible. It's in waiting. Its unveiling will come to pass in only a few months.

'And on west side, we must go to Rondo, outside cultural centre,' says the local man.

We set off, carrying our instruments, four music stands and a chair for the cellist. It's about five o'clock, and the sun is preparing to change its colours, an optimal time for photographers. Our first port of call is at the top of the street that runs alongside the river, just before it turns away. The view to the bridge is perfect. The cobblestones are rather less than perfect with regard to the stability of the music stands, but soon we are all ready, the Reuters man clicking away and the local man monitoring his recording and video equipment.

It is not easy, playing Haydn here in the open. The sounds dissipate almost as soon as we make them, evaporating into the air, snatched away. But we play with spirit and warmth, trying to shape the phrases even as they fly from us. There are not many passers-by. Only a few stop and listen.

We play several movements, then, 'Must go to Rondo,' says the local man, and he packs up his equipment. The man from Reuters says he has what he needs and will now drive back to Sarajevo. '*Hvala, hvala*,' we say, '*ciao*.'

It is a fifteen-minute walk to the west side location, and there is a lot to carry. The Rondo is a large roundabout and there are even fewer people here. 'Maybe we should go to a busier place,' I suggest.

'*Ne, ne*, here *dobro*. But need light,' and the local man sets us up under a street lamp. Since he knows the area better than I do, I defer to him, especially as this will all result in good publicity for the Sinfonietta. Again we play and again we are filmed. Hardly anybody walks by. It's disappointing. If we do this again, we must choose our locations more carefully. The cameramen were obviously more interested in getting their shots than in the venture itself.

Frustrated and tired, we pack away our instruments, and I say to the local man that I hope he is happy with what he has on film. But he replies by asking, 'What I do with film?'

I'm perplexed. Belma has told me that he has an arts programme on local TV.

He repeats, a little louder, 'What I do with film?'

I have no idea how to answer, so I mumble something about how I'm sure he can make a nice programme with it, and he can mention our concert tomorrow night, and if he wants, I'd be happy to do an interview for him.

He rounds on Belma and starts talking animatedly, waving his arms and raising his voice. She tries to speak but is continually shouted down. After a seemingly interminable period of shouting and gesticulating, he finally turns on his heel, and I look at Belma questioningly.

'He kept saying, what am I going to do with the film? Why has she dragged me all round Mostar? I could have been home with my wife!'

I'm dumbfounded.

'I don't understand,' I say. 'What does he mean? He has his arts programme. And he could have gone home whenever he wanted – it was his idea to come to this spot. What on earth is going on?'

Belma thinks. 'Maybe he wanted you to buy the film.'

'Buy the film?!'

'Maybe not,' she says and shrugs.

I'm incredulous. And angry. This little adventure has not at all turned out as I'd hoped, and now I'm the butt of an incomprehensible tantrum. It's frustrating that my Bosnian is not good enough to understand what was being said, that I couldn't answer. Not that it would have made any difference. Belma and the others don't seem much perturbed. Perhaps this is normal, how things are here. They don't commiserate. I'm standing in the fading light of the deserted Rondo, feeling misused and frustrated and furious. And I'm also concerned that I have somehow jeopardized the Sinfonietta's relationship with the television station. So I feel guilty too.

It's all so incomprehensible. It's the first time I've been angry in Bosnia, but I'm tired of things going wrong at the drop of a hat, with no explanation and no apology. I'm tired of not understanding, and not being understood, tired of the volatility of this place, of the lack of co-operation and communication and empathy and respect, of the waste, the absurdity.

Between me and Bosnia is a cultural chasm, and I've lost patience with it.

As for Reuters, I make numerous phone calls but never manage to ascertain if the story is taken up by any newspapers. The only article I see comes out a few days later in a British paper: it's about Mostar and the bridge, and there is a large photograph of Stari Most in all its scaffolding, taken from exactly the spot where we played. Some of the passers-by are in the shot, but there is no sign of the quartet. And no mention of the Sinfonietta.

It's hard work. We rehearse every day, and there are the lessons with Rada's and Suzana's pupils. This time some of the violinists in the Sinfonietta also ask me to teach them. And I have to find time to practise – the violin as well as the conducting. Plus the tambourine! No-one wants to play the tambourine for the Glazounov dances, so I'm left having to fill the vacancy myself. I've never played the tambourine before. Borrowing one from the music therapy office, I practise various ways of holding it and tapping it and shaking it. I've no idea what I'm doing . . . and how am I to play it while conducting and turning the pages of the score at the same time?

There is the usual chaos with the orchestra. Like last year, there is always someone missing, often several players, so I have to keep on top of the scheduling. And it's not easy for us to rehearse when some of the lines or harmony are missing. Why is this chord so bare? – ah yes, two of the winds are missing. Why are the strings having trouble playing together? – it will be easier when they have both horns to follow, so let's not spend time on that now. Whereas it's possible for me to imagine the missing lines, the orchestra has no idea of what's in store.

It's not until the last rehearsal that we all hear the full sound of the music; although at the beginning, the bassoonist, who could not come to any of the other rehearsals, is nowhere to be seen. I start without him, and we have just finished rehearsing the Adagio when he walks in, an hour late, and seats himself in the empty chair. I say to the orchestra that we have to go through the Adagio again and there is an audible sigh. I don't want to embarrass him, but since his arrival has not been noticed by everyone, I mention that he has just arrived and would they prefer to take a break now, or just get it played and take a break afterwards. They choose to get it over with, so we play it once more and the bassoonist manages his part tolerably well.

At the break, he comes up to me and apologizes for being so late. He is tall and dignified.

'My wife was driving,' he explains.

I'm speechless.

'She drives slowly,' he adds, as if this clarification makes his case indisputable.

Many replies jostle in my brain, but as I look up into his lined face, I just nod. Or maybe I shake my head. Or maybe I smile. I've no idea any more. As far as excuses go, this is one of the best.

The first performance is in the northern town of Zenica, where Belma grew up and where her family still lives. The two of us go there early in the day because a local school has organized a master class. I don't remember anything of the town, or indeed much else of the day: just a delicious lunch that Belma's mother cooks for us; rows of delightful eight-year-old violin students (and a couple of cellists) overpowering a small school-room with their enthusiastic attempt at a little minuet, all slightly out-of-tune and out-of-time; and an impressive concert hall. Even the concert itself is lost to memory, having disappeared into the general Bosnian haze. We leave Zenica straight after the performance, driving back to Sarajevo where I spend the next day teaching. I see Marina only briefly and she cries for five minutes while telling me that she fears her marriage is over.

I do remember the concert in Mostar. I've chosen to start the programme with the Adagio and Scherzo, then the Haydn Symphony, and end with the dances. A kind of Glazounov/Haydn sandwich. Putting the violin solos first means that I can warm up and get my brain and fingers into playing mode before we begin. I also know that the Adagio will create an immediate mood of intimacy in the space, a direct way into the heart.

When we walk out into the hall, it is packed to overflowing, as last time, and moreover, everyone is smiling. Playing the Adagio is a dream. The clarinet and horn weave their lines around mine with sensitivity, allowing the music to breathe and soar. It's like floating on an ocean. Or a cloud.

I remember Nureyev.

Alma tells me afterwards that she cried all the way through it. 'Angelic,' she says.

When we get to the Glazounov dances at the end, the orchestra ignites. They have enjoyed the challenge of tackling these pieces, with their vital rhythms and exotic harmonies, their brashness and their brilliance, and now they give themselves to the excitement of the music. I exchange my baton for the tambourine and try to conduct with my whole body while rattling and rapping away, raising it high above my head for the climax as everyone bows and blows with all their strength. The orchestra envelops us all in its huge sound.

There is so much applause that we repeat the last two dances as an encore, and I mouth to the players '*piu presto*' before launching into the *Danse des Garçons Arabs* again. The triplets in the *Sarrazins* dance race up and down like the wind, any residual inhibitions dissolved because now the concert is officially over.

The post-concert party goes on for hours. The usual crowd of friends joins us and there is singing and dancing, drinking and eating, laughing and hugging. Afterwards I walk 'home' through the deserted streets feeling happy and relieved. It was a terrific concert. And despite my anger and frustration of the previous days, I have been able to retrieve my positive, encouraging self, have been able to deliver the music and inspire the players.

I remember something that Suzana said: that they like the way that I rehearse, that I work with purpose and am clear about the detail, that I'm tough with them but not harsh, that I don't treat them with kid gloves like so many others. It's a hard balance to achieve, and no doubt I don't succeed all the time, but I'm encouraged by this comment.

And grateful.

May 2005

Since the financial state of the Sinfonietta was somewhat sensitive, we decided to dispense with the winds this time and just have an orchestra of strings. I found an early Mendelssohn string symphony with a great sense of humour; some Elgar pieces for violin and orchestra; and to finish off, the Vivaldi Double Concerto. It would be nice to share the platform with one of the younger players, so we invited Siniša, a good violinist who is determined and ambitious. I've always loved the Vivaldi A minor. Of course, whenever anyone thinks of a concerto for two violins, the Bach Double springs to mind. But this Vivaldi has a simplicity and freshness that's immediately captivating.

The Elgar would be really unusual. Probably a premiere in Bosnia. I have been performing unknown Elgar pieces for violin and piano for many years and have a great affection for them. A few have been orchestrated by Elgar himself, though without the violin solo. So my preparation this time was the opposite of last year's: instead of cutting down the number of lines, I had to recreate the violin solo line, teasing it from the texture without leaving a hole. Again it took weeks to prepare the parts, and again I promised myself to buy a music-writing computer programme for next time.

Of course, what excited me the most about this trip was the prospect of seeing the new bridge; and seeing how Mostar would feel with the symbol of its integration renewed in stone, solid, before Mostar itself was actually integrated. Maybe the symbol has to come first. There had been a lengthy, formal ceremony to mark the opening, with an impressive guest list of heads of state and royalty. Bosnians were proud of their new Stari Most, and so was the outside community who had enabled the rebuilding.

Rows of chairs had been set up on platforms by the river from which the guests and locals could watch the performances of dance and music. The Sinfonietta was not invited to play. The Sarajevo Philharmonic contributed a Beethoven Ninth that was notable for the addition of a pop-beat, and there were speeches from the politicians most closely involved with running the country. Much was made of the symbolic reuniting of the communities, with hope expressed that this would spur more progress in actual co-operation. The presence of the international community ensured that the world was watching. Black clouds gathered and the wind rose.

As darkness drew in, the crowds waited for the last event. For centuries, there has been a tradition of young men diving from Stari Most. It is twenty metres high above the river and there are deadly rocks. Mostarians hold the divers in special respect. There is a nervousness in the air as lightning flashes across the sky, and the first diver climbs onto the parapet. He stands motionless for a few moments, concentrating. Then he stretches his arms and executes a perfect dive, the crowd cheering as he slices the waters of the Neretva.

Reconstruction of Stari Most

Crushed stones cut for filling in the back of the arch.
Filling of space between abutment walls and back of arch with stone conglomerate, limestone and mortar.
Injection of ground foundations behind abutment walls on both banks to connect old and new parts within construction.
Before assembling the last three rows of arch, five hydraulic presses placed to prop existing stone rows.
Final arch stone placed.

I get off to a bad start. The plane in London misses its take-off slot through waiting too long for an errant passenger, arriving in Vienna at about the same time as the departure of my Sarajevo flight. No information about connecting flights is offered, and the buses taking everyone from the plane to the terminal, instead of leaving as soon as they are full, wait, while the level of anxiety rises, until the very last person has disembarked and the last wheel-chair has been carefully stored in the wheelchair van, before rolling slowly away. Once at the terminal, I run through the long, highly polished corridors to find the flight to Sarajevo still listed on the board but no-one at all at the gate.

I have a seven-hour wait until the next flight. Ermin is supposed to meet me at the airport soon to drive me to Mostar, so I phone him and Belma to tell them of my late arrival. Then I put some rather disgusting canteen food onto a plate and sit down in front of a huge window. And as I'm staring sightlessly out onto the runway, a bus with 'Airport Tour' painted on its side catches my eye. Who on earth would want to take a tour of the airport? On the other hand . . . my mind wakes up – would there be time to nip into Vienna, go straight to Stefansplatz and drink a coffee in Demel's? It has been years since I was in Vienna. And so I do. The bus ride takes half an hour, the sun shines, and the blue Danube is decidedly green.

Restored by this little adventure, I arrive in Sarajevo to be told that Ermin has already driven back to Mostar because his car was leaking water and he had to keep filling the tank and it would not be very safe, or possible, to do that in the dark. So Belma takes me to her flat where I stay the night before catching the bus to Mostar the next morning.

It is a beautiful journey. The day is bright, and as we pass through the villages, there is washing hanging up everywhere. And there is snow on the mountain peaks.

It is lovely to see Ermin and Alma again. They invite me for lunch and we chat like old friends. Ermin tells me of his continuous frustration in trying to persuade the Ministry to fulfil its promise of funds for the orchestra. It has already taken years of application-filling and petitioning to get to this stage, but it seems that it's one thing to be approved for funding, quite another to elicit the money itself. He speaks with patience, but I wonder how he, and the orchestra, keeps going.

I ask Ermin about the Pavarotti Centre, and he tells me this lovely anecdote.

Ermin

I can tell you one story actually, it happened with us, in my house. It was one summer '94, no electricity and still no water in the house, and it was very hot, and I was working for War Child, and two directors of War Child they becoming good friends of mine, they're coming to visit us, every month, every two months. And this evening it was so hot in the house and I give them idea to go on the river, Neretva river bank. Let's sit there, it's cooler, nothing else. And they bring some drinks, they bring some candles, and they bring some backgammon, that we play.

And we start to play one game singing a song. One of us had to sing some song and the other had to tell us what's the name of the song. And that's the way how we start, and it was so romantic evening. It's nice full moon, and we have drink, cooler, singing, whatever, and it's coming idea, oh it will be nice to make discotheque on one of these houses next to the river. And it's starting, oh it's nice, it's beautiful. And then some months after that, these two directors are coming with Nigel Osborne and some other people and they start to talk about this music.

Because you thinking, people need food, after food, what they need, need to be happy, how you can make them happy? – with music! And actually this idea of Music Centre is started.

⌘

The bridge. I hurry along the familiar street and turn the bend, and there it is. Stari Most, small yet spectacular, brilliant white, a jewel with a perfect curve. I lean on a wall high above the river and gaze at it, finally freed of its scaffolding, painstakingly reconstructed stone by stone according to how it was originally built in 1566 by the Turks, this time built by a team of many nations, a concerted effort to restore Mostar's pride, its history, its identity. Oh, there are many other bridges in this town, but this was Mostar's Old Bridge, a construction of real beauty, that crashed into the river twelve years ago amid heavy Croat shelling, the spume flaring up to close an unclosable gap. After years of waiting, years of planning and building, it is now back, Mostar's beautiful arch, pristine, finally risen again.

The sky is a clear blue, the Neretva a luminous green, as I make my way towards it, keeping my eyes on its graceful form. I'm so used to the surrounding streets being blocked off, full of building materials, that it feels like walking through a dream, where movement is effortless and there are no obstacles. The approach widens and then narrows as the gradient rises steeply to the highest point of the bridge.

Its surface is slippery. Protruding stones are laid horizontally in strips, presumably to provide a foothold, but they are placed too far apart for me. I hold on to the iron railing on top of the parapet, but there are no cross ridges here near the edge and my feet slip. Walking down the other side feels even more precarious. I watch how other people cross, some setting their feet in between the crossbars, some placing their feet on top of them. I'd not imagined that Stari Most would be so difficult to navigate.

It feels as if the bridge is harbouring its own traditions that outsiders cannot be privy to. We foreigners will always be discomforted by it. But as I perch at its highest point, and see how the locals cross, head down, at an inevitably measured pace, I regret that this is not a bridge for running over, that nobody will be able to race across Stari Most, hair flying, to meet their lover.

Aidan is here! He's living in Berlin now where his girlfriend has a good job, and he's come specially to play these concerts. Everyone is thrilled to see him and as we walk in the streets, he is stopped every two minutes by old friends. I'm really glad of his presence. We go out at the first opportunity to a good restaurant for dinner.

He tells me that after he left Bosnia, he spent six months with his girlfriend's family in Bolivia. 'Most of the time, I just slept. I don't know, I couldn't do anything, couldn't think, had no energy for anything. I just needed sleep. Those six years here sort of got to me, and I couldn't get it out of my system. You know, it's so intense here and . . . tense as well, I was so involved with stuff, trying to do everything, the organizing and teaching and playing and everything. I was being worn down and worn down. I'm the kind of guy who springs up in the morning and is positive and I get things done, but here . . . Everyone feels trampled on by everyone, and they've lost their identity, it's like, "We don't owe anyone anything, we're not going to go to any trouble for anything . . . " It was just too much I suppose.'

I ask him what he's doing now. 'Well, not much at the moment. I'm not sure what I want to do. I'm thinking about going into teaching, youngsters, and maybe do a bit of playing, but . . . Maybe I'll take a teaching course to get a qualification for Germany so I can teach in a school. I'm learning German, going to classes. But I want to keep some connection with the Sinfonietta, you know, come here every now and then.'

Aidan strikes me as being more thoughtful and focused than when he was living here. But after a few days, he confesses that he's feeling the same strange Mostar effect that seems to creep up on the internationals. 'It was brilliant seeing everyone for the first three days. But on the fourth day, I was a wreck – not a wreck . . . drained, it was all I could do to just sit and have a drink. I didn't have any energy to do anything.'

'It was you who warned me about the fourth day here, remember?' I say.

'Yes,' he laughs, 'it's true. It's something to do with the energy here. You're having a nice day, and in the space of half an hour, suddenly everyone's getting wobbly and stressed.'

Having Aidan back in the Sinfonietta makes it feel like old times. But I'm sorry that Ivica is no longer playing with it. Evidently there has been a long-smouldering difference of opinion about whether his instrument, which was donated from London, belongs to him or to the orchestra; and a general antagonism, not entirely related to this, has been developing between him and some of the other players. Thankfully his wife Suzana is not drawn into the argument and feels she can still play with us. But Selma is taking Ivica's side and is also no longer involved, though perhaps this is because she has found a good position in an educational project. All ensembles have a somewhat fluid membership, particularly when they are part-time and the players have to earn the bulk of their living elsewhere. And the Sinfonietta has had fairly stable personnel up till now. Which is remarkable considering the circumstances.

Of course, Selma has her baby, Hana. When I pay her a visit, she is a proud and doting mother, showing me round her new, compact flat on the west side. Hana is a sweet child and I'm so pleased that Selma seems content with her life. The only thing she mentions that makes her, and me, uncomfortable, is her reaction to hearing the baby cry. She says that she cannot bear any crying, 'even for a second', and must rush to do whatever is necessary to comfort her. She's aware that this is not good for Hana, but she's unable to act any differently. I imagine that many people who have suffered greatly have trouble distinguishing between degrees of distress, the same alarm bell sounding for a scraped knee as for a heart attack. It makes living a fraught affair, adrenalin pouring out at the least sign of trouble. And anxiety easily passes to the next generation. There must be many mothers in Mostar who cannot bear to hear crying.

Undaunted by last year's disastrous attempt at bringing music to the streets, I decide to try again, this time taking advantage of the reopened bridge and the busloads of tourists and locals usually milling around it. I gather some of the orchestra and suggest we play the Vivaldi Double Violin Concerto, Vivaldi being the one composer who can be depended upon to set a merry tone, even out of doors. I do not alert the press!

At midday, we arrange our music stands close to the approach of the bridge, placing an open violin case on the ground strewn with concert leaflets and a few coins to encourage the passers-by. We tune up and dive into the bright, confident concerto. This time, many people stop to listen, especially the elderly. And the children seem fascinated too. They gaze transfixed, shy, their faces showing bemusement and delight. One child makes some drawings of us and gives them to us. Another child presents each of us with a red rose. We are all touched. As we pour the lively rhythm into the street, I know that this is what I'd wanted, this is more than what I'd wanted.

The day is overcast, and rain threatens. So after we have played the first movement a good number of times, we tempt the elements no longer and retreat into our favourite café near the bridge. Our takings are not generous, but they are enough to furnish a coffee for each of us. We are content, elated even. And when I hear English being spoken at a nearby table, I surprise myself by getting up and, still in extrovert mode, approach the two middle-aged women sitting there.

'Excuse me,' I say, 'I heard you speaking English. Would you be interested in coming to a concert tonight?'

They reply that unfortunately they are leaving Mostar in a few hours, but what concert is this? I explain and they comment on how unusual it is for an English woman to be doing this work. Their accent is familiar.

'Are you from the north of England?' I ask.

'Yes, Newcastle.'

'That's funny. My mother's from Newcastle.'

'Oh really? What's her maiden name?'

It turns out that they are friends with one of my cousins.

Apart from the occasional bright spot, I am not enjoying this visit as much as previous ones. I can't quite put my finger on it. The rehearsals are progressing as expected, with the usual obstacles and challenges, but no more problematical than before. The weather is lovely and warm so we can spend time outdoors.

But I'm hearing more complaints – that so-and-so is not doing his work, that someone else is not pulling her weight, that those people over there are two-faced. One westerner shakes her head and says that everyone here lies. Several say that the Dayton Agreement is unworkable and needs to be renegotiated. One says, 'Revenge is the Balkan way.' I feel a general despondency.

Perhaps it's because I had a serious bout of cancer last year that took the wind out of my sails, and left me feeling a little disconnected to everything. I have the impression that the locals look to the internationals to be strong and reliable, but I don't know how strong I can be this time. In any case, they are not weak and I am not superhuman, and a more normal relationship would be healthier for everyone.

Perhaps it's something to do with the bridge being open. Last year, there was an anticipation in the air, of completion, of change, of a future. That is missing now. 'We thought things would be different, better. But it's not. When will it get better?' people ask.

Ermin

Now this new bridge for me I don't like it, because it's missing its oldness. Four hundred year missing. He's beautiful, he's new, but he's not old bridge, his name is Old Bridge, for me it's not same thing. But fine, I understand how is bridge connecting two paths, two banks. This bridge should also connect two people. It's trying, that's a good message.

This celebration I didn't like. For me it's look like when you broke glass for water and have you ever celebrated when you buy new glass? Why they celebrating the bridge? – they should be sad about it. They should be very criticize any civilization who make this damage. For me it not right spending millions and millions euros for celebrations. They should spend it in factory, to employ some workers. That's more intelligent than celebrating . . . It's very nice to open this but I'm afraid for this celebration of opening they forget what they celebrate. They celebrate one historical crime. Fine, I understand the message. But if you're not finished something, like criticism why they blow up this bridge – I don't even know who is blow up this bridge – just for me it's not civilization to destroy something what is four hundred years old. This is for me, I'm not talking about any sides, I'm talking about who is make this damage, and after that make celebration. For me . . . it stays in my mouth. I cannot understand why is people destroy something what is valued, really historical valued.

And now is situation very bad, because is not enough employment in town. Our country's economy is very low, no industry, no can't find any job here. The first when the war stopped the people was very happy because no more shelling. And after that, year after year it's coming worse and worse here. And I feel thinking we don't have good enough government. What worries me is lots of political crime, people from government is the main crimes. We are very small country, we are not part of Europe even, we have not got a protection. You know, who can guarantee us tomorrow a war it's not come again?

Alma

You can't overnight here forget all things what's happened in the ten years. Even if you have a magical something, a powder or something, and say I like everything perfect. Because I understood, unfortunately, that we cannot finish everything and it sort out everything overnight, in one, two, ten minutes, one hour, we need unfortunately now another decades, to first change brains.

Because we were before war better and more developed in the brain than now I find. Generally talking, people were very normal, very European-thinking, very open, democratic. But now when demographically it's been changed this area, it means people who was here, they leave mainly, or die, or something, change places. Lot of other people who're coming from rural area with other habits, with something else.

Woman have to work for whole family almost because man cannot find a previous jobs in factories where they used to do because factory is destroyed, you know. So women is now in very very difficult situation, and because of all this bad life what we had in last years, ten years, man and children also have a bad time and heavy time. We have a lot of drugs in the streets, and alcohol and lots of criminals and mans cannot find a job, and historical role of man actually is not like any more provide the food and bring . . . have a job . . . And then women like that is there to try to save a family, they are pushed to do many things, like cleaning, and a lot of educated women is just doing everything to provide food for family, to keeping family around.

And then I'm so disappoint, still I'm disappoint, maybe more than in war. Because I say look this is peace, but I'm still disappoint, this is not what I thinking that we can make it and create it in peace.

Alma, Suzana and I are talking one day, and I ask them what they think of the bridge. There is silence. Alma looks over to Suzana who tries to speak, shaking her head and looking down at the carpet. After a few long moments she finds her voice, 'Of course it's not our bridge. Not our bridge.'

Alma explains. 'Physically, it doesn't look like before. I mean it is for shape and for materials, but how to explain . . . Something what's been make by man and then maked-up by nature across four hundred years, you cannot make again of course. I mean for us we can see these small points that's missing for us and we can be very sad because of that. My husband he says, "Oh, I don't like this new bridge". But when I look, I say doesn't matter in the end, after everything that's happened, how he look. We have a bridge.

Because this bridge has to symbolize something. Because when you look at this view from before, when young people kissing on the bridge, when only nice things happen on the bridge, and when we have a peace, we didn't know that some things can happen to us like happened.'

Suzana tries to speak again, her face pained.

'And then if you look how many people we're missing, we can't get back people, we can get back bridges and buildings and streets and towns but we can't get back people.'

Alma adds, 'I have a view from two sides. People you cannot bring back. But we have a bridge again.'

It's the first time it's rained all week and it's concert day. This afternoon when I arrive for the dress rehearsal, there is a sizeable plastic bucket positioned exactly where the podium would be, if we had a podium. A small amount of water is sitting in the bucket. I look up towards the ceiling. 'Yes, ceiling drips when it rains. Maybe rain stopping before concert.'

Having to perform while standing next to a bright green bucket and dodging drips is the least of my worries. However, as I move to the left, I mentally instruct myself not to wander over to the right, and not to kick the bucket . . .

After the rehearsal, I forget all about it, and when I come out to take my bow at the beginning of the concert, I'm astonished to see a large green plant set into the bucket. It's all I can do to stop myself emitting a peal of laughter. As it is, any sensitive soul in the audience might suspect that my broad grin is not entirely due to their enthusiastic applause. I turn round and beam at Belma and the others, wondering who was responsible for the bright idea. A wonderful way to begin a concert.

It wasn't until I arrived in Bosnia last week that I was informed that the concert in Sarajevo would be at the National Museum, the first concert there since it reopened, and that it would be televised. Evidently Siniša, my *secondo violino* in the Vivaldi, has pulled out all the stops to arrange a special occasion for our performance. I just wish that I had been told beforehand, possibly even been asked for my agreement . . . I'm not sure that it would have affected my choice of programme, but I would certainly have brought a different concert-dress! And I'm not too keen on this kind of surprise being sprung on me as a *fait accompli*.

The Museum is closed on the day of the concert, so I'm not able to see any of its exhibits. I only recall a grey atmosphere, and a broad gallery with one large case in the middle and a few smaller cases on the sides. Our cramped changing room is in the basement, more of a dusty storage room, with hardly any chairs and no mirrors. There's nowhere to put on make-up, and no quiet place to collect one's thoughts and prepare to perform.

A rectangular-shaped hall is ideal for acoustics, but two rectangular spaces are definitely too much of a good thing. The Museum's performance-space is L-shaped, with the orchestra set up in the bend of the 'L'. This does not pose any difficulties when I'm conducting, but when I'm playing the Elgar solos, I'm torn between facing the audience to my left or the audience to my right. After some discreet swivelling, I end up in an unhappy compromise by playing to the wall in between.

Immediately after the concert, a woman from a local radio station interviews me, and as soon as that's finished, Siniša pulls me away saying there's a photographer from a women's magazine who wants to do a photo shoot of us.

A women's magazine? A photo shoot? Maybe twenty years ago, but now, at my age?

'Come, my *primo violino*,' and Siniša guides me to an ornate staircase where we are instructed to sit next to each other. He is young and virile with just the right amount of dishevelment in his hair, while I am . . . I try to drape my long skirt fetchingly over the stairs, nudging away his shoe which has wandered onto it. Flash bulbs go off alarmingly. Now what is it one is supposed to do? The word 'pout' comes to mind. I don't think this is for me.

My one moment of attempted glamour is, in the end, only a moment: the magazine decides not to publish any of the photographs.

☙❦❧

Siniša has a string quartet and he invites me to accompany them to a school where they will give a little presentation for the children. The school is in a suburb on one of the hills above Sarajevo, and on our way we pass through some poor neighbourhoods. The people don't look to me like townspeople any more. 'No, they don't going to Sarajevo. They stay here. Even it's close.'

The school is housed in a fairly large, concrete building with anonymous corridors. We are led into the director's office where espresso is handed out on little trays and the young headmistress, her beautiful face framed in a white headscarf, talks animatedly in Bosnian about her work. After twenty minutes or so, we make our way to the assembly hall. There is a stage and rows of benches which are soon filled with about a hundred and fifty children, aged from seven to twelve, who file in quietly under the gaze of their teachers.

The quartet has prepared a programme about Mozart and has brought a delightful singer to introduce it. She is dressed in a Mozartian costume which intrigues the children and she walks among them so that they can examine it more closely. She has a lovely informal style and talks about how people lived at the time and about Mr and Mrs Mozart and about the music itself; she asks questions and the children shout out their answers; she sings some Mozart songs, accompanying herself on an upright piano, and the quartet plays some movements. There is a friendly atmosphere and good participation.

At one point she asks if anyone can play the piano. One child comes up to the front and stumbles around a bit on the keyboard. Then another comes up and plays the A minor Rondo perfectly and musically. He looks to be about seven years old and has a quiet confidence. What a surprise that even here, in a forsaken suburb of Sarajevo, there is a talent that is being nurtured.

⚜

On my last night, I stay in the little *pension* in Sarajevo where I had stayed two years ago after the conference. I am almost asleep at around 1.30 a.m. when a man and a woman enter the room next door. There are loud noises, thuds and slams. My annoyance quickly turns to something else.

It's not that he's shouting, this is worse. The man has a booming voice, naturally fortissimo, and when he raises it, which he does frequently, it seems to be without any effort. Like a lion that roars because that's the only sound it can make. I have never heard a voice like that. It's the voice of a giant.

His words are not articulated. He speaks very slowly, controlling, menacing, as one who knows his power. Occasionally I hear a frightened female voice, but the man growls and seems to be trying to comfort her. A giant's comfort . . .

My bed is against the wall. And the wall seems to be getting more and more insubstantial. I am holding my breath, listening, my pulse beating too quickly. The sounds stop for a moment. They start again.

I sit up and put my feet firmly on the floor and try to breathe. Should I phone the police? bang on the wall? There would be no-one at the desk at this time of night, and to get to the stairs would mean passing their door. Probably the police would be no help and if he hears me phoning or opening my door . . . I must do something, but I feel trapped.

I'm suddenly, excruciatingly afraid. Terrified of the force on the other side of the wall. I feel helpless, unprotected, incapable of helping the woman, cowardly. The sounds stop.

I am useless, the world is full of people like this, and I'm not making a dent. Here I'm meeting only with like-minded people, playing music while thugs and war criminals run rings round us. I put on the television very softly and cannot turn off the light until 4 a.m.

I wake early the next morning and am greatly relieved to hear the woman's voice next door. I dress quickly and go down to the reception desk. 'Yes, we heard, last night. Woman is OK, yes. Police would have done nothing. Yes it was terrible, these people, they are not from here, terrible. But we were aware.'

I have an urge to hover in the small lobby, to see for myself that the woman is all right. I drink some tea but no-one comes downstairs. I have to leave for the airport in half an hour, and I'm desperate to get some fresh air. I go outside and walk a little, then pack my case and wait in the lobby for my taxi.

There are not many people about. A tall woman pays her bill and a handsome man in his thirties says good morning to me and bows slightly. That kind of courtesy is not common here. Or anywhere.

They leave and the woman at the desk nods at me. This was the couple. This was the man who has the voice of a giant at night and is soft-spoken in the morning.

I think of Jekyll and Hyde. Of werewolves. Of madness. How close we all are to darkness, our own darkness.

At least he is not a monster always. Again I feel the volatility, precariousness, underlying threat of this place. I'm skating on thin ice, that can crack at any moment.

∽✣∾

Belma and Siniša are in the taxi to accompany me to the airport. We have time for a coffee and a chat before my plane leaves and I'm glad of it. We talk about future plans. There's a festival in September, and the new Director of the British Council might arrange a tour, and Siniša wants me to play *Fiddler on the Roof*, and maybe the Mendelssohn Octet, and I've met a Turkish diplomat who is interested in doing an exchange with an orchestra in Turkey. Lots of possibilities. In this country where possibilities seem to be narrowing, it's good to be with people who are trying to keep the doors open.

Last night's experience is still with me. It still feels that I'm skating on thin ice, but here and there, there is a tree to hold on to. And the work that I'm doing may not reach people like the man last night – though who knows? – but it does affect the musicians themselves, and their families, and students, and the audiences and their families, and maybe a little thread of peace and joy and safety weaves just a little further into the fabric of the community.

June 2006

I suppose I was not too surprised that all the ideas discussed at the airport came to nothing. The Turkish diplomat never replied to my emails, the British Council suffered a budget cut that put paid to any tours, the September festival came and went, and Siniša's plans were somehow overtaken by other plans. So my next visit took place on exactly the same basis as the previous ones – just me and the Sinfonietta. This time though, it was going to be the full orchestra and perhaps it was time for something special.

As the emails went back and forth, the orchestra configuration crystallized into two flutes, one clarinet and two horns. I discovered that there is just one Mozart symphony that does not have any oboes, No. 27, so I ordered the score and parts. It would be lovely for the Sinfonietta to play a Mozart symphony, and surprising that I'd not heard this work before. Perhaps it doesn't get aired often because normal orchestras, of course, have oboists who may as well be utilized, considering that they are paid whether they play or not.

I myself was performing at that time a virtuoso piece by Tchaikovsky, his Valse-Scherzo, not the type of repertoire I naturally gravitate towards, but it's delightful, coquettish and elegant and it regularly explodes into fireworks. I went to the library to check whether our reduced winds could carry the weight of the entire section, and was plunged into a mystery: the beautiful old Russian edition that was before me contained a spectacularly difficult cadenza and a middle section that dallied with exotic keys, all of which is missing in the violin and piano score. It seems that a shortened version has become standard. I was goaded into action, giving myself even more work than usual in having to write out extra bars as well as re-orchestrate them. And of course I had to learn to play them as well.

So I had a Mozart Symphony and a short Tchaikovsky work: what else would fill out the programme? What would end the programme? It was then that I thought of *Swan Lake*. It is not a work to bring to a country straight after a war – that's the time for Beethoven's Ninth, or Mozart's Requiem, for music that replenishes courage and hope, that offers solace and a deep understanding of suffering. *Swan Lake* speaks of waltzing and leisure and abundance, of long gowns and sparkle. Was Bosnia ready for a taste of serious frivolity? I ordered the Mazurka and the famous Waltz. And to provide a still centre to the programme, I chose Fauré's beautiful Pavane.

Just as I was beginning the laborious work of doling out the oboe and trombone and trumpet parts to the other instruments, Belma emailed that she had found two Serbian oboists who were willing to join the orchestra for these concerts. Oboes, finally! And from Serbia, which means the Sinfonietta is crossing even more boundaries. If only I'd known earlier, I would have chosen a different Mozart symphony – what a shame to have two prized oboists sitting out for a third of the concert . . . perhaps I could choose an encore that would feature them specially. But there was no time to consider that now.

Belma also had an unusual request. Would I please send an email to the new British Ambassador to Bosnia because he plays the double bass and maybe he could play with the Sinfonietta. 'How does he play?' I emailed back. 'OK, he's good. But maybe he can't come to most rehearsals.'

Hmm. In my imagination I saw myself turning to our new bassist and saying, 'Mr Ambassador, would you kindly consider the possibility of paying a little more attention to your intonation?'

I emailed Belma, 'Since he can't make all the rehearsals, and maybe his work will prevent him at the last minute from even playing the concerts, I think we should have another bassist as well.' So the bassist who had played with us last time was hired, and I sent an email to the Ambassador. He said yes, he'd be honoured, and could I send him the music, just the difficult passages? One *Swan Lake* bass part went into the diplomatic pouch.

Reconstruction of Stari Most

Lower cornice assembled.

Repair of wing walls.

Monitoring system permanently installed to measure and register bridge stability.

Final assembling of spandrel walls with lightening voids and drainage pipes.

Cutting and laying of pavement with protruding cross-ribs.

Assembling of upper cornice from blocks 70cm wide, of which 14–20cm protruding from the arch. Cramps connect top of blocks.

Construction of stone parapet.

Manufacture and placement of metal fence in parapet.

Removal of centering and its concrete pillars.

Wednesday

On the plane to Sarajevo, I am sitting next to a young Bosnian who lives in Sweden. He tells me that the Croatian football team was beaten in the World Cup yesterday 1–0 by Brazil (not a bad score, I'd say, but I know nothing about football); and that after the match, there was fighting in Mostar. He doesn't know any details. He also fills me in on the local football situation in Mostar: two teams, one from the east, one from the west, which is a problem for supporters who find themselves on the wrong side of town, and now the team from the east has just been promoted into the first division so they will be playing each other next season. He is afraid of continual violence following the games.

There hasn't been any violence in Mostar for years, so I'm feeling apprehensive when we touch down in Sarajevo. Ermin and Belma are there to meet me with warm hugs. It's as if I were here only last week.

Belma has decided to travel to Mostar tomorrow, rather than to come with us now as planned. This will allow her to give the music that I've brought with me to the Sarajevo players who will follow later in the week. 'They want to practise it before first rehearsal,' she says. I like that. They know what to expect from me and they want to be prepared. So here we are in the middle of the airport, sorting out a sheaf of orchestral parts.

Then Ermin and I set off in his new minivan. He tells me he has a job driving people around Bosnia and he's been up today since 6 a.m.

'You must be very tired,' I say.

'It's OK, I like driving,' and as he negotiates the winding road, he starts to tell me of how he drove a bakery van during the war.

Ermin

In the war here, many dead I saw, dead people around me, and I was start to be worried about myself. I getting crazy, I getting mad in this. I couldn't leave the country because I didn't have passport and the government didn't give us any permission to go outside. That was wrong, and I tried to find what's the best solution for me. I couldn't go, I have to stay but I don't like this atmosphere, war atmosphere around me, I had a headache about that. And I looking the first international organization I can be part of them, just because I thinking that was my therapy in this time. These international people not gonna talk about war, they talk maybe about sport, art, culture, music, whatever, that's my therapy.

And I volunteered for one year for War Child, who was coming I think '94. And they coming with mobile bakery taken from British army from Second World War, mobile bakery. But fine, we organize everything and we start production of bread, people need it. We got the flour from UNHCR – United Nations for Refugees – and we were very involved together with their office here and they support our project and they supply us with all these things that we need.

We making bread and deliveries in town, in many organization because this moment in town never be shops, you cannot buy anything, no shops at all. And we supply a public kitchen, kindergarten, hospital, old people house, this kind of thing. We make a bread and delivered it, personally, sometimes between grenades. By bike I go south of Mostar in industry zone, it's five kilometres south of Mostar. It's not all the time shelling but from time to time. So every time who knows what's going to happen? And we had from beginning like fifteen workers working for free, working just for bread, for bread.

And it was interesting times we producing the bread, but for starting this machines, for heating this machines, take two or three hours before start. And once, we in the middle of production, it start shelling. And I ask these people, if you like we stop to work and we can go somewhere but I don't know where because there is no basement around. Or we . . . whatever we like to do. I feel responsible for these people.

And you know what they told me? 'Put the music on higher, and we can keep to work'! Local music, Bosnian music, sevdah. Because the people doesn't want to hear this sound of grenades! But I respect that they know if they stop we need two or three more hours to start the heating again. So they said put the music on. We had radio and cassette player. But we didn't listen radio because this radio it was full of this war emotional . . . bad things let's say. Yeah, propaganda. I didn't like it and we just used the tapes, that's great.

And this bakery working for fifteen months. And I make all calculations every day how many breads we produced and where we delivered. I still have these lists. And we produced around one million three hundred thousand loaves for these fifteen months. Can you imagine? With delivering. In box-van. We had a box-van, specially for bread, the War Child bring it, and we driving two, three times during day and deliver bread to these public kitchens, people's houses, many things. That's starting this humanitarian work, feeling human feeling when the people need something and you make somebody happy, smiling, this feeling my heart was full, even for nothing.

A wonderful story. Bread and music. And when things get rough, put the music on higher!

I ask about the trouble last night.

'Yes, there is fighting. Near front line. Some Bosnian Croats were drunk, they broke shops and windows, cars, anything they finding. Then I don't know, or they went to the east, or some east young people went to the west and they fighting. Police didn't come for one hour. One hour! Used tear gas.'

'I'm sorry. Was anybody killed?'

'*Ne*, one person shot, but not dead, and six policemen injured. Today was meeting with Mayor of Mostar. Everyone unhappy with police, that they not coming. Why they not coming? They are afraid. But that's their job, no? They must come.

'In meeting decided that all people who are arrested must pay for a damage. That's good, very good, it's first time they doing this. But whole thing terrible. We need peace.'

At least Ermin feels that something positive has emerged from this violent episode.

As we come into Mostar, it all looks very familiar. The non-descript outskirts, the bus station, and then turning into the little street where 'my' lodgings are. When my host opens the door, he gives me a brief hug. I am surprised. It's unusual for him to be anything but formal. I'm glad to be back.

As I enter 'my' room in the attic, I promise myself I'm going to keep a diary this time.

Thursday

Breakfast is a bowl of cherries, an omelette, toast and cheese, and peppermint tea.

After a short practice, I walk over to the Pavarotti Centre. The little square along my way is now fronted by an enormous, glass-sided building, a hotel I think, and on the main street there are a few more huge buildings that have discarded their scaffolding. I'm glad of the rebuilding, but the architecture seems brash, uninteresting and rather insensitive to the surroundings.

Vassili has asked me to hear one of his students. She is sixteen years old and already plays with a solid technique, testament to his good teaching and to her dedication. She plays me some Bach and then Vieuxtemps 5th Concerto. After I make a few comments, we go downstairs into the lobby for a coffee where Vassili tells me, in a scattering of Bosnian, Russian and English, that he can't play the concerts and that his student will play instead of him and will I please teach her? She seems a little nervous – she will be by far the youngest player in the orchestra – but I assure them that she will be fine and I will help her with her part. She will sit at the back of the second violins and Siniša, my *secondo violino* of last year, will take Vassili's place and lead the orchestra.

Vassili has to go to Moscow tomorrow for two months, something to do with arranging his mother's pension. The conversation wanders on to Vladimir Horowitz, one of the greatest pianists of all time with a uniquely individual style, and Vassili asks me if I know that Horowitz had a sister who was also a pianist. She was 'just as good', he says, but her career was stunted because she stayed in the USSR. Two Horowitzes? Isn't that an oxymoron?

Rada joins us. She is even more beautiful with a new spiky haircut that makes her look still younger. Soon Suzana and Miro arrive but we can't begin without Belma who has all the music. Eventually Belma enters bearing cello and music and apologies, and we find a studio and work through some of the programme. It's going to be an uphill struggle. Again.

After the rehearsal, Belma, Rada and I sit outside in a café overlooking the river. It is hot. Each visit of the last few years has inched towards summer, pushing further away the snows of my first encounter with Mostar. I look over towards Stari Most, poised high and white above the green Neretva.

Belma relates how hard it's been to gather an orchestra for these concerts because many musicians have dropped out at the last minute. In addition to Vassili, one graduate student has to rehearse all this week for an examination concert; another's wife has just had a baby; our horn player is with the Sarajevo Philharmonic in Dubrovnik; and the Mostar Symphony suddenly organized a concert, taking three of our players.

'The Mostar Symphony? What's that?' I ask.

'An orchestra on West side. They play only at Christmas and Easter, not really classical music, carols and things, and maybe one or two more concerts in a year. Three of Sinfonietta's players are members of Symphony. It's full-time. It means they *have* to play with the Symphony.'

'But they had already agreed to play our concerts.'

'Yes. But they have to play with Symphony.'

I think about this. 'Didn't the Symphony know about the Sinfonietta's concerts this week?' I ask.

Belma looks puzzled.

'Can't they co-ordinate the dates?' I continue. 'There are so few concerts for musicians here, it's a shame if there is a clash and they're deprived of playing one of them.'

Belma is incredulous. It's out of the question, she says, nobody co-operates here. I want to ask if the conflict of dates is just a coincidence, but I think better of it.

The other discomforting news is that the Sinfonietta will not perform in Mostar this time. The first concert will be in Banja Luka in the north and then we'll repeat the programme in Sarajevo, but there is apparently no money for a performance here. The musicians are paid for each concert and rehearsal and that's how it should be, but it feels sad, and wrong, not to be playing in Mostar. So I suggest we do an open rehearsal in the courtyard of the Pavarotti Centre, just for students and friends. If everyone agrees, we'll plan it for the last afternoon here and Rada says she'll spread the word among the students.

As we get up to leave, I ask Belma where I can buy a SIM card. I'm not a mobile phone fan, resenting the thing most of the time, but I've brought mine with me from England because, with plans changing so frequently here, I could see that it might be useful to be easily reached. So now we find a little kiosk that sells postcards and cigarettes, and I get myself a SIM card and a Bosnian phone number. To have a Bosnian phone number suddenly seems a big step, and I am ridiculously proud of it.

There's time for a leisurely supper, and as I let my eyes wander over the largely empty restaurant that I've entered, I recognize that I'm anxious. About whether the programme is too difficult for the musicians, that maybe I'll have to conduct the Fauré in four beats to the bar instead of two which will break it up too much, that spending a week in Bosnia rehearsing will tell on my own playing and that I should have chosen an easier piece to play than the Valse-Scherzo. Vassili had said that this is a compulsory piece for the Moscow Tchaikovsky Competition, and it's very difficult and why am I playing it? I'd replied, because I'm a Bach player, and a Mozart and Beethoven player, so it's great to play this kind of piece for a change. But now I'm having second thoughts.

Back in my room, I paste together the final wind parts of the Fauré, thankful for the air-conditioning unit. It's 12.15 a.m. before I switch off the light.

Friday

I work all morning in my room, marking parts, practising conducting and then practising the violin for two hours. The Valse-Scherzo is rippling along now. If only I can keep it like this . . .

Lunch is a potato *burek* with a Turkish coffee, and then it's back to the Pavarotti Centre. There are very few people on the streets – they must be watching the football. Now that Croatia is out of the World Cup, there shouldn't be any more trouble. Though I think that Serbia is still in the running.

I find Rada practising *Swan Lake* and we talk about the recent violence. 'When I heard about it, I cried,' she says, 'I thought it was happening all over again.' A fight between football fans is ugly anywhere, but here it has the potential to revive old – not-so-old – animosities. And fears. 'It has been very upsetting for many people. We are very shaken,' she adds.

Then she shows me some presents that her students have given her over the years as graduation gifts, including a hand-carved music stand and a painting of herself. I'm not surprised that her students love her.

I have promised to teach Vassili's student, Irena, so we go through the Mozart Symphony. She has a lot to learn but she learns quickly. She's a sweet girl, earnest and shy, and I reassure her that she can do it and will even enjoy it. In fact it will be wonderful for her to play with older and experienced musicians, and to get her first taste of orchestral playing with Mozart, Fauré and Tchaikovsky.

There is just one problem that I haven't solved. And that's the small matter of the triangle. We can do without tympani and percussion, though I dearly wish we had a bass drum for the *Swan Lake* waltz; but the triangle has a solo and is essential. No other instrument can substitute for its tiny bell-like sound. And I don't want to repeat my jack-of-all-trades trick of two years ago. Maybe one of the music therapy team can help . . .

'Triangle? I've always wanted to play the triangle!' Alpha can play the Sarajevo concert, but not the one in Banja Luka. I'll have to find someone else up there. I give her the music so that she can practise.

We are again a small nucleus of players for today's rehearsal. We have no bass section at all, the Ambassador being otherwise engaged, and the other bass player unfortunately unable to fit his bass into the van that was sent to pick him up from Sarajevo. They will try again tomorrow with a different van. Ogi played with us last year, so it's not the first time they've had to find suitable transportation. And now I'm told that he will be two hours late for tomorrow's rehearsal, which means I will have to reconsider the running order . . .

This afternoon I work with the musicians on the nuts and bolts of entrances and notes. Every now and then, the pieces fall together and it sounds clean and unified and that's such a joy. Rather like a wiper clearing the windscreen for a brief moment after you've been peering through a torrent of mud and rain.

During the break, Belma tells me how things have changed from the time when she was a student in Sarajevo.

Belma

I came to study in Sarajevo in 1999, fresh after the war. And I can tell you it was great. It was more energy and more enthusiasm . . . and we played a lot. I played that time in a chamber orchestra which had very good manager, and he's politically very active, and he has connections, he's really good as a manager. And that time they made good deal, co-operation with Swedish Royal Academy, so lot of money was coming from there. And we were travelling.

When Swan Lake Comes to Sarajevo

We went to Sweden to rehearse, and make concert in Dubrovnik. So it was twice a year, in summer in Sweden and winter in Dubrovnik, and it was always great. And bringing teachers. I mean we had master classes – so many master classes for strings, and I never paid for it. Manager was organizing scholarships and everything. So it was really great.

And then with years it was getting worse and worse and worse, and then now, I mean I was earning more money as a student than now as a professional. You know what pays my bills? It is gigs non-stop, cocktails and all this stuff, playing in a wine cellars and all this . . . as somebody who studied, who had another idea of being musician, it's really terrible. But concerts, normal, professional concerts, it is so rare, this is really like killing me softly and every young musician and old musician of course.

So Sinfonietta is really the project of all of us, and I'm the person who is pushing it most of all, but when we sit together in rehearsals, although half is professional, half is completely amateur, I like that still there is some ensemble, I can feel an ensemble, I can feel same ideas, same will. Not just like we are professionals here and we sit and we play and we finish the concert – this is more than that. Although concerts are not always good, I just like that we are all together in this, because we are in the same sauce, cooking the same sauce.

I smile at the analogy. And I'm amused by Belma's comment, similar to Edo's, about professionals, implying that they just do their job, unfeelingly. As if you can't be a professional and play with love at the same time. Not always easy, when you're tired of performing the same repertoire night after night and you don't like the conductor's interpretation and your stand-partner has some annoying habits. Still, professionalism without love and commitment beggars the description of 'musician': the only difference between a professional and a non-professional is that the first earns a living from the activity. Or tries to earn something resembling a living . . .

I have dinner with a woman from the music therapy programme and we talk about the impending elections and how dirty the campaign is becoming. She fears that the political parties provoke instability in order to keep the spirit of nationalism alive and the old guard in power. An old trick. When there is fear, it's easier to force a retreat into your clan than to risk a new collaboration. Yesterday there was more violence, this time in the big school near the front line. She's not clear what happened.

We are joined by a few of her colleagues who tell us that Teo will be singing at a bar tonight. *Idemo!* We get there at 11 p.m. to be told that he's singing tomorrow night, starting at midnight. We are disappointed but I could do with some sleep, so I leave the others to their drinks. '*Dobro veče*, see you tomorrow!'

Saturday

During the years that I've been walking back and forth to the Pavarotti Centre, I've always passed the spot where the road turns towards the river and simply disappears over the edge. The first time I came upon this, I remember peering gingerly over the sheer drop to see sections of roadway lying in the river and an old rusted car smashed on the rocks below. Last year, the piles of rubble were being cleared and cranes were in place. Now there is a bridge, and suddenly it feels strangely abnormal for this place to look normal.

The musicians from Sarajevo are arriving, so after a morning's work on the scores, I get myself to the Centre for a full rehearsal. Now we have all the strings, minus the basses – there was yet another mix-up with the van bringing Ogi and his bass – and we have flutes and a clarinet. Oboes and horns are supposed to come tomorrow, the horns also coming from Serbia. There are a number of string players I've not met before, young, dynamic, and female. And they play well. The standard is definitely improving.

It's tough to play the Valse-Scherzo while giving cues, so there are many missed entrances and lost lines and we have to repeat the tricky passages over and over. This is not a piece that trips along – or gallops along – at a regular pace; I play with a lot of *rubato*, but I'm fairly confident that as they become familiar with my style, they will be able to breathe with me.

As for the *Swan Lake* Grande Valse, I try to instil the lilting feel of the waltz, though it's rather a handicap to rehearse the opening oom-pah-pahs minus the pah-pahs of the horns. Even so, we work hard on giving the downbeats a sense of lift and lightness, so that the offbeats have something to rebound from. Once the accompaniment is waltzing, I encourage the violins to introduce the famous tune as smoothly as possible, meltingly, like chocolate, or like a soft breath on the ear. Everyone knows the melody, and the dawning of familiarity is all the more welcome when coupled with a most tender warmth. They love it.

The Mazurka, though also in three-in-a-bar, has a completely different character and a different lilt. Bold and flamboyant, it demands a strong downbeat and a strong, delayed second beat. It's harder for the players to feel this rhythmic gesture, so I bounce an imaginary ball on the downbeat, watching its high trajectory before landing on the second beat. When we've had enough of bouncing balls, we troop down to the lobby for the break.

The café there has been recently taken over by Rada's husband, who is hoping to make a success of it though past attempts have failed. It's a good space but just far enough off the beaten track that tourists don't pass by. So it's a big risk, but we all want to support him, and it's nice for us to feel it's 'in the family'. We spill out into the courtyard and relax in the warm air. The sandwiches are very slow in coming, and after twenty minutes I see someone rushing in with lettuces and tomatoes and bread – they obviously haven't planned for a sudden influx like this.

While we wait, Rada's husband tells us of how once, during the war, when he was on fire duty, he was called to put out a fire in a cinema. 'When it was finished and fire was out, we sat in the burned cinema, very tired, very dirty. We resting, we smoking cigarettes in the dark. Nobody talking. Then someone says, "Lousy film, this".'

Rada laughs. 'You see, not everything terrible in war. Sometimes funny.'

After the second rehearsal, I manage to rest a little, and then take Ermin and Alma out for dinner. They choose a restaurant on the other side of the river which has a huge garden with trees and grass and widely spaced tables. And a large television screen where the football is being shown. We pick a table furthest away from the screen, but there seems to be no way of avoiding the mosquitoes, which appear to regard my legs as dinner.

Apart from that, the quiet and the green and the wine and the good company all work their magic and soon I am beautifully relaxed. Alma tells me she is involved with a summer camp.

'Summer camp is my love. By accident I meet this lady six years ago, seven years ago. We just have a coffee and talk about everything and she said that she like me if I like to come in her summer camp, in Croatia, to be a volunteer, my son can come and be a camper. And then we start, and for the beginning I have to collect some children from both sides of Mostar and organize buses, transport and everything. It's kids from you know, from both sides of Mostar. So I somehow find children, all national groups, and they really enjoy. I was afraid in the beginning how they all respond to be with each other, to have a fun, but you know, children is beautiful, they are so honest, they are so open and they just after two days they just like old friend. It was beautiful in the end, last day we cry everyone, all . . . and the young ones. It was beautiful twelve days, I couldn't forget these twelve days, even though we work hard with the kids.'

Ermin adds, 'Work, any kind of work with children, that's the good. Show them how any life is beautiful, they should be happy, not sad, not think anything wrong, not negative, and that's the only way they can organize their lives in the future. It's opened one door for me after war – I respect human being. And I concentrate my life and my work for humanitarian work, to help people.

'The last ten years for my age is the best ages in life actually, and I lost them. And I never gonna catch them again, but I believe younger generation could do something better. I hope, I hope, it's future for this country, new generation without any hate. That will be something what will give me energy for rest of my life. This is the most important thing now. I not afraid about myself, I afraid about some crazy people who is still thinking like ten years, fifteen years ago, still.'

The waiter comes with coffee and then retreats to the football screen.

'Will you tell me what it was like straight after the war?' I ask. 'After the fighting stopped, what actually happened?'

Ermin

We were very careful in this period, but day after day it's coming less and less shelling. That was Spring 1994 because the Washington Agreement make peace between Croats and Bosniaks, but there's still Serbians fight, shelling from the hills, and then Dayton Agreement coming, they are forced by big countries, power countries in the world, like United States, and we feel very comfortable and safe because everybody respect this.

And after these years of war and our afraid for our lives and looking every time where is danger position for us, and this peace coming, and give us freedom, let's say, freedom to go to walk on the streets, and these people I can tell you because I know from this town, feel so much happy. They have this freedom to walk, they have this freedom to talk, they have this freedom to meet each other. And in this period is coming European Community administration in Mostar, they will build now repairing the houses, repairing economy, and they coming with lots of money and they start lots of industry in this town, and that's the first time money is coming in this town. And I feel the money's around and you can drink, you can buy something, what we can do something, it looked like normal, and the people was very happy about that.

Very slowly is coming returning in the houses, people coming, cross the front line to visit families. A year after Agreement. The people afraid go before that. Like my wife had parents on the other side and it's about five hundred metres between their apartment and us. They didn't see each other for ten, eleven months. And she went to see them on other side and it's really emotional. Afraid to be not only shot but bad treatment on other side. They starting first to cross when the Agreement coming in Spring '94. The internationals make tents between lines, in these tents could meet families. They're not going across the line, they meet in the tents. They have three hours to meet each other. And then after that is coming slowly, by day, they have permission to go one day there and back in the evening, and after that is coming three days. And then is open line. You know, step by step. Organized by the UN. Crazy it was crazy.

After the meal, we stroll over to where Teo will sing and we share some vodka. He sings from midnight to 3 a.m. on Fridays and Saturdays. I'm certainly an owl rather than a lark, but these hours would be too much even for me. Tonight he starts with pop songs, and when I'm struggling to keep my eyes open, I ask him if he would please sing some sevdah. The husky voice with the wide vibrato curls around the notes of *Moj Dilbere*, my favourite, the one I played in Sarajevo, and immediately all the tables of young men join in. The place comes alive, in an instant. More sevdah follows and Alma sings all the lyrics. She tries to find a definition for the word sevdah, coming up with phrases like 'a state of bliss', 'a connection to your own heart', 'at peace with oneself'. 'You can fall into sevdah,' she says. No wonder it is so alluring.

On our way back, we stop on Tito Bridge to listen to the nightingales.

Sunday

Today the British Ambassador comes to rehearse. Before he arrives, I casually mention our expected guest to the orchestra, and there is a general excited rustle of '*Ko? Who?*' He looks much younger than I'd anticipated, tall and fair-haired and fresh-faced. He's wearing shorts and his informality endears him quickly to everyone. And as soon as we start, I'm relieved to see that he plays perfectly well: I didn't relish the possibility of embarrassing an ambassador. It must be unusual to be a bass-playing ambassador, but I can imagine that playing the bass is a good respite from the tensions of diplomacy, or of any job. (Oh yes, there were many occasions when I was younger, mainly in the US, when an audience member asked me after a concert what my 'day-job' was. This is it, my day-job and my night-job, I'd say.)

Today holds an abundance of riches, since we also welcome our prized oboists. As rare as gold dust! Two young women, one small and slight, the other tall and substantial. They are both good players and oboe number 2 seems to be someone who can find humour in anything – I think she will be an asset to the Sinfonietta.

So with only the horns missing – I'm assured they're arriving tomorrow – we work through almost the whole programme and now the orchestra is beginning to come together. Everyone is more comfortable with the music and it shows. The new flute player is excellent and her solos in the Pavane are beautifully phrased. The impressionistic harmonies of Fauré are refreshing, especially in contrast to the classical style of Mozart, and it's good for the Sinfonietta to have the chance to play music of this era. And I might after all be able to conduct it in two, subdividing into four only if things threaten to pull apart.

After four hours, I suggest that they rehearse tonight without me, in their individual sections. I think this will be more productive than a general rehearsal, as each section will be able to co-ordinate itself and ensure that everyone is clear about everything and is pulling their weight, something that is not appropriate for me to do. It will also give them more sense of involvement and responsibility.

I meet Alma and we have a cup of tea.

'How was rehearsal today?' she asks.

'Much better, thanks. They're doing really well. But we still don't have the horn players. Anyway, I just want to relax for a bit and not think about the concert.'

'OK I understand how it's nice to just relax and talk about something else. 'Cause you know how stressful can be now, it was before as well, of course, last fifteen years, this kind problems what we have, social, no job, economic, like this, and you know I think that our key is actually go have a fun with people. Ermin and I we never thinking have a fun, just bring people, be together with people.'

I nod.

She continues, 'Between people you can't be sad, you can't be in bad mood – the situation doesn't give you opportunity to think, it just has to be, to socialize with people, to talk, because many people coming . . . and they have different theme, they like to talk about different things, and then you forget your problems. That is very important if you're in situation that you have depression or something. Just go out, or bring people in your home or . . . just don't be alone. It's probably instinct. Now I know that this is it, but from this period we didn't know that's what we had to do. Only what we know that we had to have our friends around us. You know we just . . . we were really socialize with people, we just don't want to stay alone at home, yeah it help us a lot.'

Monday

This is the day the horn players arrive from Serbia. One of them walks in half an hour after the start of the morning's rehearsal, having travelled all night by bus from Belgrade. He is young and eager to play, turning down my offer of drinking a coffee first. The other horn player will not arrive until much later. Very frustrating. I can't rehearse everything again just for him.

Today's rehearsals do not go well. In fact over the course of the day, the playing seems to get progressively worse. We are all extremely hot. It's about 38C and the air-conditioner is not working. The horn players find it hard to fit their notes into the general texture and it's not an instrument that easily hides. So I have to stop frequently to explain the subtleties of rhythm. They are probably not very experienced, as one of them asks, when I've indicated that they are out of sync with the violas, 'Isn't it in time?'

I know of hardly any music that I'd want to hear 'in time'; and in any case, it's impossible for two human beings to play 'in time' at exactly the same time, without some kind of communication. So I suggest that they listen to the violas and try to stay together. Now they actually look over towards the viola section and I know we are making progress. I'm saying '*zajedno*' a lot today.

During the breaks, the atmosphere is very friendly and relaxed, the new players made to feel at home. Oboist no. 2 keeps everyone laughing and I see that Irena is getting on well with the clarinettist, and that the clarinettist likes to chat in Hungarian with one of the violists.

I organize a fairly long lunch break, so that we can all cool off, and I go 'home' to sleep for an hour. I'm tired of walking back and forth, the violin getting heavier each time and the heat more oppressive and the way longer. So I return by taxi, but the taxi driver makes a fuss about taking euros, even though all the cafés and shops take them, and I'm completely out of KMs. In the end he has to accept them.

We thought it would be cooler in the courtyard in the late afternoon, but it's still stifling. A number of students and friends have gathered to hear the open rehearsal, but we decide to keep it short. The flute players need to leave, and a cellist and violist have already left, one in order to teach, and the other in order to get divorced! (I'm assured that she is happy about this.)

Before we start, I have a brief one-on-one rehearsal with Alpha, the new triangle player – how hard can it be to play three notes on the triangle? – at the right moment? – ah, there's the rub. I tell her not to worry, that I'll cue every entrance. Then we embark on the Valse-Scherzo and the horn players keep getting lost. I don't play my best and the whole event feels messy and unfocused. I've noticed in the past that the Sinfonietta tends to rush when it is not completely concentrated, and this is very noticeable now. However slowly (or quickly) I beat, they are ahead of me, straining for the finish instead of immersing themselves in the journey. It's not an enjoyable experience, but it's better that this happens now rather than later. I'm used to fluctuating levels of playing: it just indicates a lack of security, and it's no bad thing for the players to realize it at this point. Alpha does tolerably well, achieving about half her entrances; there'll be more time to rehearse before the Sarajevo concert.

Our impromptu audience is very appreciative. I sit with some of the teachers who are full of compliments. 'It was wonderful. You treat them with a gentle authority. It was lovely to watch.' I try to absorb the comments but it's not easy. They also remark that the orchestra was smiling.

'They don't usually smile,' they say.

Perhaps it wasn't as bad as I thought.

On my way home, I bump into Jasmin, the son of Alma and Ermin. He's about seventeen years old and strikes me as a normal teenager, with the occasional bout of teenage lethargy. He's grown a lot in the four years since I first met him, in height and in confidence.

Jasmin

I've just been playing football with my father behind my school, and Croat kids my age came and we played together. My friends, I know them. Majority of my generation is not interested in those kind of confrontations like nationalism and those kind of things. But there are still children that are raised in their family with a strong sense of nationalism. And they are very, very . . . not good.

I got friends on both sides. Like this is eleven years after the war, twelve almost, still we call it 'the other side' in our language. We say 'I'm going to the other side'. 'Where do you bought that? On the other side'. 'Where is that? It's on the other side.' So we kind of call it 'on the other side' and they call it on 'the other side'. So it's kind of in the dictionary, stuck. It's stuck there. When you say the other side it means . . . it's like Berlin, like Germany.

We have a chance every day in the school to talk, because we are all in the same school. We're segregated by classes, not by floors. So on the first floor you have, I dunno, a Croatian class and a Federal class. We call it Federal class because we are Federation of Bosnia. Stupid, but what can you do. So you have Croatian, Federal, Croatian, Federal, and in the recess we all go out from our classes and you can't miss each other, we meet all the time. It's still kind of early to jump to joint classes. I feel so, I don't know, I think it would be best if we could all mix up, you know what I mean. But I feel it's still a bit . . . But we do extra-curricular activities and then we go outside on weekends and we drink together, we socialize together. Well, we are the first generation that are starting to do something. Maybe even my children won't like . . . live up to my expectations. But maybe I'll have grandchildren one day and maybe they will. Who knows?

When Swan Lake Comes to Sarajevo

During the war, say I was four, and five, we had actually a very good time. You learn after, I dunno, after a year, I can't say you get used to it but you kind of figure some things out. Some things are important, some things are not. For example, why should I keep worrying? I am concerned, but why should I keep worrying and growing white hairs? I don't have any, but my father and my mother do. And then after a year of worrying you just kind of figure out, oh why should I keep doing this any more? Let's have fun, you know, let's get the best out of the situation. And then I remember some good things when all of us were together and we shared lots of things and we laughed, despite the war. And we had pretty good times sometime. Like not looking at the shelling and you know, wounded people, dead people.

The parties were like drinking coffee, we had this home-made coffee, it actually wasn't coffee, we called it coffee, it was made out of, I don't know how to say . . . grain or something, I'm not sure . . . And you just hang around in the dark, with those small candles we made out of oil. We didn't make candles it was like small lamps. You put oil in a small cup, in a jar. You put it in jar and then you pierce the lid and then you put small string inside and you just light it. And the flame is so small. But in the morning, we were all black in the face because of the oil and everything. The smell was very not pleasant. It was oil from the car was basically what we had. Maybe we would share a can of food, like fish. We used to have these cans of fish. It was disgusting. And I remember like six people ate one can, like shared. I dunno where we got the can, like some humanitarian aid, you never know, like from the army my father used to bring something.

I didn't have any friends. How could I? I was locked up with my mother and a couple of other people there. I played in the bath, it was the safest place. I played with cars and stuff, I know I had cars. There was nobody my age. I didn't know what it was like having young people round. I was just watching my parents' parties and jumping around. Yeah it was fun, everybody was laughing, that's the best part of it.

During the summer you know how hot it gets here? We used to have open windows, which is completely normal, and gunpowder you can feel it in the air, you know, it's heavy smell. That's one more thing you get used to it though. And the noise . . . my mother tells me and I know, I could have slept with the shelling for ages and I didn't wake up. You know when you have a cuckoo clock in the house then you don't hear it after a week.

And when it was a bit calmer situation, we moved out from this building. We went to Mahala. And we went to an apartment there and it was a big change because it was a suburb, kind of. And then we had water on tap, which was a big surprise. And we had water in the toilet, you know? That was a very exciting part of my grow-ing up. I went like every ten minutes and flushed. I didn't even go to pee, I just went to flush, it was fun!

And then I started going out. And then I dunno, my father started working for War Child. And I was still too young to go to school, a year before school, so I was six. War Child headquarters was basically my house. So I listened couple of months, and I just started speaking English, aged seven. I went to school first grade and I knew English better than my mother tongue.

I don't have those post-traumatic syndromes, and those post-war stuffs. Dreams no, none of those things. Everybody's kind of stayed normal after. You have to move on. I mean you can't just stick to the war.

I play the guitar. Music, when it comes to art, music is number one, and it's my relaxing, my process of relaxing goes through music. My process of saying something goes through music. And basically when I'm angry, I turn to music, and it affects my life in lots and lots of different ways.

We formed some kind of band and we practise weekly because of the school now. But hopefully during the summer we'll practise more often. It's just kind of basic rock music, normal one. It's just something to learn, we hear some music and we try to make it, it's good that way because you try to learn, and then you socialize and you have people who have the same interests with you.

I definitely want to leave Mostar to get some education some-where else. But I can see myself living here as a very, very rich man, and very powerful! Because I see that the only way that you can live actually here, full meaning of live, is that you have a lot of money. Because, I mean I don't want my parents' life. I really don't want their life. They're kind of hardly fixing up. And I don't want to be afraid for my future, and for my children's future. I don't know, I'm confused now. I don't want to pull my hair for worrying about will I have anything to eat tomorrow. And I want to afford everything to myself.

My friends are not interested in anything. People my age in Mostar are very, very passive. Not motivated, and poor. Through the student council and all these organizations I'm involved, I've been starting to see what the real situation is in town and I started thinking about myself and that I became an egoist. Egoist, big egoist! Well not that big. I mean exactly, I want to contribute to society as long as I know that that society's going to give something back. So I'm not working anything for free. Free not as in I want to get some money, but free as in just goodwill. I want some goodwill back. It's very hard to get. Well they say, oh thank you very much, please do that again, but you can hear it in their voice that they don't appreciate it that much.

Tuesday

My mobile phone rings at about 8 a.m. It's Belma saying that the vans have picked up all the musicians and could I please be at the little square in fifteen minutes. The phone is proving worthwhile. Three white vans have been provided by the OSCE (Organization for Security and Co-operation in Europe) to take the orchestra to Banja Luka. I squeeze into the first van with the instruments and luggage and we set off in a convoy.

Our driver is a jovial man who listens to his radio or chats with Ogi who's in the front seat. He's a brilliant driver. The road winds across fields and hills, and there's very little traffic, but inevitably we get stuck behind slow-moving lorries. As soon as there's a clear stretch ahead, we overtake and I notice that he stays in the middle of the road, or even in the left lane, long after he's overtaken the lorries. I wonder what on earth he's doing, gaily travelling down the middle of the road and nipping back to the right only when there's oncoming traffic. It takes me quite a while to realize that this is a signal to the vans behind us that the road is clear and they can also overtake.

Sometimes there are many bends and if there is no oncoming traffic as the road weaves and rises and falls, our driver will get onto the intercom and yell to the other drivers, '*Hajde, hajde*', come on come on, the road is clear. It must be pretty terrifying to the others when their vans pull out and drive on the wrong side of the road into blind corners. Great system. Exhilarating.

It's a long journey, and we stop a couple of times for cigarette breaks and a bite of lunch. I'm sitting next to Irena who says she's nervous when she plays and what can she do about it? We talk about the pressures of performing. 'I practise a lot so everyone expects me to play perfectly,' she says.

The pressure to be perfect. It can't be anything but debilitating. And it's so common.

I talk about envy and about kindness and why she plays music at all. She understands quickly. I'm reminded of a student I'd met in Sarajevo, also hard-working, who had complained of feeling disconnected, fragmented, his technique separate from his feelings. And that his friends make fun of him when he rocks back and forth. It's involuntary, his rocking when he's eating or reading or even practising. He will grow out of it, I'd said to him, it doesn't matter at all. And now I think about how the focus and discipline of these young people enable them to feel somewhat in control of their lives in this fragmented society.

Republika Srpska. I suddenly see two signs, one in Roman, one in Cyrillic script. I didn't realize that this part of Bosnia uses a different script. This region is firmly stating its own identity in opposition to the rest of Bosnia. And it's using language, our main means of dialogue, as a means of differentiation. I wonder how some of the others are feeling.

My parents had no desire to go to Germany. The first time I went was on a concert tour. I just remember having to take a deep breath. Crossing into erstwhile enemy territory gave me a slightly sick feeling in the stomach even though that was long after the war. Since then, my work has taken me often into Germany and my stomach no longer responds. Reason, familiarity, friendships, good experiences all make their mark.

Here, the dust has barely settled, question marks remain, and for my companions, the memories are personal, and fresh.

Belma has arranged for me to stay in a flat belonging to her cousin, but first we go to where the orchestra will stay – an orphanage surrounded by lawns and trees. Four or five children come out and sit on the steps, looking us over. Inside, the building is institutional rather than comfortable. The musicians will sleep six in a room. Siniša decides to find somewhere else. While everyone is getting settled, I walk outside for some air and find one of the new violinists in tears.

'Melika, what is it?'

Melika spent the war years studying in the US and has good English.

'I'm sorry, I'm sorry,' she says, 'I can't stay here.'

'All right, it's all right, I'm sure we'll find a place for you somewhere else.'

She continues to cry.

'I'm sorry, it's the orphanage. I can't stay in an orphanage.'

She explains how she had visited one when she was eleven years old, and how it had upset her so much that she'd had nightmares for years. Perhaps it had something to do with her mother being orphaned at an early age, and Melika being terrified of losing her own mother.

She is distraught. 'Why do I have to feel like this? It was so many years ago. Why does it all come back? It brings it all back to me. Why? Why?' The tears keep coming and I put my arms round her, saying that this is what it is to be human, to remember, to be affected by the past, it's part of being human. I feel my own tears pricking at my eyelids.

One of the other musicians has wandered outside. I'm sure he can't hear what we are saying, but he can see that Melika is crying, and after a moment, he too brushes away some tears. They are so close to the surface. We are all sitting on an emotional volcano.

Five of us climb back into one of the vans – Belma, Rada, Melika, Siniša and myself – and we are taken to our respective dwelling-places that Belma has miraculously found for us. My flat is in a series of identical apartment blocks, grey monstrosities, with washing hanging out of barely existing balconies. Inside, there is the usual overconfident, dark, heavy furniture, linoleum, Formica, and plastic tablecloths.

I walk into the bathroom and pause. Something is missing but it takes me a while to realize what it is. There's a toilet, a bath, a washing machine . . . no sink! I check the sink in the little kitchen but there's no water. I'll have to wash my face and brush my teeth under the bath tap.

It is extremely hot in the flat. All the windows and shutters are closed. Tonight when it has cooled outside, I'll open a window, but the window handle is very high, well beyond anyone's reach. Maybe I can climb onto the radiator . . .

But these are small things. I'm lucky to have my own place for two nights and I'm glad for the privacy. I find a little grocery shop outside and stock up on bananas and cheese and nuts and water – I'm drinking gallons of water every day.

Belma has drawn a little map so that I can find my way to the concert hall. My walk takes me along some leafy residential streets; Banja Luka is an elegant city with wide boulevards and many trees. The hall is in a distinguished, Viennese-style building, and it has a wide stage and excellent acoustics. A concert hall to grace any city. At the stage door, a security guard nods me through while barely taking his eyes off the ubiquitous football on the little television set.

Our rehearsal starts at 6 p.m. I approach Melika to see how she is feeling. 'Yes, I'm much better now thanks. And you know what? This place has such good memories for me because I won a competition here a long time ago. And I played a big concert here, in this hall.' She smiles. One bad memory and one good memory, all in one day.

The orchestra plays well – it's amazing what an inferior performing experience can do to the concentration – and I'm able to add more subtleties. But there is a lot of talking and some of the younger players are a bit wild. The concert is tomorrow evening, and I think that we can profitably cancel the morning's rehearsal to allow everyone to have some free time to let off steam. Belma thinks otherwise. 'We must rehearse tomorrow,' she says firmly.

'Let's ask the orchestra,' I say.

She does. They choose to rehearse. The first time I have ever heard of an orchestra choosing to rehearse!

When Swan Lake Comes to Sarajevo

We have all been invited to a bakery next door for something to eat. We're tired – it's about 10 p.m. – but the promise of freshly baked pastries is irresistible, and the baker and his wife welcome us into their courtyard with trays of savoury and sweet pastries and crates of cool beer. The baker is a jolly man and loves music. I understand that he has arranged the accommodation for the players and that he's involved in an orchestra here. He says proudly that Banja Luka was a cultured place during the Tito years and received many illustrious musicians, including Prokofiev and Rostropovitch.

Prokofiev! I've just embarked on a project regarding his violin sonatas and have had Prokofiev on the brain for the last few months. And I spoke to Rostropovitch about him only recently. Strange how paths unexpectedly cross, how dormant thoughts can be jolted awake.

While I munch on pastries, I chat with one of the wind players. She is young and has recently graduated. Her Bosnian boyfriend has lived in Australia since he was a child. He is an artist and she is insisting that he get a degree. 'I want him to study, and I'm trying to persuade him,' she says. 'We have been together a long time, but I don't want to be with someone who can't fit into my world.' She says this with sadness but determination, and the conversation reminds me a little of the one I had earlier today on the journey. It occurs to me that, in general, Bosnians tend to adopt one of two courses: they either skate on the surface, avoiding effort and commitment, proving to themselves that they have nothing to prove, letting the days slip by because so many days were lost; or, more rarely, they develop a tenacious discipline to make the most of their lives.

It is almost midnight when I walk up the three long flights of stairs to my flat. It is still very hot. Just as I finish negotiating the bath tap, I suddenly realize that I've forgotten to photocopy the triangle part in *Swan Lake*, which is in Mostar with Alpha. A percussion student has been found to play the concert, but even someone who is an accomplished triangle player needs music.

I take some paper and write out the part by hand from the score.

Wednesday

Sleep is fitful because I know that I have to get up at 6.45 a.m. to do a live TV breakfast show. Bleary-eyed, I drag myself out of bed when the alarm sounds, shower, wash my hair and put on full make-up. I don't like putting on full make-up at the best of times, and early in the morning is the worst of times. I've arranged to meet Belma for a coffee at 7.45 a.m. – the interview is at 8.30 a.m. I turn on my trusty mobile phone and Belma calls – 'I'll be there in ten minutes,' I say, glancing at the clock which says 7.30 a.m. I get to the bottom of the stairs and remember that I've forgotten my earrings – must have earrings for television! – and climb up the stairs again. A woman comes out of the neighbouring flat wearing a typical 1950s housedress and I feel ridiculously dolled up. She looks surprised to see me and says something in Bosnian. I don't think she's commenting on my appearance, so I say *'ne razumijem, dva danas,'* hoping she's asked me whether I've moved in. I wonder if she'll be watching TV in an hour . . .

Belma is in the café waiting for me. I order a coffee. 'I was worried,' she says.

'Why?' I ask.

'Because it's 8.30.'

I look at my watch. 8.30! My alarm clock must have stopped! We must run!

Belma says, 'It's OK, have your coffee.'

This kind of sang-froid I don't have. I stand up, take a huge gulp, and say, *'Idemo!'*

The television studio is in the next building, an office block that seems to specialize in hiding its offices. The main entrance has no mention of any studios among its tenants, and the workers we ask don't seem to know anything. 'Try round the back,' they say. We are breathless now, looking for any door that might offer hope. Eventually we come across some lifts snuggling behind a wall and enter the studios trying to look cool and collected.

The presenter is a glamorous young woman wearing a tight skirt and so many layers of make-up that I'm not sure where her face is.

She holds out her hand to me and says, 'So, do you come here with prejudices?'

I'm taken aback. What kind of welcome is this? Of course it's also a minefield: it says a lot about her expectations of me, and possibly about the general feeling here that the West is prejudiced against the Serbs. Thank goodness we're not on air.

I hesitate. I say that this is a complicated question but isn't the programme about to begin? – and I'd be happy to answer it after the interview.

I'm relieved that she doesn't ask this question on air, nor afterwards. The interview is pretty normal, except that it's cumbersome to have everything translated from Bosnian into English and back. I know that this is not Belma's favourite occupation, but she seems to do a good job. I'm asked about how I came to be involved with the Sinfonietta and what I think of Mostar and Bosnia, and am I enjoying it and what are we playing tonight?

Afterwards we walk out onto the street, suddenly relieved and giddy and feeling like stars. So why is nobody asking for our autographs? We wander round a pedestrian shopping area. I've no idea why, but I feel like I'm twenty-five years old. 'Let's have breakfast,' I say, thinking that some food will settle the giddiness. I order 'toast', which turns out to be a ham and cheese toasted sandwich. Belma has no appetite.

Then it's back to pick up the violin and on to the hall for the rehearsal at 11 a.m. It's lovely for the players to be able to spread out comfortably on the ample stage, and it's nice to see a whole orchestra in front of me. 'We're just missing the British Ambassador,' I say, 'he's coming this evening.' '*Ko? Ko??*' exclaim the two horn players, incredulous.

I start the rehearsal by saying that this is the first time in my long experience that an orchestra has chosen to have an extra rehearsal. As I wait for Ogi to take out his bass and get set up, I say a few encouraging words and then fill in the time by telling a story that I'd heard from the manager of a concert hall in Stockholm. That a lunchtime concert was about to begin but there were builders on the roof, making the noises builders make. The manager had gone up to the roof and begged the foreman to take a break while the concert proceeded. The foreman had refused – 'We have our job to do,' etc. The manager had tried to explain that the hammering would disturb the concert, but received the same answer. In frustration, the manager pleaded, 'You must stop; we're playing Mozart.'

'Ah, Mozart? Why didn't you say so? OK chaps, time for your lunch break!'

Ogi is moving slowly and does not seem at all well. He looks about forty and is very thin. I've been told that he is ill and is on a course of strong medicine for a year that makes him tired. He plays very well and has a ready smile, but in unguarded moments, his eyes show suffering. I'm suddenly aware that the effort to be normal is not confined to Bosnians; that I too am affected by everything around me and that I too am trying to be normal. And at this moment, I'm close to feeling overwhelmed by the pervasive tension and pain that has insidiously seeped into me, that has reminded me of my own painful memories. The past becomes more intrusive in a place like Bosnia, insecurities welling up like buried strata during an earthquake. I wish I could be whisked away – I'm an outsider here, my own experience not shared, and I feel terribly isolated.

Ogi is tuned and ready now. During the rehearsal, I work with Siniša on how he, as leader, can help to keep the orchestra together, how he can cue the winds during the violin solo, and have eye contact with the other sections. It's a tough job, being the leader, a kind of middleman between the conductor and the players. An active leader can make all the difference.

When we're finished, I go straight to the flat and straight to sleep. On a concert day, if I have any choice, my main meal is a late lunch since I can't eat immediately before a concert. So when I wake up, I allow plenty of time to find a restaurant near the hall, but there is nothing except pizzerias. I choose a table outside under a shady tree; nearby is a screen showing a match between Mexico and Portugal. A gypsy boy of about five years old hovers nearby and is continually shooed away by the waiters. I'm happy to give him half my pizza, but the waiter discourages me, saying that all the gypsies will come here if I give him anything. At one point when the waiter is inside, the boy rushes up and I offer him the pizza but he refuses. He wants only money.

It's very quiet on the streets. Whenever there's a football match, the streets empty. Tonight Serbia is playing. Because Montenegro has just voted for independence, it means that Yugoslavia will finally be dissolved, and tonight will be the last time that the Yugoslavian National Anthem will be played or heard. The significance is enormous.

Maybe this is contributing to my general distress today. I've not had enough sleep. Every night has been the same, and every morning I've felt short of sleep. It's too hot for me: I can't think. The rehearsing has been difficult, with the arrival of new players every day making it repetitive and illogical for everyone. And I've not been able to have a decent practice myself for five days, so I'm nervous about the Valse-Scherzo. There is something strange about the morale that is bothering me. It's too intense all the time. I desperately need to relax.

It's nice to be the first to arrive at the hall. There is something very special about the quiet of an empty concert hall. It seems to hold its breath, to know that this is unnatural, that there should be music filling the space, and people. My eyes pass over the red velvet seats and the pale plastered walls and the deserted stage and I think of all the vibrations of all the concerts that have been absorbed and still linger.

I go to my dressing room. It has a tall ceiling and dark wooden furniture, its shutters closed against the heat. It's 7 p.m. and the concert starts at 9 p.m. I lie on the floor and try to relax. After a while, I phone Belma about recording the concert, and she says she's been trying desperately to reach me for the last two hours. My phone had been turned off.

'The manager of hall thinks the concert starts at 8 p.m.,' she says.

'What?'

'Half of publicity says 8 p.m., and half says 9 p.m. There are even two posters outside hall, one says 8 p.m. and one says 9 p.m. I didn't notice.'

Neither did I.

This is crazy. Even for Bosnia.

'So when *are* we beginning?'

'Well, I couldn't reach you, and if we made it 8 p.m. and some people arrive at 9, they will miss the concert. So we decided 9 p.m. because that's what orchestra expects and when audience arrives at 8 p.m., the manager will go out and explain and tell them to stay.'

I doubt it. The football begins at 9 p.m.

'And one of the violinists is sick.' The man who brushed away some tears yesterday. 'He is throwing up all day.'

Belma says that she was hysterical. She tries to explain how the misunderstanding about the start time came about, but it's all too complicated.

'OK,' I say, 'never mind. I'll see you in fifteen minutes for the sound check.'

I try to warm up my fingers but they are perspiring so much that they simply slide around the instrument. I keep washing my hands with soap to dry the skin.

We have a very brief rehearsal. It's the first time that everyone is present, including the Ambassador, the ill violinist who's feeling better, and the triangle player. I'm surprised to see the young women dolled up in so much satin and glitter and beautiful make-up. Much more dressy than previous years. It's nice to sense a new pride in their appearance. Even Belma has put on her best dress. 'Everything was going so badly today,' she says, ' I wanted to look really good. To feel better.'

The orchestra is excited. This is the most beautiful hall it has played in since I've been coming to Bosnia, with proper backstage facilities. It does make a difference. It's bound to be a struggle when changing rooms are dirty storerooms or dark instrument rooms tucked miles down a corridor. Here they can be professionals.

It's five minutes to concert time and I can't find the woman from the British Council who has promised to record the concert. So I give my recorder to the triangle player who's not needed until towards the end of the programme. There's always something to arrange at the last minute.

We walk out on stage to the polite applause of about thirty people. Almost all women. The hundreds of empty seats look very empty. But it could have been worse. I banish thoughts of football and turn round to face the orchestra who look at me expectantly. We are ready.

The Mozart sounds clean and well characterized. Everyone is concentrating. The Fauré is beautiful – what a gentle world is created in seven minutes. The Valse-Scherzo is not bad but it is very difficult to play the violin after conducting for more than half an hour. I knew it would be a challenge to perform in the middle of the programme, when my fingers are no longer warmed up, but no other order would sound convincing.

The morale feels good as we embark on the two pieces from *Swan Lake*. The Mazurka lacks poise and grandeur, but the Waltz takes off, gliding and sparkling and building up to a triumphant ending, the triangle glistening high above. The players have put everything into it, and the small but enthusiastic audience doesn't let us go before we've repeated the Mazurka as an encore.

Backstage everyone is buzzing. The tension has poured off them like water pours off a diver bouncing up from a dive. I congratulate them all individually. Then I ask them to go back on stage after the audience has left so that I can take some photos for their publicity. They are hilarious, playing a dreadfully comic performance of the Mozart Symphony and laughing uproariously. Unfortunately I'm not used to my new digital camera and don't find the right settings for the dim indoor light, so the photos come out too dark. I don't want to take the time to work out how to do it properly as the players are eager to get out and celebrate. I'll ask the Ambassador if he can provide a photographer for the concert in Sarajevo.

The recording also doesn't work, the mini-disc showing many takes but all of them silent. 'I dropped machine,' the triangle player says apologetically, 'I hope I didn't break it.' No, he didn't, but it erased the recording. At least he played his triangle part perfectly.

We all leave our instruments locked up in the hall and proceed to a bar across the street. I stay as long as I can, but the music is intolerably loud, so after chatting a little to the Ambassador, I say goodnight to everyone and leave them to drink the night away.

Thursday

I wake up at 7.30 a.m., pack, and make my way to the vans that are waiting outside the hall. The concert in Sarajevo is not until tomorrow night, so one van takes the Mostarians back to Mostar, while the other two vans take the rest of us to Sarajevo.

I'm sitting next to Ogi. I've been told that he is well known as a TV actor – that's two bass players leading double lives! He left Sarajevo during the siege and tells me how it happened.

Ogi

A few weeks after the war began, I had a phone call saying there's a plane going the next day and I said yes, because I saw that there is no future somehow. That people are really, how to say, people very polluted with the atmosphere of nationalism. They started to speak about that, how it should be more without that people, without that people, I mean . . . separated. I couldn't find myself in that atmosphere so I decided to, in one minute, actually in one second, to go. And tomorrow morning we left. Me and my brother.

And my mother and father they stayed. You know it was beginning of the war, we said yeah maybe it will stop, actually I didn't think it will stop, but people are really you know . . . hopeful. My parents were really 'you go, you need to have future'. So we left. We were quite young. I was twenty-six maybe, my brother seventeen maybe. We didn't tell our friends, that was some kind of rule. And actually the organizers, they also said don't tell to anybody. Because there was a mood if you go you are traitors, you are leaving this town, the town needs you and in the past gave you everything, and you are just now leaving . . .

That was organized by the Jewish community you know. The plane, maybe four hundred people in that plane, and that was army plane, you know, the big one. There were all people, all kinds, all nationalities. I took my guitar, a bass guitar, and bass bow, and maybe one small bag. That was everything. That was some kind of beginning of a new life. We went to Belgrade and it was seventeen minutes, the army plane, it was so fast. And then we decided to go somewhere else. Because in Belgrade it also seemed that in ten days a war will start, it seemed like that. We have some family, we also have some arrangement, some hotel or something, for few days. And then we decided to go and we left, fifteen days maybe, we finished all the papers, documents, and we emigrated, to Israel.

Even before, I was interested in spirituality, but when something like that happens in your life, then you become serious about these things. Maybe before that, I only read about it and I had some desire to practise it but you know, you have your life. But this was really special arrangement, you now live somewhere else, you don't know anybody, how to say . . . like a new life. Life after life. Completely new life. So I found a chance for that, how do you say, 'I will start now'. So I started and I decided to take it seriously. So I spent the last seven years living in a different temples in India and in Europe also, with some kind of Vishnu temple or Krishna temple. I decided that is my way I can find myself there. And I had a very nice time, I learned many things, something completely new.

Actually my father had died of a heart attack, I didn't know for three or four months. He died in December, I heard maybe March or April about it, three, four months later. No contact, you know, no telephone, nothing, no post. I have one aunt in Belgrade. She phoned me one day and she say you know, seems like your father died. And I had a dream about it maybe seven days ago so it was not so heavy for me, I was somehow prepared. My mother had a really hard time because she lived until a few months before with three – with two sons and a husband – and now no-one is there. She was . . . her friends told me that she was really, really upset for a few months. And then she decided to live, she decided to fight.

I came back immediately after the war, maybe a few months later. But I found the town really . . . destroyed. Look really sad and old. Like old person, like somebody who, how do you say, in a *few years made like thirty years . . . aged like thirty years. It was very sad, I even cried in a taxi when I came here. And then I wanted to stay but I couldn't really. I was only here for few days, and then I left again. But then maybe two years after that, something appeared like I should go. Because my mother was here and my brother also came back from Israel. And somehow I felt that we should be together again. So I came back and that's it. Then was better, somehow.*

Some of my friends, they say you are lucky you left because here was really hell and we were fighting for three and four years in a forest somewhere. Or other way, in town they were all time grenaded, they were all time . . . you don't know what is worse. And most of my friends they were in something called the artists' brigade. It was nice. They did something on TV, they made some TV show, playing music, I mean, it was better than to go somewhere fighting. Most of my friends were there.

Since before the war I played in a Philharmonic Orchestra for eight years, nine years maybe. And after that I left without double bass and somehow I didn't have desire to play. I chose a new life, I mean new kind of life. So I stopped playing, you know. Only when I came back six or seven years later, I started to play again. And I started also to play in Philharmonic Orchestra. But somehow I found it not for me any more, everything changed. Before that, I knew everybody, everybody knew me. But later when I come, that was complete other atmosphere in the orchestra. That was one of the reasons I left, not the only one. So I'm not really actively playing, only sometimes.

But I'm playing some Indian music, you know that's what I found interesting. That's maybe my main occupation now. And I wanted to start now some Eastern music from Iran, China, India, Bosnia also. Bosnia is also part of Orient. I will play bass guitar.

I like to play classical when the music is nice, when the people are young and enthusiastic for playing. Therefore maybe I don't like to play in these big orchestras where everything is more like professional . . . not professional, I don't know what is real name for it. Like this concert last night with Sinfonietta, that was really nice to play, I enjoyed playing. One guy who is playing in Slovenian Philharmonic – and Slovenian Philharmonic is maybe the best orchestra in whole region – he said that maybe last night concert we had here is at least twenty per cent better than concert of Slovenian Philharmonic! Because they're young people here, they are playing . . . into it, you know, and they are really good.

The scenery has changed to coniferous forests and meadows bobbing with wild flowers. Some of the mountains still have snow on their peaks.

The van drivers stop outside their favourite place for lunch – a chalet in a tiny village. Wooden tables have been set up beside a stream and there's a picturesque little waterwheel. The local dish is *pura*, which I'm ordered to try. I don't need encouragement – I love trying local food.

Several wooden dishes on a wooden tray are placed in front of me: an enormous bowl of corn mush, rather like polenta but coarser, a huge mug of yoghurt, a large plate of *sir*, the local crumbly cheese, and a saucer of raw onion slices. 'How can anyone get through all this?' I ask. Surprisingly easily. The combination of tastes works and I manage to polish off a good deal of it. Belma and Ogi leave not a crumb.

After another couple of hours' driving, Ogi points out that we are in Pyramid Valley. 'On the right,' he says, 'you see pyramid. It was discovered only last few months. They have now found the entrance.'

A very large tree-covered hill comes into view, definitely pyramid-shaped.

Ogi says, 'We have jokes already. We say that Egyptians who built pyramids in Egypt were all refugees from Bosnia!'

The vans drop us off at the OSCE headquarters in Sarajevo, and I take a taxi to my hotel. I couldn't face returning to the *pension* where I stayed last year, so Ermin has booked me into the Hotel Relax, which sounds vaguely promising. Its main selling point as far as I'm concerned is its offer of a free massage for every guest. In my present condition, that will be a godsend.

The taxi driver doesn't know the hotel but I'd seen it once last year, just up from the old town square with all the pigeons. He drives up one of the roads and then says, 'Not here, *ne*, turn back,' but I say, '*Da, da*, further up *molim*.' This is reminding me of a previous visit to Sarajevo.

There it is, a few yards up, just a door with a sign on a fairly run-down street. Inside, it is clean and modern. My room is extremely hot but there is an air-conditioner standing on the floor. And a sink in the bathroom. I have no appointments today, so without even unpacking, I climb into bed and fall asleep.

Friday

I haven't been able to reach Marina by phone so I walk to the Academy, only to find she is not there. Just inside the entrance is one of our posters for tonight's concert, but the violin solo is not mentioned and, perhaps to compensate for being the only part remaining on the noticeboard for the last two years, my name is missing altogether. The students will be disappointed if they discover too late that I've played here, since they don't get many opportunities to hear foreign artists.

Yet another relatively simple thing that is not right. It's so annoying that so many mistakes are made, and then not corrected. I remember the fiasco in Banja Luka about the start time of the concert, and wonder how it was that nobody noticed the discrepancy. Apparently the radio announcements had all stated 8 p.m., and the newspapers, 9 p.m. Not to mention the two contradictory posters displayed side by side outside the hall itself. It's a vicious circle, the tension caused by constant mistakes leading to fatigue leading to more mistakes, more tension, more fatigue. And in the end, an enveloping apathy setting in.

Back to the hotel to work on scores and to practise. I had brought an encore with me from England, the score of the famous slow movement from Bach's 3rd Suite, but without the parts we haven't been able to play it. Miro, who is in charge of the library, has promised to bring them today, so now I devise an arrangement where the two oboes take the melody during the repeats. I had wanted to put our valuable oboists in the spotlight, and I override my reluctance to alter any of Bach's scoring by telling myself that

I'm just following his own example. He often rearranged his works according to whatever instruments were to hand; his compositions frequently seem to exist independently from the instruments themselves. And I know that in this case, as in many of his cantatas, the clarity of two oboes will enhance the two closely woven upper lines of the melody. Tonight's concert is to be in a church, and after the Tchaikovsky, I can't imagine anything more perfect than ending with Bach.

Alpha, my triangle player from Mostar, arrives at midday. She's Canadian, middle-aged, and has a quiet and kind demeanour. She's staying at my hotel, so we have a quick *burek* while talking over the intricacies of playing in an orchestra. And then it's time for my complimentary massage. The hotel has made an attempt at a fitness centre downstairs, which seems somewhat gratuitous, but I'm grateful for the massage.

Slightly more relaxed, I ask the young, friendly receptionist how to walk to the Svete Ante Church, where the concert will be. As I turn to leave, something puzzles me.

'Svete Ante Church, not the Cathedral,' I reiterate.

'Oh,' she says and proceeds to send me in the opposite direction. Strange.

Svete Ante is home to the wonderful Pontanima Choir which had so moved me a few years ago. The priest responsible for its creation and success is Fra Ivo, who greets me warmly. He tells me about a church service at six o'clock so please, we must finish rehearsing by 5.45 p.m., and also the altar cannot be moved until after the service and so we'll have to set up the chairs in the space behind. '*Može?*'

Yet more obstacles. The space is as resonant as a swimming pool, and there will be no time to test the acoustics from our actual performing place. And the truncated rehearsal means that there's only enough time to rehearse the Bach Air and to begin each movement briefly. I limit my comments to not forcing the sound and, at the other end of the scale, to playing really *piano*. Mostly, I talk about enjoying the concert.

The orchestra leaves as a storm breaks. The rain will cool the city. I sit quietly in the refectory and then coach Alpha who still hadn't been able to understand my cues. As soon as the service is over, I return to the church where the male musicians are moving the heavy wooden boxes that will form the stage. (They tell me afterwards that their arms were shaking from the weight.) It is a tight squeeze. Their chairs are three inches from the edge and I am concerned that a chair leg will stray too close. In normal halls, wooden strips are routinely fixed to the edge of risers to prevent accidents. There is also very little room for me. I'll be waving the baton almost above the heads of the seconds and violas, and if I step back . . . What a contrast to our last concert in Banja Luka.

The backstage facilities also couldn't be more different. The orchestra squashes itself into the vestry, and I take the room on the other side used for storage. It's dusty and I must step over a rolled-up carpet by the door. I'm startled by a life-sized statue of a saint, draped in plastic sheeting. It looks like a ghost. 'Hello,' I say to it.

At 7.30 p.m. the orchestra steps out to substantial applause. I follow, to see an enthusiastic audience filling about half the pews. Two young children with their mother are on the front row, looking very English, no doubt the Ambassador's family. There are also many television cameras, presumably also attributable to the presence of the Ambassador.

As we start the Mozart, I hear immediately that the acoustics are excellent. The sound reverberates off the walls to just the right extent, bright but not harsh, burnished. The orchestra relaxes, smiles, makes eye contact with me and each other. It feels very good to be making music together. I try to dispense with showing beats, allowing myself to simply express the music, but an occasional waywardness makes me snap back to precision beating until they are comfortably on track. Siniša and Belma exchange glances when something goes particularly well, Alpha gets all her entrances right, and everyone knows that this is a good concert.

Swan Lake is pure enjoyment. Creamy indulgence. Utter eyes-closed pleasure. As the final stretch approaches, I make a big *accelerando* and urge the basses and horns to blare out their solos, the high strings rising ecstatically to the final rapturous chords.

There is tremendous applause. The audience is beaming, the orchestra is beaming. I wish more Sarajevans were here, that the church were full to bursting. The applause rings round the pillars and we take repeated bows. When I think I've allowed enough energy to dissipate, I turn round and mouth 'Bach' to the orchestra.

It is exactly the right music to play, though the musicians struggle to find enough calm after the Tchaikovsky. I listen to the oboe lines unfolding hypnotically over the steady careful strokes of the cellos. This is music that speaks to our small, still centre, that makes us feel whole, and quiet. When we reach the end, I let the long last sound fade slowly into the silence, the sweet D major chord lingering in our ears.

The church bell chimes and the concert is over.

I go back to my changing room, glance at the statue again and pack away my violin and baton. When I emerge, Fra Ivo is waiting for me, smiling broadly. 'You must come again,' he says, taking both my hands. 'You must conduct our choir, will you?'

The Pontanima! Of course! '*Naravno! Hvala.* It would be my pleasure.'

'We will make a tour, yes?'

'Yes!'

Marina is here. And some of her students too. They have grown so tall! How wonderful is the growth of children. 'When is master class?' they ask. I am staying a few more days, so I say, 'Tomorrow?' OK, I'll go to the Academy in the morning.

The post-concert celebration takes place nearby and I let Alpha carry my case as we walk along the streets. It's lovely to have some assistance for a change. We are the last to arrive at the restaurant and I add my violin case to the pile of instruments that has accumulated in one of the corners.

'Was there a concert tonight?' A man on a nearby table is curious. I tell him about our performance.

'I'm so disappointed to have missed it. There are hardly ever orchestral concerts here. I didn't see any announcements.' I'm not surprised.

He has a German accent and I ask him what he is doing here.

'I help to train the police,' he says. 'Stabilization.'

I nod.

'Like you,' he says.

That hasn't occurred to me.

But it's a nice thought, and maybe he is right.

Ermin and Alma beckon me over to their table. They are sitting with some Americans who run the children's summer camp which Alma helps to organize. They are effusive in their appreciation of the concert. 'Was this the same Sinfonietta?' Alma asks, 'it was so different standard, expressing, you live the music, you bring life.'

And then she turns to the others and adds, 'Ruth comes to Mostar and everyone wakes up!' and she hands me a little gift – a fan! Perfect. And now Alpha comes bearing a glass of wine. I'm feeling very pampered. And full of energy. I give her a hug, and Alma, and Ermin, and drink to them all.

It always seems too abrupt when it's time for the goodbyes. I thank each musician and hug them all. I feel such warmth from them, from the new players, from Irena and Melika, Ogi and Siniša, Rada and Suzana and Miro. We have worked so hard and spent so much time together. It's hard to part.

I will see Belma first thing in the morning, since we have another television interview.

Saturday

It's 7.15 a.m. and time to get the mascara on again. I meet Belma by the old ruined library and we cross the river to a small run-down building that houses the television studios. This time it goes smoothly, there are no provocative questions, just some chat about my reactions to being here. 'Will you come back to Sarajevo?'

'*Naravno*,' I reply and the interviewer gets confused and translates into English, 'Of course!' So we're agreed.

At 9.30 a.m., we are finished. I pick up my violin from the hotel and walk with Belma over to the Academy where she also will give some lessons. We stop short at the door and Belma peers at a notice pinned onto it.

'It's closed,' she says disbelievingly. 'Closed for painting.'

She says that in all the years that she's been there, it has never been painted; and now this is one week before exams and the teachers are giving extra lessons and the students need somewhere to practise, and moreover, nobody had said anything about it being closed.

A few students arrive and look questioningly at us.

'I can teach my students in my flat,' Belma says, taking out her mobile phone, 'but you . . . ?'

'I'll see if I can teach in the hotel. Maybe downstairs in the fitness room,' I say.

I lead a small procession of students to the Hotel Relax. On the way, one of them says how frustrated he is here. 'I really hate people here, they think only of themselves, they are unfriendly. Look how they drive, how they park their cars on the pavement – there's no room to walk.' It's true – if there is a pavement, there's often no space to walk on it, and you take your life in your hands walking in the road.

The receptionist in the hotel is gracious and understanding. 'Of course you can teach downstairs. What do you need? chairs? tables?' Here's one helpful person at least.

She shows us into a large mirrored basement, the type of room where ballet or aerobics are taught, and switches on the fluorescent lights. 'Is this all right?'

'Perfect, *hvala puno*.'

Three students play for me. The first was almost a beginner four years ago, and now he is playing fairly advanced repertoire. Marina must take a lot of credit as his teacher. The second student plays Kabalevsky and then one of the violinists from the Sinfonietta plays the Sibelius Concerto. He is about to take his graduation exam so we work hard on making his playing musical as well as secure.

'You know,' I say, 'it can be very boring to be on a jury listening to one violinist after another who is simply nervous and playing safe. Jurors will always appreciate a musical performance, something that wakes them up. You must play with your soul. Don't hide.'

I will hear him again tomorrow. Now I go up to my room, and I think my clock must have stopped again when I see it says only

2.30 p.m. – it feels much later. I rest for a while then spend the remainder of the day wandering the streets with Alpha, pausing at various coffee shops. We dine at a Mexican restaurant and it's disorienting to be eating one of my favourite Mexican dishes, chicken *mole*, in Sarajevo with a Canadian. But the conversation is firmly centred on Bosnia, as Alpha relates how stressful it is to live here as a foreigner. It's hard to find a sympathetic ear, she tells me, although there is a great need to talk about the pressures and tensions of being here. I completely understand what she is saying.

I say that some of my friends here have been so honest with me over the years that I've felt I've wanted to talk about myself, share some of my own difficulties, make the relationships less one-sided. 'I told one of them that I'd had cancer. She looked briefly concerned and then said that a relative had had cancer twenty-five years ago and is all right. And then she changed the subject.'

Alpha nods.

I continue, 'I must have misjudged her – there's still not enough emotional space for others.'

As we wander back to the hotel, we pass a large, grand building, with steps leading up to a colonnaded entrance. For some reason, I stop.

I don't know what I'm looking at but I'm staring at the building. And then my eye settles on a banner stretched across the top, and a small figure of a ballet dancer comes into focus. The words on the banner say '*Swan Lake*'. My heart jumps; there was a performance of *Swan Lake* here? When? Last week!

So the Bosnians had decided for themselves that they are ready for *Swan Lake*.

And not just the Mazurka and Grande Valse.

The whole ballet.

And now I remember what I'd heard someone say – who was it? when was it? – that they'd overheard a woman in the street saying, 'When *Swan Lake* comes to Sarajevo, it will mean we are getting back to normal.'

Sunday

I sleep past the alarm and wake up at nine o'clock; my student arrives in half an hour. I'm quickly dressing when the phone rings. It's Belma. This is the beginning of an extraordinary day, even by Bosnian standards.

'Can you come on TV at four this afternoon?'

Another television appearance? Marina has invited me for lunch today, but there will be plenty of time for both.

'Yes, fine,' I say.

'They want live music, a quartet.'

'Well, can Siniša's quartet play?' Belma plays in his quartet, the one that I heard at the school last year.

'Yes, but they want you to play too.'

Impossible. For a multitude of reasons. I say that it's better that the quartet plays, and I will do an interview.

I go down to the mirrored basement, from where I can hear Sibelius being practised. Sounds like a conservatoire in here. We are hard at work when there's a knock at the door. The receptionist tells me there's a phone call. I run upstairs.

'The TV really wants you to play. Maybe you can play with us a Mozart Divertimento. Is OK for you to play second violin? We've already explained to the second violinist.'

'Second violin?'

'Siniša says he is used to playing first violin part and doesn't want to practise new part. *Može?*'

I don't like virtually sight-reading on live television either. At least the second violin part is not as exposed as the first.

I'm afraid that the quartet will lose their chance to play if I don't agree. Still, it's madness.

'*Može,*' I say, 'but we have to rehearse somewhere.'

'Where?' asks Belma.

'Here in the Waterman Conservatoire?'

I don't know what we would do without this remarkably co-operative hotel.

I resume coaching the Sibelius.

The receptionist interrupts again. Phone. I excuse myself and dash upstairs. Belma says that everyone will come to rehearse here at 1.15 p.m.

Downstairs again. The student is very patient. I explain what's happening and say that this is very much what it was like to be taught by my distinguished teacher in the US, Dorothy Delay. One interruption after another. Her schedule would get so far behind that lessons would start two or three or four hours late.

What are we going to wear? My thoughts have gone back to the television programme. They will be bringing their clothes here and we need to co-ordinate.

I excuse myself again and phone Belma.

'Informal,' she says.

This will be my third unscheduled TV programme in a week and I've only one possible outfit left. Or rather I did have, before those trousers got wet and spotted in the rain last night. Maybe no-one will notice if I appear in the same skirt. Over the years, I've learned to travel with the fewest clothes in the smallest suitcase, and this is the first time that I've been caught out.

'And TV programme starts at 3 p.m., not 4 p.m.'

Marina and lunch! I phone her – thank goodness her phone is now working – and lunch is postponed until 4 p.m.

More Sibelius, then a viola student playing Stamitz, after which I nip out to the nearest grocery and buy some fruit and sunflower seeds. Anything to keep my energy up for the next few crazy hours. As soon as I return to the hotel, the phone is handed to me.

'It's Natasha,' a young voice says.

Natasha?

'Don't you remember me? I played for you last year.'

I try to put a face to the name.

'Can I play in master class?'

Word about the Waterman Conservatoire has spread. I explain that unfortunately I have a rehearsal now, but she should come and listen. When she arrives, I remember her as the girl to whom I'd given the nuts.

I say goodbye to Alpha who is leaving for Mostar, and go downstairs. The quartet is setting up the music stands. Siniša sits down in the second violin chair.

'I thought you wanted to play first violin,' I say.

He waves his hand with a little smile. 'No, you play first,' he says.

'But . . .'

I sense there's no point in discussing it.

I sit down in the first violin chair.

'So how much do we have to play?'

Belma says we need two movements, so we read through the Divertimentos of Mozart, abruptly eliminating movements that pose too many difficulties. We have less than an hour and time is going fast.

'I don't like this movement,' says Belma.

'And I don't like *this* movement,' says one of the others.

We finally agree on a fast and a slow movement. I haven't played this repertoire for about twenty years and I don't think I have ever played the slow movement we've chosen. My mind races to find fingerings, to understand the harmonies and structure, and to mould an interpretation. All the players are alert, and as long as I lead strongly, it might be respectable enough. I still can't believe that we will shortly be playing this on live television.

Just as we finish, Alpha pops her head round the door.

'Hello, I thought you'd left,' I say.

'Yes, but I can't leave because I can't get my car out of the yard,' and she proceeds to explain that five huge motorbikes, Harley Davidsons no less, are blocking her car in the hotel's tiny parking area. All the hotel staff, comprising two women and one man, have been trying to move them to no avail. The bikes' owners are five young Italians who checked in last night and are out on the town, goodness knows where.

Alpha is supposed to be at a meeting in Mostar in a few hours. She won't make it. Stymied by five Harley Davidsons. It's beginning to be comical.

As we go up to the lobby, the hotel phone rings. And rings. We hesitate. Alpha slides behind the desk and picks up the phone – 'There's nobody here, please call back,' she says in Bosnian. We start to laugh. Here we are behind the reception desk and there's not one member of staff anywhere in the building. It's like landing on a hotel in Monopoly, except that this is real life.

I desperately need a coffee. We exchange glances. No, we don't think we should go into the kitchen and make it ourselves.

I go up to my room to change, and when I come down, Alpha is still standing in for the receptionist. She's surprisingly sanguine about the whole thing. But then, this is Bosnia.

'Hope you find the Italians! If you're still here tonight, let's have supper!' I say, setting off for the TV studios.

Psychedelic. That's how I would describe the studio. Splashes of diagonal reds, whites and purples to wake the dead. I don't think Mozart will feel at home here. And what are these white plastic things? Our chairs? Four stools looking for all the world like urinals are placed in a row. And they revolve. Revolving urinals. I imagine playing a particularly energetic phrase and finding myself spinning round.

In any case, my feet don't reach the floor.

'Sorry, I don't think we can use these,' I say. 'Four ordinary chairs are all we need.'

Not possible. They don't have four ordinary chairs. They have one, plus these four urinals.

I leave the negotiating to Belma. There's nothing for it but for her to sit in the normal chair and for the rest of us to play standing.

The sound check proceeds in the same vein.

'We don't need three mikes. We would prefer to have just one microphone and we balance ourselves,' I say.

Not possible. Three mikes is how they do things here. Even though there are four of us.

'Then we'd like to hear the balance.'

Not possible. We can hear the balance through the monitors.

'Monitors?! We don't want monitors,' I exclaim, imagining trying to blend and balance our sounds while being blasted by our own playing from the speakers. This is pop music procedure, not classical music. Classical music seems to be a first for them, and they finally admit that these are not even music mikes!

'We need to hear a balance,' I repeat. 'Just record one minute so that we can listen. It won't take long.'

They reluctantly record one minute. After spending five minutes searching for the spot on the tape, they play it for us. Boom boom! – the cello is loud enough to be heard in London.

This is all becoming too much. And time is flying.

'We're not a rock band,' I say under my breath. Or maybe not under my breath. 'The bass is far too loud.'

The engineer consults with the sound-man who looks about sixteen years old. He emerges from the sound booth saying, 'Let me hear how you play.'

Perhaps he is realizing that he has broken rule number one: to listen to the performers' own balance first, before hiding away in the sound booth and twiddling knobs.

'OK, I understand now,' he says. 'You can go, and come back in twenty minutes.'

'No,' I say, not even wondering where my sense of tact has gone, 'we need to hear the balance again to make sure it is right now.'

Not possible. No time.

The teenage sound-man approaches me.

'Trust me,' he says.

Woe betide him! The worst words he could have chosen to say.

Two little words guaranteed to raise my hackles. In any circumstances.

I turn on him.

'No. No! I don't trust you!' I say very slowly, 'that's the problem. *To je problema.*'

My eyes must be blazing. If this is being a prima donna, so be it.

Why do I bother? Does it matter if we play Mozart and it sounds ridiculous? Does it matter if another twenty, hundred, thousand people are driven away from Mozart – are driven away from classical music altogether – because it's made to sound utterly ridiculous?

We record another minute. Now it's acceptable, so we pack up the instruments and I go downstairs to the studio café, while the others go out to smoke. It's ten minutes to showtime, and there is no-one in the little basement room that's trying to pass itself off as a café. I'm desperately thirsty, and pretty hungry too. Am I supposed to make coffee myself? Where is everyone? Is all the world out searching for five Italians with Harley Davidsons?

I've just found the kettle when a woman arrives and makes me a coffee.

It's two minutes to four – in the midst of everything, the start time had changed again, to four o'clock, though I've no idea where the extra hour went. Marina's lunch has been postponed yet another hour.

The studio lights transform the studio into a sauna.

Now I understand why all the pretty presenters wear pancake make-up. This one continues to appear cool and dry while the quartet pours sweat as soon as our bows hit the strings.

It seems to be a general arts, or rather entertainment, programme and we are given the sign to begin on the heels of some anodyne jingle. We play one movement and then the presenter asks questions. Only one or two are directed at me, so while Siniša is speaking and the sweat is dripping off his nose, I stare at the video monitor and, praying that the camera will stay on its close-up of Siniša, I take the opportunity to wipe some rivulets of perspiration from my face with my sleeve.

Our spot ends with us playing the beautiful slow movement. The sounds have barely faded before the same anodyne music sweeps away the purity, and it's over. All considered, we've probably played well, though at this stage I don't trust my judgement.

We walk out into the warm air and allow ourselves to be seduced by the nearest coffee shop and its generously sized, seriously sweet pastries. We're all punch-drunk on the day's events.

Marina picks me up from the café and drives me to her home in her bright pink car. She loses the top of her gear-handle on the way. 'Oh, I wonder where it goes,' she says. 'Should I stop and look for it?'

I think it's a good idea.

She finds it has rolled behind the seat and puts it back on.

She has moved into a new flat. 'Everything is good. There is water, electricity and no violence. I can't be sad because nothing is bad.'

'And you and your husband . . . ?' I remember her tears of last time.

'Oh now everything is fine,' she says. 'I know, when I saw you I cry. I'm sorry. But after, we worked hard and talked a lot. It was a bad time. Now it's good, everything good. I want to tell you something about my husband.'

Marina

My husband is a lawyer. And there was one guy in the jail – he's a Croat and he was accused as a Croat soldier that he was a war criminal, but it wasn't truth. And later my husband found out that he helped people to get out of prison and of concentration camp and just a few times he kicked somebody, that's all, but he didn't kill anybody and he tried to help as much as he could. But the people, the other really war criminals accused him because he's so poor and insignificant and other people who did committed crimes, all of them accused him, that it was him.

And then he asked for Croat lawyer of course, but every Croat lawyer has some better thing to do because they don't want to defend somebody without being paid. Because when state is paying you, it's symbolic. And then he looked on this paper with list of lawyers' names and the only name he recognized was my husband's name. Of course we didn't know why.

One summer two years ago one paper came, of course you cannot refuse that if court is already written to you that you have to do that. So my husband went there and he asked that man so why you chose me? And that man said don't you remember me? And my husband told no, this is the first time I see you in my life.

Oh you don't remember that one time I took you to prison during the war?

And my husband said, oh you must be some great guy because I remember all of those who were torturing me and then beating me and telling me bad things, so you must be very nice one when I cannot remember you.

And of course my husband helped and found witnesses who would tell that that man was helping them. Yes he's free now. They are pretty poor, they have some sheep you know, and they don't have jobs and money, but they have a big part of land, near Sarajevo, and they want to give us some part of land to have for us, just in a way to say thank you. So you see, everything is good.

The flat is in a new building with a lift, and is light and modern. Four of her students have been there since midday, helping her to cook, and then passing the time by watching the football. 'I hope you've eaten something and have not waited for me,' I say to them as we walk in, well after five o'clock. They shrug. 'Maybe a little,' they say. Marina's children are out, and her husband is away.

So today, her students are her family, and they busy themselves in putting out the food and being generally useful. She has made a feast again – soup, lasagne, salad, and ending with pancakes with chocolate sauce and fruit. My first meal of the day – I'm ravenous.

Marina creates a lovely atmosphere, and after the meal she tells the students they can go back to the television. 'England playing Ecuador!' they shout from the next room.

We chat about students and teaching and life in general and I say I'm so glad that everything is going well. 'You seem really happy now, it's wonderful. One day I want to meet your husband. Do you have a photograph?'

Marina shows me a photograph of a calm and kind man, and says, 'I want to tell you something that happened during the war here. It's funny. Many times when my husband and I were walking through the streets when we, you know, stopped for a second to kiss or something, for a few times it saved our lives. Because first time when it happened it was in 1992, May or June, I think June, my husband just moved head twenty or thirty centimetres to kiss me, and then in that same second a bullet came through his hair and one or a few hairs was like this you know of that bullet, because it ran through his hair.'

She lifts some strands of her beautiful long hair.

'And you know, something else . . .' She hesitates.

'Yes?' I ask.

'I don't know whether to say this, but every time we made love, the fighting seemed to stop and there were no grenades and it was really silent. It's really funny because every time, of course, when you're doing that you're not paying attention, and then after that, when we're finished, in seconds, bam! And oh, it was so silent, let's do it again! Great really, like some divine sign that we are really made for each other.'

And on that note, it's time to leave.

It's been an enormously long day, and I've arranged to see Belma, to say goodbye. She meets me in the centre of town and we search for somewhere to have a drink that does not have a huge screen showing the football. Easier said than done, but eventually we come across a quiet courtyard and share a bottle of wine and a rambling conversation. She is frustrated with life here. There are too many obstacles, too much suspicion, too much everything.

Belma

Life is like hell here! It's really bad and I really, every day, dislike it more and more. And find it difficult more and more. I mean I think the main problem with this mentality here is, the Bosnians lost identity completely. And I think that is the source of all bad things that are happening here. In politic, in every segment of the life. And there is this stupid saying in Bosnia like, 'If you are laughing a lot, smiling and being happy, then put a stone in your shoe.' It's so sick ... or 'Don't laugh or you will cry later.' So this is this kind of mentality. And after the war I think it is even worse.

If I think about the people here, I'm so like contradict ... how do you say, so opposite thoughts. Like it's nice and it's not nice, people are hospitable and friendly and then again they're not, this is just cover. Of course you can meet in Bosnia beautiful people.

But general thing is this losing identity, and people lost strength to fight for the right. If you say I'm Bosnian, that doesn't exist, then you are something else. So you are either Croat, either Serb, either Bosniak ... And all these things ... trying to get money for Sinfonietta, and all the organizing ...

In the last moment I remember I do this because of music! Somehow I forget that. So, I just like when we sit and play together. I like that part. Like this time, it was really difficult for me, first this terrible mess in Banja Luka, but the Mozart pushed me, helped me to forget every bad moment in organizing. So that is the thing, that I really enjoy playing.

I pour some more wine. 'To music then!'

'To music!'

The past ten days have been exhausting for us both. And to live with the contradictions of life here is also exhausting, everything changing in the blink of an eye, from heaven to hell and back in five minutes.

Now the air is pleasantly cool and the wine is good and we begin to relax. I suddenly remember Alpha and wonder where she is. Belma phones her. Yes, she's in Mostar – a cleaner from the hotel had spotted the Italian bikers having lunch in the old town and had told them to move their bikes *pronto*. Of course they'd finished their leisurely lunch before making a move.

So everyone is where they are supposed to be.

We find a couple of taxis to take us to our separate destinations. 'Belma,' I say, 'take good care of yourself. Thank you for everything. We'll do something next year yes?'

I'm soon back in the hotel. It feels like three days since I got up this morning, and as I fall asleep, I have a surreal vision of five motorbikes and four revolving urinals . . .

Monday

Bosnia is impossible. It's difficult to do the simplest thing. I'd like to pay my hotel bill, but the hotel doesn't take credit cards and the cash machines don't give out cash. I have to go from one bank to another before finding one that even takes travellers' cheques. And then they need my passport which of course is being held by the hotel. I'm definitely ready to go home.

On my way to the airport, I drop in at the British Embassy

to thank the Ambassador, and am immediately struck by the courtesy there. It's nothing special, just common courtesy, but it takes me by surprise. As soon as I'm shown in by the friendly English assistant and handed a cup of coffee, I feel I'm in a little oasis, away from the stress and negativity, denial and haphazardness outside. The Ambassador is attentive and kind. 'Did you have a relaxing weekend?'

I laugh. 'No, not at all,' and briefly describe the goings-on of the last two days.

I thank him for playing with the Sinfonietta and say that it raises the morale. I also let him know that I'm happy to help if he thinks of other ways I can be of use, even to do similar work in other countries. We shake hands and as I leave, he gives me a set of press cuttings. His presence in these concerts has certainly stimulated the media.

The Embassy photographer did not after all come to the concert; neither did anyone record it. I've tried to get photos from the newspapers and videos from the television stations, enlisting the British Council in the pursuit, but as usual, nothing seems to be forthcoming. The orchestra could do with these for their publicity as well as for their archive; photos and recordings help to form a history and an identity. And the musicians – everyone living here – struggle with history and identity. Even with reality.

I take a taxi to the airport. The driver asks, 'Are you flying to England?'

'Yes.'

'I like Beckham,' he says. 'And Newcastle United. I play football once a week, with my little son too. Bosnian team is not in World Cup so we supporting England.'

The World Cup has run through this visit like a motif. I ask him about being a taxi driver. 'My father was taxi driver. I just finished school in '92, and then was in army, and after war there was no money for study, and I was married, so become taxi driver.'

This is my chance. In all the conversations I've had here, everyone has spoken of being a victim. Not one person has spoken of committing violence themselves. The taxi driver will almost certainly never meet me again – perhaps he can tell the truth.

June 2006

Taxi driver

I don't know, your question . . . Look, we were defending our city. We were in, how you say, the hole, yes like trench. And when they starting shooting, I'm very afraid. They coming and running towards us shooting, so we have to defend, yes? We must defend, we have to shoot too. I was on front line for a year. Twenty-four hours on front, then home for twelve hours. Like that for a whole year. I was wounded twice, shot. But it was safer than being at home. My house was hit by two grenades, it was destroyed. I would have died, with the others. It was better on front line. No, I don't think I shoot anyone. No.

Now I drive taxi, ten hours each day. It's good to work. Many people they don't have work. They have too much time, to think, to remember. For me, life is good, I have two children, I like work.

It's hard to admit the possibility of having killed. Even in self-defence. *They have too much time to remember.* The time isn't ripe yet.

Rumbling beneath the surface of Bosnia must be an ocean of guilt. Mingled with an ocean of grief. Denying it, suppressing it to keep it safe, siphons energy.

Isolates emotionally.

Disturbs the peace.

If the arrival of *Swan Lake* into Sarajevo was to herald the return of normality, then normality is dragging its feet. Yet it must come, since the pull towards it seems to be instinctive, almost as strong as hunger and thirst. In ordinary times, normality is ignored, even belittled, but as soon as it vanishes, its absence is intolerable and unforgiving. Who knows how long it will take to reappear, and what shape it will assume?

We are approaching the airport. I say goodbye to the driver, go through customs and take a seat in the departures area. There are not many people around.

As in the past, I am drained, but I am also filled up. Bosnia has allowed me to glimpse an interior world quite different from my own.

Bosnia has given me the chance to experience new reactions, think new thoughts, ask new questions.

Something Alma said flits through my mind: that when I am here, everyone wakes up. I hope that this is what they want. The scent of possibility.

And now in my mind's eye, I see Stari Most, not defiant, not sturdy, but shimmering in the light of the sky and reflecting the light of the waters beneath, providing a simple crossing between east and west, connecting cultures and centuries, peace and war, the present with the past and the past with the future, the dead with the living. Its colour and curve are delicate, its proportions fine. It almost seems to float.

Stari Most, the twice-built bridge, is beautiful.

My flight is called.

I'm leaving again.

Bosnia:
A Brief History

Bosnia was ruled in turn by the Venetians, the Turks and the Austro-Hungarians before becoming part of the Kingdom of Yugoslavia after the First World War. In 1945, Yugoslavia became a Communist republic under President Tito.

The Bosnian War erupted in 1992 when Bosnia declared independence from Yugoslavia, which had begun to break up following the weakening of Communism. Slovenia and Croatia were the first to split away in 1991, followed by Macedonia, and then Bosnia-Herzegovina. The war lasted for three and a half years and was fought by Serbs, Croats and Bosniaks. For most of the war Sarajevo, the capital, was besieged by the Serbs, and in 1993 most of Mostar was destroyed, including the beautiful and symbolic bridge.

Following NATO air-strikes, the Dayton Peace Agreement was signed in 1995, establishing two entities within Bosnia: the Bosniak-Croat Federation and Republika Srpska. An international peacekeeping force was deployed and a High Representative appointed to oversee the running of the country and the establishment of civilian institutions.

Full name: Bosnia and Herzegovina, Herzegovina being a small region in the south
Population: 3.8 million (UN, 2006)
Area: 51,129 sq km (19,741 sq miles)

Concert Programmes

July 2002: Brijuni

Schubert Quartettsatz in C minor
Scott Joplin Country Club Rag

December 2002: Mostar, Sarajevo

Mozart Three Pieces for violin and orchestra:
                    Adagio in E, K261
                    Rondo in C, K373
                    Rondo in B flat, K269
Haydn Symphony in G, No.88
Scott Joplin Paragon Rag, Country Club Rag

April 2004: Mostar, Zenica

Glazounov Grand Adagio from *Raymonda*
Tchaikovsky (arr. Glazounov) Scherzo, Opus 42
Haydn Symphony in C, No.52
Glazounov from *Raymonda*:
                    Romanesca
                    Danse des Garçons Arabs
                    Entrée des Sarrazins

Map of Bosnia and surrounding countries of former Yugoslavia, 2007

May 2005: Mostar, Sarajevo

Mendelssohn String Symphony in E flat, No.6
Elgar Carissima
Chanson de Nuit
Virelai
Rosemary
Vivaldi Concerto for two violins in A minor

June 2006: Banja Luka, Sarajevo

Mozart Symphony in G, No.27
Fauré Pavane
Tchaikovsky Valse-Scherzo, Opus 34
Tchaikovsky from *Swan Lake*:
Mazurka
Grande Valse